The Parlour and the Suburb

The Parlour and the Suburb

Domestic Identities, Class, Femininity and Modernity

Judy Giles

Oxford • New York

First published in 2004 by
Berg
Editorial offices:
̖el Court, 81 St Clements Street, Oxford, OX4 1AW, UK
838 Broadway, Third Floor, New York, NY 10003-4812, USA

© Judy Giles 2004

Berg is an imprint of Oxford International Publishers Ltd.

Library of Congress Cataloging-in-Publication Data
Giles, Judy.
   The parlour and the suburb : domestic identities, class, femininity and
modernity / Judy Giles.
         p. cm.
Includes bibliographical references and index.
   ISBN 1-85973-796-X — ISBN 1-85973-702-1 (pbk.)
   1. Women—Social conditions—20th century. 2. Housewives. 3. Sex role.
4. Suburbs. I. Title.

HQ1154.G493 2003
305.42'09'04–dc22

                                                                    2003020918

British Library Cataloguing-in-Publication Data
A catalogue record for this book is available from the British Library.

ISBN 1 85973 796 X (Cloth)
      1 85973 702 1 (Paper)

Typeset by JS Typesetting Ltd, Wellingborough, Northants.
Printed in the United Kingdom by Biddles Ltd, King's Lynn.

www.bergpublishers.com

For Alexandra

Contents

Acknowledgements

This study owes an enormous debt to the Leverhulme Trust, without whose sabbatical funding in 2000/2001 the research would never have been completed. I am also indebted to York St John College who released me from teaching and administration in order to complete this project, and to those colleagues who found themselves with a heavier workload due to my absence.

My involvement with this research has extended over many years and some of the material contained in this book was originally published elsewhere albeit with a different focus. Material in Chapter 1 was published in *Signs: The Journal of Women in Culture and Society*, Autumn 2002, 28, 1 and material in Chapter 2 originally appeared as an essay 'Help for Housewives: Domestic Service and the Reconstruction of Domesticity 1940–50', 2001, *Women's History Review*, 10, 2. Mavis Kitching's story in Chapter 4 was first related in my *Women, Identity and Private Life*, published in 1995 by Macmillan, Basingstoke.

I am also greatly indebted to the number of people with whom I have shared the ideas contained in this book and who have, at different times, commented on or made suggestions for improvement. The anonymous readers for the essay in *Signs* helped me to think more clearly about women and modernity. And the anonymous reader for this manuscript stimulated me to consider suburban gardens as well as interiors (that I have probably not done justice to this idea is due to constraints of time and space rather than a lack of interest in the idea). Treva Broughton, Laura Potts and students at the staff graduate seminar run by the Centre for Women's Studies, University of York, provided me with thought-provoking insights; Penny Tinkler generously shared her work on modernity and smoking; and Alison Creedon's ideas about late-nineteenth-century suburbia greatly helped me with writing Chapter 1.

Kathleen May at Berg Publishers has been an exemplary editor. She has been consistently encouraging and helpful and has taken an interest in the project from the very start. Thanks are also due to Lisa Wellington who helped me to prepare the manuscript for submission. My greatest debt, however, is to Barrie Linfoot, without whose love, patience and support, the writing of this book would have been a far more onerous task. Finally, I dedicate the book to my grand-daughter, Alexandra, in the hope that one day she may be as fascinated as I have been with the experiences of the millions of women who lived in that other country we call the past.

Introduction

Two very different representations of domestic identity led to the questions I explore in this book. The first is a photograph of my mother, taken sometime around 1950 and the second is a popular fiction of the 1970s, *The Women's Room*. The photograph was taken by our next door neighbour, an amateur photographer who submitted work to competitions and exhibitions. It is not a family snapshot but a glossy posed composition. In it my mother is wearing an apron, a 'pinny', round her waist, on her feet she has a pair of carpet slippers and in her hand a cigarette. She appears to be presenting herself through an iconography of the 'working-class housewife' that is found in documentary photography and films of the period. Why? My mother was extremely conscious of her class and intellect: she took a law degree at Manchester University in the 1930s, her husband was a solicitor, and her father was partner in a legal firm. Throughout her married life my mother struggled with the tensions produced by the demands of housewifery and mother-hood, and the aspirations generated by her education and background. Intellect-ually and socially snobbish, why did she choose to be represented as 'just a housewife' at this specific historical moment? Asking why a proudly middle-class woman would willingly present herself in the garb and dress of the working-class housewife in this period immediately after the war led me to think about the cultural meanings and identities that attached to the figure of the housewife in the first half of the twentieth century.

The second trigger for the ideas in this book, Marilyn French's *The Women's Room*, was first published in Britain in 1978. It quickly became a best-seller and, according to the blurb on the back cover, was 'the most important novel yet written about the realities of life experienced by today's women . . . a landmark . . . of our developing consciousness' (French 1978). The novel, endorsed by Betty Friedan, as 'the best novel yet about the lives of women', tells the story of a group of women who reached adulthood in the 1950s, bought into the American Dream of marriage and motherhood, but, through education and politics, gradually come to understand the ways in which this dream is oppressive to women (French 1978). The novel traces the development of a feminist consciousness in the narrator, Mira, and explores the tensions that result from attempting to live outside the orthodoxies of the time. Along with Friedan's *The Feminine Mystique*, *The Women's Room* attacked, what it saw as, a stifling suburban domesticity that was entirely damaging to women, particularly college-educated women. At a crucial moment in the novel

Figure 1 My mother, myself and my sister, circa 1951

the narrator decides to cook a meal for her estranged sons, her lover and her new-found women friends:

> Smiling, she stood at the kitchen sink, holding a bunch of string beans in her hand, letting herself be part of it: part of the gold streaming over the kitchen, part of the mellow surge of the waltz, part of the green of the trees bowing outside the window. It was beauty and peace, the child noises outside, the delicious simmering aroma of the soup, the fresh liquid green smell of the string beans. Her home was humming happy and bright and Ben – sexy, exciting Ben – was coming at six. It was happiness.
>
> She brought herself upright. My God! She dropped the string beans, dried her hands, sank into a chair, and lighted a cigarette. It was the American Dream, female version. Was she still buying it? She didn't even like to cook, she resented marketing, she didn't really like the music that was sweeping through the apartment. But she still believed in it: the dream stood of the happy humming house. Why should she be so happy doing work that had no purpose, no end, while the boys were off playing and Ben was off doing work that would bring him success, work that mattered? (French 1978: 457)

Mira has, she believes, liberated herself from the outmoded and constraining conventions of the past. She sees, or wants to see, herself as a 'modern' woman, engaged in 'work that matters' rather than the chores of domesticity. For Mira at this moment the seductive appeal of domesticity is dangerous and frightening. It has, she believes, the power to entrap and to limit despite the security and belonging that it represents. The consciousness expressed here is one that, while it is obviously gendered because of women's particular association with domesticity, can also be traced back to the late nineteenth century when the Victorian cult of domesticity, so revered by men like the art critic and social commentator John Ruskin, came increasingly to be seen as stifling, oppressive and old-fashioned. The 'modern individual' in late nineteenth century accounts of modernity is unconstrained by family or domestic obligations, free to roam the city streets, observe the modern world, create art and engage in 'work that matters'. Mira's struggle for liberation is a struggle to fit into this version of 'modern' consciousness, as well as to rid herself of a certain version of patriarchal oppression, and one that, it could be argued, is doomed to fail because it is limited to a paradigm produced and constructed by masculine subjectivities. 'The American Dream, female version' is as much a manifestation of modernity as the consciousness that sees domesticity as suffocating, and for millions of women in the West it offered opportunities for a 'better' life. The imagination that created Mira's dilemma is shaped by narratives that are historically and class specific, in the same way that my mother's way of representing herself could only have taken place at the particular historical moment that it did. In this book I want to ask what happens when we look at the relationship between class, feminine subjectivities and history, and what happens when we problematize the classic narratives of modernity that link the private, domestic sphere with a non-modern and ahistorical femininity?

At the end of her essay, 'The Invisible *Flâneuse*: Women and the Literature of Modernity', Janet Wolff complains of a lack in this literature of any account of 'the experience of "the modern" in its private manifestations' (1985: 45). The paradigmatic public space of modernity has been the city whether approached through sociology, historiography, geography or literary criticism. However, narrating the city as a public stage upon which the spectacles of modern life are performed can reinforce a rigid distinction between public and private spaces. The realm of the private and its metaphoric and spatial manifestations have all too often been set in polarised dichotomy to the public with the result that the private sphere has frequently been understood as a refuge from the modern, a repository of traditional values, a haven from the excitements and dangers of living in the modern world. My starting point is that responses to 'the modern' are to be found not only in narratives of the public city but also in stories of, for example, the home, consumer relations, married sexuality, domestic service. Such spaces are, of course, both material and imaginary, both actual and metaphorically described. When we speak of home, for example, we are often speaking about something else. That 'something else' is linked to our most utopian dreams and thus articulates profound needs and desires that are themselves the products of modernity. This book is about the ways in which modernity was lived, expressed and imagined in the private worlds of women as well as the ways in which public discourses about domesticity shaped those experiences and imaginings.

Equally important to this project is historical and cultural specificity. I have chosen to examine the early years of the twentieth century and, mainly, British society. As Rita Felski has argued, there are dangers in 'the relentless generality' that attempts 'to claim that an extended historical period [for example the last 300 years] can be reduced to the manifestation of a single, unified masculine principle' such as the emergence of 'modern man' (1995: 17). It has also been argued that women have been rendered invisible in modernity or that modernity is antithetical to the values of femininity and that therefore the modern world is no place for women (Felski 1995: 17, 58–9). Both these arguments, as Felski recognises, are predicated on ahistorical dichotomies that fail to account for the historical specificities of modern development. To understand modernity as simply a masculine project 'effectively writes women out of history by ignoring their active and varied negotiations with different aspects of their social environment'. (Felski 1995: 17–18). Certain aspects of modernisation at particular historical moments have been beneficial for women or offered them opportunities to see themselves differently or enabled them to become active agents in the process of historical change. Moreover, benefits, opportunities and agency may be seized upon or experienced differently by women of different classes. I am proposing that the first half of the twentieth century was a moment when the forces of modernisation that swept across Europe and North America transformed domestic life and, in doing so, produced opportunities for change that were beneficial for millions of women. At the same time, of course, these changes also brought anxiety, loss and insecurity. In the words of Marshall Berman, 'to be modern is to find ourselves in an environment that promises us adventure, power, joy, growth, transformation of ourselves and the world – and, at the same time, that threatens to destroy everything we have, everything we know, everything we are' (1988: 15). The writings and words of the diverse women represented in this book express 'power, joy, growth, transformation' but they also express anxiety, loss and confusion. In this these women are as recognisably 'modern' as their male counterparts and the forms in which they choose to represent this modernity are equally diverse.

At this point it is helpful to define certain terms that frame the argument I am proposing. Modernity, modernisation and modernism are all terms that will recur throughout this book and it is important to be clear at the outset precisely how these are being used. Modernisation denotes those social and economic transformations that originated in the Western world but which have since spread to every corner of the globe. These include: scientific discoveries that have changed ideas of our place within the universe; technological knowledge that has both led to and been created by industrialisation which in turn has generated new forms of corporate and social power; the rapid growth of urban environments; demographic upheavals resulting in increased geographical mobility; mass systems of communication that have the power to bind together (and some would argue stifle) diverse individuals; the development of powerful nation-states; and a vastly expanding, but often volatile, capitalist market (Berman 1988: 16). Modernism refers to the specific cluster of artistic practices and ideals that emerged in late-nineteenth-century Europe and America in which aesthetic self-consciousness was valued over moral purpose, representation and reality were problematised, and disjuncture and fragmentation were the preferred modes of stylisation. Modernism was ambivalent in its relationship to the processes of modernisation: modernists (but by no means all) were frequently critical of the effects of modernisation while simultaneously seeking to imagine and express a modern consciousness understood as radically different from what had gone before. Finally, modernity is often deployed as a term of periodisation to identify a particular historical epoch. However, as Lawrence Cahoone observes, 'the historical starting point [of modernity] is impossible to fix; any century from the sixteenth through the nineteenth could be, and has been, named as the first "modern" century' (1988: 1). I am not using modernity in quite this sense. Instead I have chosen to work with Berman's concept of modernity which foregrounds experience and cultural negotiation. For him, modernity denotes 'a mode of vital experience – experience of space and time, of the self and others, of life's possibilities and perils – that is shared by men and women all over the world today' (Berman 1988: 15). Modernity, thus conceptualised, is a structure of feeling that enables women and men to make sense of the social processes of modernisation in light of the responses, visions and ideas generated by these processes. Modernity, as Alan O'Shea puts it, is 'the practical negotiation of one's life and one's identity within a complex and fast-changing world' (1997: 11). In the context of this book domestic modernity refers to the ways in which women negotiated and understood experience and identities in terms of the complex changes that modernisation provoked in the so-called private sphere.

Crucial to the argument I am developing is the issue of agency. To return for a moment to Mira's dilemma with which I began. French constructs Mira as struggling against imposed structures that define what is acceptable behaviour for women. To free herself from these structures she must reject domesticity and all it stands for. The established structures, in French's vision, are what hold Mira back from autonomy and liberation and all that is needed is for these to be dismantled. Berman, elaborating on Marx's famous dictum, that 'people make their own history but not of their own free will: not under conditions they themselves have chosen but under the given and inherited circumstances with which they are directly confronted', suggests that what also limits agency can be the 'structural *processes* pulling us along pell-mell' (Marx 1973: 146; O'Shea 1997: 11). Mira's dilemma will not be resolved by a simple rejection of established norms, she also has to negotiate the processes of change that pull her with them whether she wishes this or not. French's imagination couches Mira's history (and by extension that of other educated women) 'in terms of struggle for change against imposed structures' whereas it could be more fruitful to read this history 'in terms of understanding [women] . . . as trying to keep abreast of imposed *changes*' (O'Shea 1997: 11–12). What might limit a woman's agency are, not only the past that has to be dismantled, but a present that may require careful negotiation, and a future that can appear vague and uncertain. Negotiating the processes of social change that swept through British society in the first half of the twentieth century was, I shall show, achieved differently by different groups of women. To suggest, as French does, that all forms of domesticity are oppressive and non-negotiable is to ignore the diverse ways in which different groups of women responded, at different times, to improved housing, suburban domesticity, the demise of domestic service, and the growth of domestic consumerism.

Britain and Modernity

The structure of feeling, identified by Berman as modernity, has characterised a general Western experience that can be applied to the USA and to Europe. While the historical forces of modernisation that changed the Western world in the twentieth century can be generalised as scientific rationalism, urbanisation and suburbanisation, and the volatile and expanding nature of industrial capitalism, these forces were experienced differently. For example, as O'Shea points out, any account of German or Italian modernity would need to give a central place to fascism (1997: 26). The particular form of modernity that is considered in this book is a specifically British (or perhaps more accurately English) form. The British experience of modernity was fashioned from specific forms of class that were distinctive to Britain and had their roots in the past, from Britain's position as the first industrial nation, from it's wide-scale colonisation that created an enormous world empire, and from its, often difficult, cultural relationship with the USA. The survival of a monarchy and an aristocracy, albeit with limited political power, and its industrial and imperial history gave Britain a large urban working class, which, despite unrest in the early part of the century, chose to deal with a changing world through the discourse of material betterment rather than militant political activity. At the same time attempts to buttress xenophobic and imperialist discourses focused on the superiority of 'Englishness'. This often required looking back to a 'glorious' past as well as distinguishing what was 'English' from what was American or European. Berman's modernist heroes were European not British. British intellectuals, unlike the American Berman, did not always embrace the 'adventure, power, joy, growth' that he celebrates as one aspect of living in the modern world (Berman 1988: 15). Many, from diverse political positions, tended to be highly critical of the forces of modernisation and, as we shall see, these critiques were often as much about shoring up a certain privileged position as about conserving a fast disappearing past:

> In sum, the particular force of this structured conflict between 'English values' and 'Americanism' has made the kind of modernism represented in Berman – a vigorous, uninhibited but critical embrace of the new which spans intellectual and popular culture alike – difficult to sustain in Britain. We all manage, and make sense of, change in relation to the representations we encounter. But the social groups which have tended to be dominant in producing such representations in Britain have tended to move into the modern world looking backwards. (O'Shea 1997: 31)

However, while there were undoubted differences between the ways in which modernity was understood in Britain, the rest of Europe and the USA, the British experience cannot be entirely dissociated from that of America or Europe. It has to be read in relationship to the experiences of the West more generally, and particularly in relation to America which was, in many ways, the paradigmatic example of modernity. Hollywood cinema, American broadcasting, and Fordism all influenced the British experience, and entrepreneurs like Gordon Selfridge, the founder of Selfridges, brought 'American' innovation to the vastly expanding retailing sector (Baren 1996: 122–6). So, although this study focuses on Britain in the main, I have tried to locate my discussion in a wider understanding of modernity that encompasses both America and Europe as well as Britain. For example, in the final chapter, 'Legacies', I discuss the American feminist Betty Friedan and her analysis of suburban domesticity. Although Friedan's analysis is drawn from a particular version of post Second World War North American suburbia, it was her ideas that offered a popular feminism to many women outside academia in Britain. I am aware that I have not attempted to engage with the histories of black or ethnic groups, nor do I consider the Scottish, Irish or Welsh experience. Immigration from Britain's former colonies was, of course, a major aspect of the demographic upheavals that constituted one aspect of modernity, particularly after, but not exclusively so, the Second World War. The experience of such groups would require a history that is beyond the scope of this book to offer. My focus is on those white women whom national culture of the time addressed as 'English'. And, as we shall see in Chapter 3, gender, domesticity and national identity came together in specific forms during the Second World War. I am also aware that this study tends to focus on personal subjectivities rather than collective organisations. Sadly there is not space to explore, in the detail they deserve, the ways in which groups like, for example, the Women's Co-operative Guild or the Women's Institutes engaged collectively with modernization and used domesticity in their campaigns on behalf of women. Such explorations have been carried out with more depth and rigour elsewhere and I hope that insights from this study will be of interest to those who research women's experience of the public sphere (Andrews 1997; Scott 1998a, 1998b).

Women and Modernity

As I have intimated above, the starting point for my analysis is Felski's question '[h]ow would our understanding of modernity change if instead of taking male experience as paradigmatic, we were to look instead at texts written primarily by or about women' (1995: 10). Felski has argued that the modern as a conceptual category of cultural consciousness has been produced from metaphors, symbolisations and figures that are always gendered. In her study of gender and modernity, Felski looks at the nineteenth-century *fin de siècle*, as a particular determining moment in the history of modernity, and at the culture that produced expressions of this moment. The figure of woman, she claims, 'pervades the culture of the *fin de siècle* as a powerful symbol of both the dangers and the promises of the modern age' (Felski 1995: 3). At the same time as representations of women carried powerful messages about modernity – for example Felski discusses the figure of woman as voracious consumer but also as New Woman, symbol of an alternative, utopian future – patterns of modernisation shaped the ways in which the so-called private sphere was experienced and understood (1995: 1–4; 61–90). The importance of family relationships to forms of modern consciousness was enshrined in culture by the psychosexual theories of Freud and his followers; the significance of the inner life of the psyche with all its irrationalities and repressions was as important in narratives of modernity as the socio-economic phenomena of capitalist expansion and scientific innovation. At the same time, the first half of the twentieth century witnessed technological advances that were to have a radical impact on the organisation of domesticity. For example, the provision of electricity resulted in domestic labour-saving devices and homes that could be brightly lit during the hours of darkness; artificial methods of birth control enabled smaller families; and new forms of mass entertainment made the home a site of leisure for both sexes. Women's lives were transformed by industrialisation, urbanisation, different family forms, new ways of organising time/space and the development of mass entertainment, although not necessarily in the same ways as men's. Moreover, gendered experiences of modernity and domesticity were further divided by class, ethnicity and sexuality as well as the myriad identities that overlapped and fractured these divisions – consumer, mother, servant, mistress, worker, daughter (Felski 1995: 21). Felski argues that it is 'these distinctively feminine encounters with the various facets of the modern that have been largely ignored by cultural and social meta-theories oblivious to the gendering of historical processes' (1995: 21–2).

As Felski argues, the paradigmatic narratives of modernity have, for the most part, been based on writings, philosophical, literary, political, by men, and on representations of masculinity (Felski 1995: 16). In standard accounts of modernity the key figures are all male – the *flâneur*, the dandy, the loner in the crowd – and the key spaces of modernity are also masculine – the nation-state, the workplace, the corporation, the city street (Berman 1988; Adorno and Horkheimer 1947, 1979). Modernity in most cultural histories is identified with masculinity. Indeed the feminine has frequently been represented as a refuge from the repressions and alienations of modernity, a symbolic space of redemption, nature and authenticity in which the injuries of modern living can be healed. In this version, the apparently timeless feminine values of intimacy and authenticity are set against the masculine experiences of alienation and dehumanisation that constitute modern history. This positioning of woman, home and private sphere as beyond the logic of modernity not only denies women a place in the historical record but also represents the private/feminine as outside and untouched by the complex meshing of modern phenomena (Felski 1995: 17–18). The social theorist Georg Simmel writing at the start of the last century saw 'female culture' as an alternative 'form of existence' differentiated from and outside what he called 'male objective culture' :

> objective culture as a formal principle would qualify as a one-sided male principle. Juxtaposed to it, the female form of existence would present itself as a different form, autonomous on the basis of its ultimate essence, incommensurable on the basis of the standard of the male principle, and with contents that are not formed in the same way . . .

two modes of existence that have a completely different rhythm. One is dualistic, oriented to becoming, knowledge and volition . . . The other lies beyond this subjectively constituted and objectively developed dichotomy. For this reason, the contents of its life are not experienced in a form that is external to them. On the contrary, it must search out a perfection that is immanent to them. (1911/1984: 65, 100–01)

In his 1903 essay 'The Metropolis and Mental Life' Simmel explicitly contrasts the modern 'metropolitan individuality' with that of the small town. The 'feminine' provincial mind 'which', he argues, 'rests more on feelings and emotional relationships' is deliberately set against 'the essentially intellectualistic character of the mental life of the metropolis' (Simmel 1903/1971: 325). Simmel's equation between masculinity and modernity is the kind of dualistic thinking that provides Berman with the framework for his analysis. Emotionalism, immanence, being rather than doing constitute modernity's 'other' in an act of dichotomising (or splitting in psychoanalytic terms) that defines femininity as non-modern, without individuality or agency, a cultural and psychic space from which to escape if the promises of modernity are to be fully realised.

In Berman's study of modernity the author recalls the coming of the expressway that tore the heart out of the Bronx neighbourhoods and, figuratively as well as literally, destroyed the place of his childhood:

For ten years, through the late 1950s and early 1960s, the center of the Bronx was pounded and blasted and smashed. My friends and I would stand on the parapet of the Grand Concourse, where 174th Street had been, and survey the work's progress – the immense steam shovels and bulldozers and timber and steel beams, the hundreds of workers in their variously colored hard hats, the giant cranes reaching far above the Bronx's tallest roofs, the dynamite blasts and tremors, the wild jagged crags of rock newly torn, the vistas of devastation stretching for miles to the east and west as far as the eye could see – and marvel to see our ordinary nice neighbourhood transformed into sublime, spectacular ruins. (1988: 292)

Berman draws on a well-established narrative of modernity: the all-devouring machinery of capitalism and materialistic greed, the loss of communities as the price of progress and the re-emergence of 'street' politics and people's protests as a response to the circumstances of modern life (Berman 1988). Berman's narrative also reveals, as do all the stories we tell, the unavoidable presence of gender: the forces of capitalism, of technology, the creator of the Bronx Expressway and the expressway itself are all rendered in ways that constitute a certain form of masculinity as rapacious, invasive, active, dominant and competitive. The lost small neighbourhoods and sense of community are rendered feminine in terms that suggest passivity, the 'natural' and the domestic (Giles 2002: 22). And, as Felski has pointed out, Berman's archetypal modern hero is Goethe's Faust with the seduced and abandoned Gretchen representing 'a sacrificial victim exemplifying the losses which underpin the ambiguous, but ultimately exhilarating and seductive logic of the modern' (Felski 1995: 2). *All that is Solid* draws on discourses of the modern that stretch back to the nineteenth century in which woman, home and femininity are conflated as more or less synonymous and seen as marginal to the (Western) Enlightenment project of producing a rational and democratic moral order.

Berman's account of the destruction of the Bronx selects certain phenomena as central to the narrative of modernity that he is constructing – the renewal and regeneration, disintegration and fragmentation of urban life and the importance of the public arena (the city, the street, the workplace, politics). In doing so he follows in the steps of his heroes, Marx, Baudelaire, Goethe, Dostoevsky, who produced a literature of the modern world that describes the responses and experiences of men but fails to address those of women. As Wolff has pointed out 'what nearly all the [classic] accounts have in common is their concern with the public world of work, politics and city life. And these are areas from which women were excluded, or in which they were practically invisible' (1985: 34). Mica Nava has challenged Wolff's thesis, arguing that women were not completely confined to the domestic sphere. According to Nava women entered the public sphere increasingly towards the end of the nineteenth century as shoppers and employees in the new department stores that targeted their marketing at women. She concludes therefore that '[m]odernity as a narrative and experience has turned out to be far more profoundly marked by the material and imagined presence of women than the classic accounts have allowed' (Nava 1997: 67).[1] Nava has shown how exploring the entry of women to the public urban world of late-nineteenth-century Britain contests the classic narratives of modernity in which women were confined to the private sphere of domesticity, feelings and personal relationships.

Nevertheless the domestic sphere remained central to many women's lives throughout the first half of the twentieth century. For millions of women the parlour and the suburb rather than the city were the physical spaces in which they experienced the effects of modernization. These were also the spaces that shaped the imaginations from which came their expressions of modernity. For many women domestic modernity appeared to offer the dignity and self-esteem that was so often perceived as missing from the lives of their mothers and grandmothers. Alison Light has argued that in the interwar period, conservative-minded middle-class women were able to enjoy a 'culture of privacy' in which the pleasures of home life offered new forms of privilege even if these were also limiting and constraining. Her analyses of writings by such women show how this 'culture of privacy' was imagined and expressed (Light 1991: 12). Many women writers were eager to propose the pleasures of the 'modern' home, frequently contrasting it with the stifling limitations of Victorian domesticity, and this at a time when, in the aftermath of the First World War, the home and the domestic were at the centre of national culture as well as increasingly claiming a place on the social and political agenda. Light has shown that it is mistaken to see domesticity and the private sphere as outside modernity: the home-centred feminine subjectivities of middle-class women were central to the construction of national identity in the first half of the twentieth century and found their apogee in the figure of the wartime housewife cheerfully doing her bit to keep Britain free from fascism. Light concludes her argument with a recognition that '[w]e still have to write the histories of the emotional and affective relations which women have with home-making as part of the histories of what we call "class"' (1991: 219). The stories discussed in the chapters that follow are a contribution to the writing of that history: the boundaries, markers and psychic formations that constituted class differences between women were produced in the domestic sphere as much as in the public world of work and politics.

Domesticity and Modernity at the *Fin de Siécle*

By the end of the nineteenth century the sentiments expressed in 1831 by John Ruskin's father, 'Oh! how dull and dreary is the best society I fall into compared with the circle of my own Fire Side with my Love sitting opposite irradiating all around her, and my most extraordinary boy' (cited in Tosh 1996: 9), were challenged and increasingly replaced by an anxiety about the consequences of female authority in the domestic sphere. Tosh suggests that the Victorian cult of domesticity that valorised femininity in an increasingly alienated and amoral world, dominated by the city and the market-place, while securing middle-class women's confinement to the private sphere, simultaneously undermined the power of traditional patriarchy in the bourgeois home (1996: 12). By the mid nineteenth century, women, in their roles as wives and mothers, had gained in moral prestige if not in public power and were able to wield considerable influence within the domestic sphere. Domestic rituals and the conventions governing personal relations were as likely to be shaped by women's moral influence as male despotism. Moreover, the domestic and moral virtues ascribed to women also enabled some to challenge assumptions about private and public space, and to create identities for themselves in public movements (Yeo 1998). Indeed, as Leonora Davidoff and Catherine Hall have argued, the formation of modern class society in Britain was shaped by the social changes and dominant ideologies that produced the domestic ideal, an ideal aimed (albeit differently) at both women and men (Davidoff and Hall 1987). So, while one strand of nineteenth-century cultural discourse constituted domesticity and femininity as a refuge from the modern, another associated the domestic ideal and woman's place within it with modernity. When John Ruskin exhorted women to become 'queens' of their domestic gardens he believed he was offering a mission and an important social role for women in the modern world, and many women who worked for philanthropic and political causes outside the home saw themselves as bringing their particular qualities to bear on modern society. For example, the Bethnal Green Female Chartist Association used the rhetoric of 'woman's mission' to legitimate their political activism: '[w]e are acknowledged to be the most useful apostles in the promulgation of religion – in this walk our claim has never been disputed. What, then, shall prevent us being useful in the mission of politics, peace, virtue and humanity' (Rogers 1998: 73).

In these circumstances, Tosh has argued, fathers, anxious to ensure the masculinity of their sons, and worried about the effects on this of too long a dependence on mothers or too much time spent in the feminine ambience of the bourgeois home, turned to the expanding public school sector. By the 1880s and 1890s a generation of middle-class men had spent the formative years of late childhood and adolescence in the all male and 'clubby' atmosphere of the public school. At the same time the inflexible authority and absolute power of the traditional *paterfamilias* had been weakened by legal changes that protected women from some of the worst excesses of patriarchy, notably the Married Women's Property Act of 1882 and the Custody Act of 1886. By the end of the century the appeal of domesticity for men was being called into question and 'The outcome was a discernible male revolt against domesticity among the established middle class. Marriage was postponed to an average age of thirty for men. Many more men now remained celibate for life . . . This was the hey-day of the gentleman's club, where the pleasures of homosocial society were available to all – married men as well as bachelors' (Tosh 1996: 12–14).

In North America where the cult of domesticity had been less readily accepted by an earlier generation of males, anxieties about its effects impelled writers like Mark Twain to create all-male fantasy worlds in which domesticity was a state and, often literally, a place from which to escape if full selfhood was to be realised. Huckleberry Finn's journey down the Mississippi is in part motivated by his desire to escape the domestic constraints imposed upon him by the Widow Douglas and Miss Watson. At the end of the novel he fears that Aunt Sally is 'going to adopt and sivilize me and I can't stand it. I been there before' and he chooses to 'light out for the Territory ahead of the rest' (Twain 1884/1966: 369). Twain's own domestic relations, particularly with his wife, were frequently felt by him to inhibit his creative independence. Even before their marriage he wrote to her, 'but you will break up all my irregularities when we are married and *civilize* me, and make of me a model husband and an adornment to society – won't you?' (Twain 1884/1966: 16). In the novel Huck tells us that 'the Widow Douglas she took me for her son and allowed she would sivilize me'. Son, model husband, adornment to society: these roles do not fit the masculine cultural stereotype of the strong, independent and assertive male. Instead they suggest that within the domestic sphere it was perceived as possible for a man to be moulded into whatever shape 'society' and his wife required. For Twain it was not so much loss of masculine power but the damage to his creative imagination that troubled him. Allowing himself to be 'civilised' required curbing that most American and masculine of phenomenon, his 'frontier' vitality and forthrightness. Twain believed that domesticity and 'civilization' would extract a high price – the loss of individual agency and a silencing or muting that would make critical protest or a creative imagination impossible.[2] The legendary figure of 'the American Adam', 'an individual emancipated from history, happily bereft of ancestry, untouched by the usual inheritance of family and race; an individual standing alone, self-reliant and self-propelling, ready to confront whatever awaited him with the aid of his own unique and inherent resources . . . fundamentally innocent' (Lewis 1955: 5), was the archetype for the American writer or artist. In Leslie Fiedler's *Love and Death in the American Novel* the quality of the 'true' American writer is to be found in a willingness 'to disavow "civilization", to escape the restrictions of the domestic family and the responsibilities of history' (Maidment and Mitchell 2000: 40). In their insistence upon the restrictions of domesticity, constructions of modern selfhood as symbolized by the 'American Adam' *de facto* exclude women who are traditionally and biologically responsible for creating, maintaining and reproducing family and domestic life.[3]

One way, at least in Britain, of escaping domesticity was through the idea of Empire. Conceived as an all-male project; a fantasy world of undomesticated freedom and adventure with 'not a petticoat in the whole history', Empire building offered a generation of young men opportunities to avoid the settled domestic existence that had so attracted an earlier generation of men, men such as John Smith, a temperance advocate, who believed that: 'The happiness of the fireside is involved in the question of temperance, and we know that the chief ornament of that abode of happiness is woman. Most of the comforts of life depend upon our female relatives and friends, whether in infancy, in mature years, or old age'[4] (Tosh 1996: 14; Hall 1992: 145). The danger of being stifled and 'tamed' by domesticity could, it was believed, be avoided by immersion in the manly adventures of Empire or frontier building. Both involved the seeking out and 'taming' of new environments, both offered opportunities for power and control that the bourgeois English home or the genteel domestic life of the Eastern seaboard could no longer promise, and both involved escape from the social and domestic mores that, it was believed, inhibited authentic creativity. In *fin de siècle* Europe the lure of new worlds was often as much about the desire to leave behind what was perceived as an older, restrictive and even decaying culture. In North America the urge to 'light out for the Territory' could be understood as leaving behind a devitalizing over-genteel tradition focused on the Europeanised states of New England. Thus, in numerous *fin de siècle* narratives, domesticity becomes linked with the traditional and the out-dated and is thereby diametrically opposed to the new and the modern. 'New Women' also attacked Victorian forms of domesticity and the domestic ideal that, they argued, prevented women playing a full part in modern society. When Kate Chopin's heroine, Edna Pontellier, seeks to escape the constraints of domesticity there is no frontier or Empire to act as an outlet for her need to discover selfhood and a free imagination. Her only escape from domesticity is suicide or madness (Chopin 1899/1993). Chopin's heroine aspires to be an artist but finds this impossibly difficult in the gendered world of late-nineteenth-century America. Virginia Woolf's feminist urge to recover and revalue women writers often conflicts with her desire to write 'modern' fiction. She berates Charlotte Brontë for too much (feminine) passion and not enough (masculine) cool rationality and Lily Briscoe in *To the Lighthouse* has many of the attributes of the modernist artist, in particular she is outside the domestic and private world of the Ramseys. Indeed, one has only to think of the impossibility of Mrs Ramsey as an artist (except in the creation of her own home) to recognise that Woolf allies herself with masculinist myths and representations of the 'modern' artist (Woolf 1929, 1927). Not only are the spaces of modernity different for men and women – and the question of this book is whether domesticity in its many forms offered discursive and concrete spaces where women might respond to modernity – but femininity and domesticity have long been proposed as inimical to the production of new forms of art and writing (Pollock 1988: 55). By the end of the nineteenth century cultural formations had been created in which it was possible to link domesticity, femininity, tradition, the past and constraint, and to understand this conceptual cluster as set against outdoors, abroad, masculinity, modernity, the future and freedom. This is not to suggest that such formations were the result of 'natural' or biological gender differences. They were culturally inscribed through sets of social relations that were historically specific and they inscribed and organised sexual difference and its relation to the modern world.

If women were seen and saw themselves as located primarily in the domestic sphere at the end of the century, this did not preclude a sense that this 'place' was changing. Katherine Chorley reflecting in 1950 on her parents' lives in middle-class suburban Cheshire during the nineteenth century represents their particular form of domesticity, and the world that domesticity represented, as something that was in the process of passing:

> I am setting out to evoke from the past my home and surroundings, my parents and their friends. And what I write will be a rendering of the swan-song of the English bourgeoise, the part of it which was sung to me from my cradle in the year of Queen Victoria's Jubilee until I was near the threshold of grown-up life in 1914 . . . The singers did not know that they were performing a swan song . . . Their world came to an end and mine was born at midnight on the 4th August 1914. (1950: 11)

Chorley sees herself, in this narrative, as a young woman crossing from an older outdated world to the new, 'modern' world of the twentieth century. Virginia Woolf and her sister, Vanessa Bell, growing up at the same time, were also acutely aware that it was in the organisation and conventions of domestic life that new ways of living and relating would be found. To this end they dispensed with the Victorian social practice of calling, attempted to live without residential domestic help and advocated, and in Vanessa's case practised, open sexual relations. They saw themselves as 'moderns', not simply in their commitment to producing 'modern' art, but also in the ways they chose to organise and live their domestic and private lives. After the death of their father, Leslie Stephen, Vanessa and Virginia moved to Gordon Square in Bloomsbury, a move that was seen by both as freedom from the oppressive domestic regimes of the family home in Kensington. In a short story written by Woolf in 1906 two young women from Kensington visit the young women living in Bloomsbury. One of the women attempts to express the differences between Kensington and Bloomsbury,

> If one lived here in Bloomsbury, she began to theorise waving with her hand as her cab passed through the great tranquil squares, beneath the pale green of umbrageous trees, one might grow up as one liked. There was room and freedom, and in the roar and splendour of the Strand she read the live realities of the world from which her stucco and her pillars protected her so completely. (Woolf 1906/1985: 24)

Later Woolf was to comment ironically on these aspirations,

> We were full of experiments and reforms. We were going to do without table napkins, we were to have [supplies] of Bromo instead; we were going to paint; to write; to have coffee after dinner instead of tea at nine o'clock. Everything was going to be new; everything was going to be different. Everything was on trial. (Lee 1997: 207)

The sense of being on the threshold of a new and exciting age was imagined by Woolf, as it was by Chorley and many middle-class women writers, in terms of the drawing room and the dinner table rather than in terms of the city street. Women drew on the spaces and places in which they saw themselves located to nourish their particular visions of modernity. However, we also need to remember that while free thinking, middle-class women like Woolf and Chorley saw, in the promises of the new century, certain opportunities, their counterparts below stairs may have entertained very different visions of a 'better' future. And, as Berman reminds us, modernity is not only about opportunity and growth but also about loss and anxiety. As we shall see in the chapters that follow feminine subjectivities are produced not only from the physical spaces inhabited by women but also from the social spaces in which they find themselves, and the imaginary spaces they create for themselves. The spaces of femininity of which the domestic is the most dominant are not historically or biologically the 'natural' place of women but 'the product of a lived sense of social locatedness, mobility and visibility, in the social relations of seeing and being seen' (Pollock 1988: 66). Finding an acceptable place in the context of rapid change was, as we shall see, about negotiating the contradictory impulses of modernity in order to create self-dignifying identities at both the social and psychic level.

So how were the forces of modernisation impacting on the domestic sphere at the turn of the century? First, increasing urbanisation and the development of industrial production had led to the phenomenon of the suburb. In 1909 C.F.G. Masterman, author, journalist and Liberal politician, famously wrote of those who had settled in the expanding suburbs of London that:

> They form a homogeneous civilization – detached, self-centred, unostentatious – covering the hills along the northern and southern boundaries of the city [London], and spreading their conquests over the quiet fields beyond. They are the peculiar product of England and America: of the nations which have pre-eminently added commerce, business and finance to the work of manufacture and agriculture. It is a life of Security; a life of Sedentary occupation; a life of Respectability; and these three qualities give the key to its special characteristics. Its male population is engaged in all its working hours in small, crowded offices, under artificial light, doing immense sums, adding up other men's accounts, writing other men's letters. It is sucked into the City at daybreak and scattered again as darkness falls. It finds itself towards evening in its own territory in the miles and miles of little red houses in little, silent streets, in number defying imagination. Each boasts its pleasant drawing-room, its bow-window, its little front garden, its high-sounding title – 'Acacia Villa' or 'Camperdown Lodge' – attesting unconquered human aspiration. The women, with their single domestic servants, now so difficult to get, and so exacting when found, find time hangs rather heavy on their hands. But there are excursions to shopping centres in the West End, and pious sociabilities, and occasional theatre visits, and the interests of home. The children are jolly, well-fed, intelligent English boys and girls, full of curiosity, at least in earlier years. (1909/1960: 57–8)

Masterman's description of those he labelled 'the Suburbans' is extracted from his study of English social life written at the turn of the century. *The Condition of England* is an attempt to assess imaginatively and critically the state of the nation at the start of a new century and to speculate on its future. Masterman is ambivalent about the benefits of modernisation and the suburban lifestyle he evokes is one of his prime concerns. He asks 'Is this the type of all civilizations, when the whole Western world is to become comfortable and tranquil, and progress finds its grave in a universal suburb?' (Masterman 1909/1960: 65).[5] For many at the start of the twentieth century it seemed that suburbia was the predominant form 'civilisation' would take in the modern world. The growth of suburbs in Europe and America that began in the mid nineteenth century had changed the physical landscape as surely as had cities like London, New York and Paris.

Although the twentieth century witnessed an unprecedented and vast expansion of suburbia, changing the geographical landscape beyond recognition, the development of residential suburban areas had begun long before. Engel's description of Manchester in 1844 notes this geographical separation, a separation that, in Engel's analysis, embodies and produces class division:

> Beyond this belt of working-class houses or dwellings lie the districts inhabited by the middle classes and the upper classes. The former are to be found in regularly laid out streets near the working-class districts – in Chorlton and in the remoter parts of Cheetham Hill. The villas of the upper classes are surrounded by gardens and lie in the higher and remoter parts of Chorlton and Ardwick or on the breezy heights of Cheetham Hill, Broughton and Pendleton. The upper classes enjoy healthy country air and live in luxurious and comfortable dwellings which are linked to the centre of Manchester by omnibuses which run every fifteen or thirty minutes. To such an extent has the convenience of the rich been considered in the planning of Manchester that these plutocrats can travel from their houses to their places of business in the centre of the town by the shortest routes, which run entirely through working-class districts, without even realizing how close they are to the misery and filth which lie on both sides of the road. (Lambert and Weir 1975: 114–115)

However, suburbs were not only the geographical spaces in which the evolving class distinctions of the nineteenth century came to be inscribed. They were also the visual expression of the spatial organisation of gender. Catherine Hall has shown how industrialisation created the material conditions in which home and workplace became separated while the gender ideology of separate spheres both confirmed and shaped the forms this separation would take (Hall 1982). Writing about the later years of the nineteenth century Chorley noted the gendered nature of the suburban landscape. She recalled that after nine o'clock in the morning, when the suburban train had transported businessmen and professionals to the city, Alderley Edge would be denuded of men except for 'the doctor or the plumber . . . the gardener or the coachman' (Chorley 1950: 149). The elements of the middle-class residential areas identified by Engels continued to be sought throughout the nineteenth century and formed the basis of the suburban ideal of the twentieth century: distance from the wealth-producing factories and industry of the nation, access to the fresh and healthy air of the countryside, efficient and reliable transport to the workplace, and a physical landscape that visibly expressed the appropriate spheres for men and women.

The aspiring English middle classes also wanted homes that expressed their newly achieved sense of status and, in recognition that the arbiters of taste and fashion continued to be the aristocracy, opted for scaled down versions of the living arrangements of the Victorian country house. Any household with social pretensions had its 'best' parlour and a small room that acted as a study for the *paterfamilias*.

Likewise external architectural features such as capitals, pediments and steps to the front door could suggest the graciousness of aristocratic residences even at the less affluent end of the class scale. In *The Diary of a Nobody* Mr Pooter's semi-detached house, 'The Laurels', Brickfield Terrace, Holloway, has ten steps to the front door and he buys plaster-of-paris stags' heads for the hall (Grossmith 1892/ 1998: 3). Robert Kerr, a well-known architect and Professor at King's College, London, published a guide to planning a 'gentleman's' house in which he insisted that this 'ought to be not merely substantial, comfortable, convenient and well-furnished, but fairly adorned . . . clinging to the grace of elegance . . . but avoiding nonetheless that poverty of dress which is not self-denial, but inhospitality' (Burnett 1986: 195). Speculative builders were quick to perceive that money might be made from such aspirations and competition to provide cheap and saleable homes was rife (Burnett 1986: 203). By the end of the nineteenth century suburban living, despite its many critics, was enthusiastically embraced for the opportunities it offered to escape the increasing pollution, disease and crime that characterised overcrowded inner-city areas. A pleasant house in a leafy suburb was also, of course, a mark of social status: its location, furnishings and style were a visual embodiment of social achievement. In the first half of the twentieth century opportunities for suburban living extended down the social scale and produced aspirations that, as we shall see in Chapter 1, were frequently viewed with suspicion by social commentators.

Second, by the end of the nineteenth century, the development of medical knowledge was beginning to make life less brutish and short. This was particularly the case for women for whom better medical care, more hygienic living conditions, the possibility of family limitation and improved nutrition at least offered the possibility of a qualitatively different kind of life. Tuberculosis remained the primary cause of mortality in women throughout the first half of the twentieth century with maternal mortality a close second. In the nineteenth century TB was frequently perceived as a disease caused by tight lacing of corsets or a sedentary lifestyle and thereby associated with middle-class women, whereas changing medical knowledge came increasingly to see it as a disease associated with poverty and malnutrition. However, rural or urban location, regional differences, opport-unities for work, differential wage levels, and diet could determine women's predisposition to disease as much as class. For example, there is some evidence that women in domestic service had lower mortality rates (Harrison 1995: 157–66). Linked to improvements in health generally was the decline in birth rates that began in the late nineteenth century and continued throughout the first half of the twentieth. In 1890 the average family size was 4.13; by 1935 this had dropped to 2.07 (Gittins 1982: 210). While middle-class families had begun to control fertility during the Victorian period, it was the decline in working-class family size that was most marked in the years between 1900 and 1939 (Gittins 1982: 33; Bourke 1994:

58). Equally important was the decline in infant mortality from 125 births per 1000 in 1911 to 62 in 1930. Again there were marked differences between classes. A woman in the middle and upper classes was half as likely to experience the death of a child as the wife of an unskilled labourer. Improvements in health and the possibility of controlling reproduction were crucial to women's sense of themselves although the implications of these changes were understood differently by different groups of women. And, while disease, botched abortions, infant and maternal deaths and exhaustion continued well into the twentieth century, developing medical knowledge made it possible for many women to begin to look beyond childbearing and childrearing, ill health and pain.[6] However, as we shall see, modernity produced new diseases and losses. Higher standards of housekeeping and suburban living led to, what was termed, 'the suburban neurosis' and the use of weapons of mass destruction in two world wars resulted in horrific injuries and deaths that impacted directly on women as well as the men who sustained them (Taylor 1938).

Scientific knowledge was also being transformed into technology and much of this technology was to benefit women in the twentieth century. As Ruth Schwartz Cowan observed 'kitchens are as much a locus for industrialized work as factories and coal mines are, and washing machines and microwave ovens are as much a product of industrialization as are automobiles and pocket calculators' (1989: 4). As the twentieth century began gas and electricity were set to transform the domestic environment. That symbol of home, the coal or wood burning fire, was to give way to the centrally heated house and streamlined kitchen made possible by the modern fuels, gas, oil and electricity. Electricity not only made it possible to heat and light homes but also enabled the rapid development of a whole range of potential labour-saving devices that revolutionised housework in the twentieth century. Vacuum cleaners were to take the place of brushes and carpet sweepers; washing machines replaced mangles, scrubbing boards and possers; refrigerators changed the way in which food was bought and stored; electric irons replaced the heavy flat iron, heated on the solid fuel fire; and cast-iron stoves and ranges gave way to cleaner forms of heating and cooking, powered by modern fuels. More than any other technology, the provision of piped water was to produce significant changes, not only in the maintenance of comfort and cleanliness, but also in the design of homes. Piped water and municipal sewerage systems enabled improved standards of hygiene and cleanliness and helped to combat diseases linked to polluted water and insanitary conditions. However, modern water supply systems not only made it possible to improve public health, they also eliminated the backbreaking work of heating and carrying water to where it was needed for cooking, laundering and bathing. We should be careful not to underestimate the importance of such changes: the availability of hot and cold running water had the potential to transform women's daily lives at the same time as playing a crucial part in improved family health. Moreover, the provision of a modern water supply led to new ways of organizing domestic space. Bathrooms and indoor toilets enabled new forms of privacy that in turn shaped the ways in which people understood their bodies in relation to others. We shall see in the course of this book that the bathroom, as much as the parlour and the suburb, could symbolise a whole range of meanings beyond simply denoting a place for washing oneself.

Third, the shift towards a consumerist economy can be witnessed from the 1880s onwards. A sense of the modern as being closely linked to getting and spending was also aligned to visions of the 'good life' and time to enjoy this. Moreover, the new forms of capitalist production that produced domestic commodities and services also produced employment opportunities in factories, offices and shops that were increasingly taken up by women. These changes were particularly relevant to lower- middle-class and working-class women who constituted a major new market for consumption as well as a pool of labour for the new stage of capitalist production (Glucksmann 1990). At the same time department stores served as a crucial conduit for the spread of middle-class ideals of domestic comfort and aesthetics. As we shall see in Chapters 2 and 3 these changes offered women new forms of identity and a changed relationship with the private sphere. However, the shift from an economy based on heavy manufacturing to one based on consumption and the production of domestic consumables not only offered new identities to women but also created tensions between the home seen as a private refuge from the demands of industrial life and the home understood as a space for the public display of commodities produced and purchased in the market place.

Fourth, at the start of the twentieth century, the home was becoming increasingly subject to the forces of scientific rationalism associated with the development of modern capitalism and bureaucratic forms of government. The wish to 'rationalise' manifested itself in the expansion of 'experts' and professionals whose task it was to organise and order aspects of the modern world. In the name of 'efficiency' members of the medical profession, educators, nutritionists, and child psychologists attempted to extend these scientific and rational principles to the sphere of personal relationships and domestic organisation (Reiger 1985: 2–3). Kerreen Reiger sees the following as the main ways in which 'scientific experts' sought to influence the organisation of and practices within the Australian home in the period 1880 to 1940:

> The strategies included efforts to introduce technology to the household and to define the housewife as a 'modern', 'efficient' houseworker; to change patterns of reproduction by placing contraception, pregnancy and childbirth under conscious, usually professional, control; to alter childrearing practices in the light of 'hygiene', seen as both physical and mental; and to bring sexuality out from under the veil of prudery and silence. (1985: 2)

A similar invasion of the private sphere can be traced in Britain as health visitors, infant welfare clinics, nurseries, and schools attempted to regulate parenting practices; as childbirth, pregnancy and contraception were increasingly medical-ised; as sexuality was discussed, monitored and advised upon; and as the definition of the 'efficient' housewife was extended to the working classes. Such activities, of course, undermined the Victorian (and middle-class) ideal of the home as 'the realm of home/family/personal life/women' that was 'the antithesis of the cold, calculative, rational world of capitalist commerce, industry and the State' (Reiger 1985: 3). As Tony Bennett has observed, women could find themselves addressed in contradictory ways 'between this "culture of domesticity" on the one hand and the "culture of science" and rationalisation on the other' (Bennett and Watson 2002: 14).

The first half of the twentieth century was one in which the home, containing the heterosexual nuclear family, was, for millions of people, the centre of their lives, the locus for personal intimacy, and the space in which leisure activities took place. Since 1960 new ways of organising and understanding home and family have contested heterosexuality as the sole locus of intimacy; have challenged the nuclear family as the only possible form; and have changed attitudes to housework. Thus the period I have chosen for this study represents a specific historical moment in which domestic and private life found particular forms as a result of the huge socio-economic changes that were occurring in Europe and North America. The forces of modernisation that I have identified as having an impact on the home and private life were, as we shall see, ambiguous in their effects. No less contradictory were the ways in which women were addressed with regard to domesticity. On the one hand they were encouraged to see themselves as agents of modernisation and scientific rationalism in their domestic roles, while on the other hand they remained caught up in conceptions of home that valued it precisely because it was con-structed as the antithesis of modernity. As a result women negotiated ambiguous and ambivalent ways of seeing themselves: sometimes pulled forward as agents of change but at others pushed back as symbolisations of continuity and tradition. At this point we need to consider how and where women might express these different versions of self and how we might explain the desires and needs that fashioned and were fashioned by the contradictory subjectivities that modernity offered.

Gender, History and the Private Sphere

Light has argued persuasively that 'modernity . . . was felt and lived in the most interior and private of places' (1991: 10). Her important study of the relationship between modernity and conservatism, and the gendered expression of this relation-ship in the writings of middle-class women, not only rescues such writers from what E.P. Thompson called the condescension of history, but, equally importantly, 'makes a preliminary inquiry as to what the past might look like once we begin to make histories of the emotions, of the economies which organise what is felt and lived as a personal life but which is always inescapably a social life'. (Light 1991: 5) As Light recognises, a commitment to making 'histories of the emotions' raises fundamental questions about the conventionally accepted boundaries between fact and fiction, history and story, public and private. The very phrase 'histories of the emotions' immediately contests such knowledge divisions, which are themselves constitutive of the gendered categories masculine and feminine. Academic and scholarly history has seen itself as the chronicler, recorder and interpreter of public events, with emotions, reminiscences, and personal experience confined to expression in literature and culture. The professionalisation of history in the late nineteenth century and its claim to act as a mirror for universal and 'objective' truth functioned to perpetuate a hierarchy in which, '[h]istorical "scientists" set up polarities between professionalism and amateurism, between political history and cultural trivia, between the spirit and the body – polarities in which the latter term was always inferior to the former' (Smith 1998: 9).

The cultural ephemera of lived experience, the province of 'amateur' historians, was set against 'historical science [perceived] as a matter of national importance, as genderless universal truth, and simultaneously as a discipline mostly for men' (Smith 1998: 10). Such formulations, in which the feminine, the personal and the everyday is constituted as history's 'other', refuses women any kind of historical subjectivity or agency: written out of the record, except as symbolisations of that 'other', and barred from participating in history's reconstructions, the role of woman is to act as a repository for all that cannot be admitted in the construction of a 'value-free' modern and scientific history (Smith 1998: 1, 11). Hence political and social history continue to see politics, of whatever persuasion, as the business of public institutions and public figures. Political effects flow downwards from governments, through institutional hierarchies to shape everyday lives. The flow is understood as unidirectional and what people do and think in their everyday lives is rarely linked to the making of national or international policy. People's lives, it is conventionally assumed, are influenced by the consequences of high policy but so-called ordinary people do not themselves shape either the thinking or the effects of this through their quotidian experiences. Academic history has, as a result, paid scant attention to the impact of modernity on the creation of political imaginations amongst those whose voices are rarely heard outside the private sphere of home, family and personal life. The significance of vacuum cleaners, semi-detached houses, and the decline of domestic service for the aspirations and attitudes of so-called ordinary people has been largely ignored, except by those fields of study frequently dismissed as less serious and academically respectable, for example cultural studies and design and technology (Light 1991: 16).[7] Autobiography, biography, memoirs, diaries, travel writing and fiction have frequently been seen as the accepted forms for expressing the so-called 'trivia' of everyday life and their authors are thereby understood to be 'amateur' historians. Life stories, letters, diaries and fiction have also traditionally functioned as a space in which women could articulate their sense of the world.

Feminist theory has drawn attention to the ways in which public and private are gendered concepts, but, as both Jan Montefiore and Light argue, to read writings by women as exclusively 'women's writing' fails to contest or shift the all-pervasive assumptions that link masculinity with the public sphere of politics and nationhood and femininity with the private domain of home, sexuality and feeling (Montefiore 1996: 20; Light 1991: 6). To see the fictions, oral histories or autobiographies used in this book as simply expressions of universal *woman's* experience is to deny the complex subjectivities from which they were produced. Many of the sources I examine are as much concerned with class as they are with gender. Published women writers did not address a universal female readership, however much they may have believed themselves to be doing so, but wrote from and for a privileged position of, albeit limited, authority, which they wished, consciously or unconsciously, to preserve. Moreover, the tendency of some feminisms to focus on 'women's experience' as if it were universal and ahistorical is to deny the multiple ways in which social differences shape experience and imagination (Light 1991: xi–xii). If we are to understand the past as something more than a backwards projection of the present, it is essential that we attempt to explore the ways in which subjectivities, memories and imagination were constituted differently – differently *then* from *now*; differently amongst groups of men and women that were never homogeneous entities but were shaped by myriad criss-cross divisions that might include generation, privilege and deprivation, gender, geographical location and education. This requires a recognition of the disjunctures, ambivalences and contradictions that constitute any attempt to write histories of personal life and an acknowledgement that the public record of history may not always match the private experience.

Culture, Memory and the Personal Narrative[8]

Any attempt to write the histories of women's subjectivities requires an engagement with the ways in which the raw materials of lived experience find expression in the construction of stories, autobiographies, and life narratives. Luisa Passerini insists that 'oral history consists not just in factual statements but is pre-eminently an expression and representation of culture, and therefore includes not only literal narrations but also the dimension of memory, ideology and subconscious desires' (Passerini 1979: 84). What I am interested in with regard to the sources I discuss is the interplay of desire and ideology that produces certain meanings rather than others. And this is informed by a body of work that understands memory as an active process by which meanings are created rather than as a 'passive depository of facts' (Portelli 1981: 102; Popular Memory Group 1982; White 1998). 'Memories' in the sense of a narrative offered to a listener or reader are constantly made and re-made as people attempt to make sense of the past in a changing present (Portelli 1981: 102). Equally important is the part played by memory in the struggle to construct social and personal identities in a world in which subjectivity is fragmented and fractured and this is particularly relevant to those social groups that modernity has rendered invisible, or despised. My understanding of memory as a process by which people shape the past into a set of meanings that makes sense to them in the present therefore necessitates a recognition of the ways in which this process involves private desires and public ideologies. The key issue here is the relation of psychic histories to social and material history and the questions this raises about the distinction between public and private which has been a central feature in the dominant stories of modernity.

In recent years there has been a rich and suggestive body of work that seeks to open up cross-disciplinary interactions between psychoanalysis, linguistics, history and cultural theory (Ashplant 1987, 1988; Alexander 1992; Dawson 1994). In particular the emphasis on symbolic and linguistic structures in Lacanian psychoanalysis has provided feminist and gender historians with new approaches to the historical construction of gendered subjectivities:

> The first wish of feminist history – to fill the gaps and silences of written history, to uncover new meanings for femininity and women, to propel sexuality to the forefront of the political mind – shares some of the intentions and scope of psychoanalysis. Whether the unconscious is traced through the familiar routes of the early Freud, via slips, jokes, dreams and symptoms; or installed in primal fantasy as Melanie Klein suggested; or inferred, following Jacques Lacan, from the gaps, silences, absences in speech, what is central to both feminism and psychoanalysis is the discovery of a subjective history through image, symbol and language. (Alexander 1992: 109)

This focus on language and symbolisation has made it possible to read private sources such as diaries, autobiographies, oral narratives and testimonies as expressions not only of individual subjectivity but also for cultural patterns of fantasy and denial, thus blurring those distinctions between private and public, fact and fiction that have functioned to silence women, the working class and the ethnically oppressed in traditional historiography.

I now want to turn to the work of Graham Dawson, which I have found particularly useful in thinking about oral history material. In his work on masculinities Dawson has developed an analysis that links Melanie Klein's theory of psychic composure with cultural theories of narrative to suggest the complex ways in which cultural resources and psychic processes come together in the struggle for

subjective composure (Dawson 1994: 48–52).[9] The organising drives of the psyche
– desire, fear, loss – and the mechanisms that 'manage' these – denial, repression,
fantasy, displacement – are experienced as social as well as psychic realities. They
are also remembered and thought about, not in some 'pure' unmediated way, but
in forms that draw on the cultural and linguistic resources available to a particular
social group at a specific historical moment. Thus private remembrance and
reminiscence engage both psychic structures and the cultural repertoire of forms
available at any point in time to the storyteller. Moreover, as Dawson emphasises,
'[t]he effort towards composure is an inescapably social process. Stories are always
told to an audience, actual or imagined, from which different kinds of response and
recognition are elicited' (1994: 23). Dawson's analysis is particularly useful for
thinking through the political dimension of using life story material in the ways I
am suggesting. Historiographical epistomologies that treat individual reminiscences as simply that – private ephemera that have little relevance for the writing
of professional history except perhaps to offer 'lighter' anecdotes to the 'heavy'
weight of documentary analysis – fail to recognise the social and hence potentially
political dimension to the active process of remembering. The cultural meanings
of individual stories, once they enter the public domain in forms such as diaries,
personal narratives, memoirs, and autobiographies, are produced from the shared
interaction of listener or reader and teller. In this sense the study of such sources
can never be a simple encounter with unmediated popular memory. It must involve
a recognition that the narrators of stories will look for points of contact with the
present and seek recognition that the story they are telling is understood or identifiable with in the present, at the same time as struggling to represent an acceptable
identity and consciousness both to themselves and to their audience.

Likewise the audience questions the story they are hearing or reading in order
to make themselves at home in it. In doing so they use their own preoccupations,
desires, and cultural understandings as resources for making sense of the past as it
is offered through any specific story. An example will illustrate the points I am
making. The following exchange is taken from an interview with Annie Stables
who lived on a farm in North Yorkshire for all her married life. She is now ninety-
five and is reflecting on the ways in which eating and cooking habits have changed
over her lifetime:

Interviewer: Why do you think a lot of women my age don't know how to do this?
[prepare fowl and game for cooking]

AS: Well because they've never been taught. You've been used to it.

Interviewer: A lot of my friends don't know how, they wouldn't eat pigeon, they
wouldn't know what to do with it.

AS: Well I don't know, I can't understand them, I mean a housewife's supposed
to cater for their family aren't they, I mean what would they have done,

they'd have hungered to death wouldn't they nowadays if there wasn't all
these shops.
Interviewer: That's it.

In response to the interviewer's questions about how and why cooking has changed
Annie offers two reasons: women are no longer taught to cook and higher standards
of living make it less necessary to do so. The interviewer and Annie are able to
share these insights despite the fact that the interviewer was not alive at the time
Annie is describing. Annie uses memory as a way of asserting her identity as a
competent housewife and the interviewer is able to recognise what she is being told
because of her 'knowledge' about housewifery and hunger in the earlier part of this
century. The interviewer is able to locate what she is being told in a historical and
cultural landscape that is familiar from books, films, TV programmes and conversations like this one with Annie, a contemporary landscape that imagines the recent
past as characterised by shrewd housewives, the ever present reality of hunger and
poverty, and no supermarkets. 'History' is one of the resources from which story-
tellers like Annie draw raw material to 'compose' a sense of self. The other resource
is private reminiscence. Specific experiences are selected or 'forgotten' by the
storyteller and/or elicited by the listener's questions. This 'memory work' shapes
the listener's response to the story being told but also demands that we attend to the
gaps and silences for in the 'forgettings' as well as the 'tellings' there will be hints
about any particular subjectivity. At the same time the listener's questions and
responses draw upon and place the story in a shared network of cultural meaning.
This shared network is produced from wider, public stories about the past, often
produced by the public media (including professional historians) but it is also
shaped by the private reminiscences of people like Annie whose stories are incorp-
orated into the complex networks of meaning about the past that we call 'history'.

If storytelling and history are less polarised than may have been thought, the
same can be argued for the disciplines of sociology and literature. As Felski has
pointed out, even the most 'hermetic of literary works alludes, however elliptically,
to the very social conditions that it strives to transcend' and those texts that purport
to explain and analyse social reality are acts of representation that use narrative,
metaphor and symbolisation: descriptive modes of enunciation that have more in
common with literary texts than is usually acknowledged (Felski 1995: 35). Celia
Fremlin's *The Seven Chars of Chelsea*, which is discussed in Chapter 2, is unusual
in that its structure and modes of expression blur the conventional disciplinary
boundaries between sociology and literature. It purports to be a social survey into
the conditions of domestic service in which the domestic organisation of the
middle-class home stands for what Fremlin believes is the antagonistic and injurious
class system in society as a whole. Fremlin begins with a description of social
reality – the conditions of domestic service – but her survey also incorporates a

variety of fictional modes to convey 'the economies which organise' the psychological experience that is as important in the relationship between maid and mistress as wage rates and conditions of service (Fremlin 1940). Berman's story of the coming of the expressway, referred to above, involves both individual trauma – the loss or end of childhood – and the social realities of economic and technological rationality that changed forever the landscape of the Bronx. Berman's imaginative use of individual reminiscences alongside one of the most powerful cultural symbols of modernity – the expressway – reminds us that social experience and psychic trauma are closely interwoven in the processes that constitute subjectivity (Berman 1988; Alexander 1994: 231).

Finally, in this introduction, I offer a brief outline of the chapters that follow. Chapter 1 explores how suburbia was represented and experienced in the early twentieth century. In particular this chapter examines the relation of space and time to modernity and considers the way in which suburbia offered pleasurable as well as limiting understandings of space and time. In Chapter 2 I turn to the system of domestic service that was in decline over the first fifty years of the century. Domestic service was a particularly potent symbol of the Victorian world that many believed was passing. It also produced classed and gendered subjectivities that required re-negotiation with the demise of the system. Chapter 3 looks in detail at the emergence of two important, and often linked, identities that women were invited to inhabit: the consumer housewife and the citizen housewife. The figure of the 'professional' housewife was a particular product of modernity that addressed women as agents of a rationalised domestic modernity. How were these identities constructed and to what extent did they offer women dignifying identities? In the final chapter the focus is on the legacies of particular ways of constructing and understanding domesticity in relation to modernity. I look in particular at Betty Friedan's *The Feminine Mystique* and I suggest that the ways in which some feminist narratives have represented domesticity have limited our understanding of what home meant to women in the first half of the twentieth century.

'Something that Little Bit Better': Suburban Modernity, Prudential Marriage and Self-Improvement

The Victorian art critic and social commentator John Ruskin disliked the rash of suburban villas built by speculative builders that sprang up on the outskirts of every sizeable English town from the mid nineteenth century onwards. He deplored their uniformity, what he perceived as their lack of aesthetic qualities and the mass production that could lead to jerry-building:

> Thousands of houses, built within the last ten years, of rotten brick, with various iron devices to hold it together . . . They are fastened in a Siamese-twin manner together by their sides and each couple has a Greek or Gothic portico shared between them, with magnificent steps, and highly-ornamented capitals. Attached to every double block are exactly similar double parallelograms of garden, laid out in new gravel and scanty turf. (Burnett 1986: 202)

Ruskin's criticisms of what he elsewhere called the 'festering and wretched suburb' have continued, with remarkable consistency, in twentieth-century attacks on suburbia (Lambert and Weir 1975: 153). In 1928 the architect Clough Williams-Ellis wrote: 'it is chiefly the spate of mean building all over the country that is shrivelling up the old England – mean and perky little houses that surely none but mean and perky little souls should inhabit with satisfaction' (Burnett 1986: 273) and in 1961 Lewis Mumford roundly condemned the mass suburbs that had been built in the past half-century, 'a multitude of uniform, unidentifiable houses, line up inflexibly, at uniform distances on uniform roads, in a treeless communal waste, inhabited by people of the same class, the same income, the same age-group (Burnett 1986: 256). It is not only the houses but also suburban gardens that have been condemned for signifying triviality and sameness. The 'little man' who painstakingly tends his rigid rows of dahlias and michaelmas daisies has been a figure of satiric fun throughout the twentieth century (Cunningham 2000: 54–7).

The connections between environment and spiritual and moral bankruptcy, between uniform houses and roads and the loss of individuality, between lack of aesthetic value (?whose) and loss of creative imagination, have featured in one form or another in twentieth-century critiques of suburbia. Suburbia's critics have frequently cast their condemnations in a form that espouses nostalgia for a lost Eden, imagined as a pre-industrial community under threat from the forces of modernisation, of which suburbia's encroachment on rural areas and an older way of life is particularly pernicious. Yet, in the same period, the city, equally rapacious of the countryside, equally inimical to traditional forms of family life and community, evoked a considerably more ambivalent response. For many nineteenth-century commentators and writers the city symbolised both the exhilaration and danger that characterised the experience of modernity. It represented possibilities for progress and freedom at the same time as housing the menace – social upheaval, disintegration and fragmentation – that was barely concealed by modernity's promises (Benjamin 1973; Berman 1988; Nava 1997; Parsons 2000; Simmel 1903/ 1971; Wilson 1992, Wolff 1985/1990). Suburbia, despite being a phenomenon of modern societies and despite its potential for the creation of new forms of everyday life, new fashions and designs, new possibilities for community and new moralities, has been represented, for the most part, as simply a 'bad' manifestation of the modernising processes that swept across Europe and America in the nineteenth and early twentieth centuries.[1]

Suburbia has never been understood as simply a geographical solution to the upheaval in living arrangements caused by industrialisation and urbanisation. It can be viewed as an architectural and social space, an ideal, a producer of cultural meanings and a psychic and emotional landscape. As Roger Webster has observed, '[w]hat is evident is that suburbia is inevitably viewed against or from a backdrop, against an "other" zone – for example geographical (country or city) or social class (working or upper)' (2000: 2). However, suburbia is not only understood as a social and spatial project, it is also associated with the temporal modalities of everyday life. At the turn of the century Simmel explicitly contrasted the tempo of city life with that of the provinces which he saw as a 'slower, more habitual, more smoothly flowing rhythm of the sensory mental phase of small-town and rural existence' (Simmel 1903/1971: 325). Suburbia, like the provinces, is frequently characterised as the temporal zone of the everyday in which people follow tedious and unthinking routines in a cyclical round of continuous repetition. One of the suburban housewives questioned by Betty Friedan for *The Feminine Mystique* describes perfectly this sense of repetition and mundanity:

> Ye Gods, what do I do with my time? Well, I get up at six. I get my son dressed and then give him breakfast. After that I wash dishes and bathe and feed the baby. Then I get lunch and while the children nap, I sew or mend or iron and do all the other things I can't get done before noon. Then I cook supper for the family and my husband watches TV while I do the dishes. After I get the children to bed, I set my hair and then I go to bed. (1963/ 1982: 25)

Miranda Sawyer, writing about suburban Wilmslow in the 1980s, sarcastically evokes the cyclical routines of her mother's life, her 'leisure time was spent in an exciting whirl of hanging out and bringing in the washing' (2000: 5). This horror of repetition is, as Felski has argued, a specifically modern response: throughout much of human history cycles, routines and rituals have been valued precisely because they repeat what has gone before (Felski 1999–2000: 15–31). In the modern era the drive is towards progress, change, and movement, forms of temporality that, as Henri Lefebvre has noted, are at odds with the repetitious nature of everyday life (Felski 1999–2000: 15). Certain discourses of modernity, however, offer the possibility that the mundanity and monotony of everyday life can be transformed or transcended. For example, Simmel's metropolis is a place where chance encounters and 'violent stimuli' produce a modern sensibility that values 'qualitative uniqueness and irreplaceability' above a '"general human quality"'. A 'better' life is one in which conformity and uniformity have been transcended and in which the free expression of an unfettered individuality is its basis.[2] An alternative discourse of modernity that sees, in the promises of modernisation, opportunities for a better standard of material life is fundamentally at odds with this desire for transcendence and, what Daniel Bell has termed, a 'rage against order'. A 'better' life in these terms means stability and order, rather than transience and random encounters. In Britain this dream of a better life has been envisioned in the promises of suburbia. Suburban domesticity offered millions of people the opportunity to realise their aspirations for material betterment and the 'decent' life that accompanied this. However, these prudent aspirations, as we shall see, could very easily conflict with the desire for excitement and adventure. And it is precisely because suburbia promises that everyday life can be lived safely and securely that it engenders rage and horror in its intellectual critics whose investment in modernity tends to an ideal in which human aspiration should be towards the transcendence of the safe and conformist. Berman recognises the ways in which these contradictory discourses pull people in conflicting directions: people 'are moved at once by a will to change – to transform both themselves and their world' and simultaneously 'by a terror of disorientation and disintegration, of life falling apart' (1988: 13).

Before moving on it is important to consider how these ideas about everyday life have been associated with femininity. Lefebvre argued that:

> Everyday life weighs heaviest on women . . . Some are bogged down by its peculiar cloying substance, others escape into make-believe, close their eyes to their surroundings, to the bog into which they are sinking and simply ignore it . . . Because of their ambiguous position in everyday life – which is specifically part of everyday life and modernity – they are incapable of understanding it. (1971: 73)

Simmel, as we saw in the introduction, believed that men and women occupied 'two modes of existence that have a completely different rhythm'; Simone de Beauvoir claimed that woman 'clings to routine' and 'is doomed to repetition'; and, more recently, Julia Kristeva explored the idea of 'women's time' in relation to female subjectivities which she argues 'would seem to provide a specific measure that essentially retains *repetition* and *eternity* from among the multiple modalities of time known through the history of civilizations' (Simmel 1911/1984: 100–1; De Beauvoir 1949/1988: 610; Kristeva 1981/1991: 445). While these formulations differ in the degree of censoriousness with which they address women's association with repetition, all three link this with the biorhythms of women's reproductive function. The biological rhythms of menstruation and pregnancy, as Felski has observed, offer the only examples 'of human subordination to natural time and a certain feminine resistance to the project of civilisation' (1999–2000: 16). At the same time, of course, to see time in these dualistic terms is to reproduce those modes of thinking that place domesticity and femininity outside the (masculine) linear, historical time of modernity. The deadening routines of the home are set in opposition to the progressive march of science and industry which is thereby (misleadingly) constructed as masculine. However, as we saw in the introduction, certain manifestations of science, industry and commerce found their way into the suburban home as well as into the public world of work and politics. Moreover, the pejorative assessment of repetition found, not only in the work of Lefebvre but in that of De Beauvoir, invites questioning. In what ways could the routines and rituals of suburban domesticity be revalued? Could they 'safeguard a sense of personal autonomy and dignity' to set against the rapid and imposed changes of modern life (Felski 1999–2000: 18)? Later in this chapter the stories of working-class women who migrated to suburbia will be considered in the light of these questions.

Suburbia, as much as the city against which it is often defined, is therefore both a product of modernity and a space in which the dilemmas and contradictions of modernity can be articulated. British forms of twentieth-century suburban development were recognisably progressive, offering hygienic homes in semi-rural areas for those previously condemned to the unhealthy dirt and squalor of the cities.[3] Yet, suburbia has suffered particularly vociferous attacks from those on the political left whom it might be assumed would, for reasons of social justice, be its champions. Why, given that many of the ideas that underwrote twentieth-century town planning originated with radical or socialist thinkers and provided improved living conditions and a better quality of material life for so many in the first sixty years of the twentieth century, has suburbia been so consistently denigrated by those who espouse democratic, socialist, Marxist and broadly left-wing sympathies?[4] Paul Oliver asks whether the dislike and condemnation of the suburban semi-detached to be found in the commentaries of architects could be explained:

Because the alternative, perhaps the truth, was too unbearable to contemplate; that the semi in the suburb met precisely the physical, material, emotional and symbolic needs of the occupants? Did they [critics] fear that the speculative builders of the Twenties and Thirties, with grass-roots values, similar origins, modest building skills and little or no architectural expertise had somehow got it right? (Oliver et al. 1981: 203)

If Oliver is right this suggests that the condemnation of suburbia is related to class divisions and anxieties at a specific historical moment as well as to gendered ideas about time and space. For many in the early years of the twentieth century (and also today) the experience of the city was one of appalling poverty, disease, noise, dirt and crime. Working-class and lower-middle-class women for example concerned to escape the drudgery of their mother's lives in inner-city areas saw in the promises of suburbia the opportunity to realise these aspirations (Giles 1995). For millions of people in the twentieth century modern life has been experienced not in the city but in the real and the imagined geography of suburbia: the parlour, the garden, the allotment, the private 'feminine' spaces of suburbia rather than the public spaces of the metropolis. Yet, suburbia with notable exceptions[5] has remained more or less invisible in most accounts of modernity. It appears either as an ugly manifestation of modernisation that has destroyed the pre-industrial communities of an 'authentic', rural past or as the city's 'other': backward and inward looking, dependent upon the city for its economic existence, a space of mediocrity, passivity and homogeneity that in its repetitive routines can sap the vitality and creativity of its inhabitants, a place, above all, to escape from.

Suburbia and the City

Berman's analysis of modernity attacks the twentieth-century re-development of cities like New York which by building expressways, out-of-town shopping malls and suburban development have destroyed what Berman calls the life of the streets and the potential therein for political protest:

> so the 1960s passed, the expressway world gearing itself up for ever more gigantic expansion and growth, but finding itself attacked by a multitude of passionate shouts from the streets, individual shouts that could become a collective call, erupting into the heart of the traffic, bringing the gigantic engines to a stop, or at least radically slowing them down. (1983: 329)

Berman's New York embodies the ambivalences of living in modern times. On the one hand the power of technology to create the city in the first place, on the other hand integral to this power is the capacity and knowledge to develop, destroy, or change that which has recently been created: 'the development of modernity has made the modern city itself old-fashioned, obsolete . . . we have the technology and the organizational tools to bury the city here and now' (Berman 1988: 307). Since the end of the nineteenth century solutions have been put forward to the problems of the modern city. Berman argues that one response to the huge, sprawling nineteenth-century cities of Paris, St. Petersburg and New York was to envisage a 'crystal palace world' in which people lived in a 'highly developed, super-technological, self-contained exurban world, comprehensively planned and organized – because created *ex nihilo* on virgin soil – more thoroughly controlled and administered . . . than any modern metropolis could ever be' (1988: 244). Against this he cites Dostoevsky's *Notes from Underground* in which the Russian writer denounces those who see in Joseph Paxton's Crystal Palace (1851) an emblem of all that is most 'spectral, mysterious, infinite' about the modern world. Dostoevsky's critique of the Crystal Palace as 'the very negation of all uncertainty and mystery, the defeat of adventure and romance' is an attack on those (like Ebenezer Howard) who were later to envisage the modernisation of the city as a project of planning and order. For Dostoevsky in the 1860s the modern city is a place of adventure – frightening and dangerous but also exciting and full of promise. As Berman says, Dostoevsky is 'affirming modernization as a human adventure – a frightening and dangerous adventure, as any real adventure must be – against a modernization of trouble-free but deadening routines' (1988: 244). In the twentieth century, according to Berman, the Crystal Palace mode of modernisation has found its expression in the 'steel and glass corporate headquarters and suburban shopping malls' of the United States rather than in the USSR. He would almost certainly have included the local authority housing estates, the new towns, and high-rise flats of twentieth-century British housing policy had he been examining the British experience, for the planned towns and the rational, functional architecture of Le Corbusier that dominated immediate post-war building in the United States were also, albeit on a smaller scale, pervasive in Britain.

Berman argues that steel and concrete skyscrapers, expressways, planned towns and glassed-in shopping malls are all attempts to impose order on the chaotic sprawl of the ever-expanding cities of Europe and the United States, the cost of which for him is 'a far more enclosed, controlled, orderly world'. He endorses Dostoevsky's vision of the city as a place of adventure and promise and condemns those who wish to replace the city which he sees as an 'heroic expression of modernity' with that 'dismal emblem of modernity as monotony' – suburbia. Berman is firmly on the side of the nineteenth-century city which is characterised in a quote from Evgeny Zamyatin's dystopian novel, *We*, as a nostalgically remembered 'deafeningly jangling motley, confused crush of people, wheels, animals, posters, trees, colors, birds'. By contrast the glass and concrete out-of-town shopping centres or 'the crystalline suburban IBM "campuses"' of our own times are condemned as sterile, mechanical, overcontrolled environments which endanger the hearts and souls of those who inhabit them (Berman 1988: 240–8). Berman's valuations of the city and suburbia are constructed through the invocation of specific oppositions that rely on a polarised contrast between the city and the suburb. The modern city functions for Berman as a metaphor for energy, activity, possibility, romance and life whereas the planned developments of suburbia stand for rigidity, monotony, control, sterility and death. The city and the suburb above all express two different ways of responding to modernisation: on the one hand the response Berman favours which is to see modernity as an exhilarating but fraught adventure or on the other hand to see it as crushing diversity and individuality by the imposition of routines, planning and controls which will 'turn into a death sentence for the spirit' (Berman 1988: 243). Berman writes as part of a long tradition of engagement with modernity and the modern city as its paradigm and his heroes concern themselves with the adventure, the possibilities, the restless activity, the speed and movement of modern life for which the city is a potent metaphor.

Felski has argued that Berman's narrative is the story of 'modernity as an Oedipal revolt against the tyranny of authority drawing on metaphors of contestation and struggle grounded in an ideal of competitive masculinity' (1995: 2). She observes that in Berman's vision modernity is represented as masculine and tradition, represented by the passive Gretchen in Goethe's *Faust*, is understood as feminine. While there is much truth in this, Berman's analysis of the city/suburb dichotomy complicates any straightforward splitting along gender lines. The teeming world of 1960s New York that Berman believes has been destroyed by the coming of the expressway and out-of-town developments is encoded with feminine attributes. Drawing on the work of Jane Jacobs, Berman celebrates the personal relations that make up the life of the city, its small neighbourhoods, its localities, its fluidity and its sprawl – this is a feminised world of personal, family and domestic interconnections. Berman comments on Jacobs' influential text, *The Death and Life of Great American Cities*, in terms that foreground its femininity:

> She writes out of an intensely lived domesticity . . . She knows her neighborhood in such precise twenty-four-hour details because she has been around it all day, in ways that most women are normally around all day, especially when they become mothers, but hardly any men ever are . . . She knows all the shopkeepers, and the vast informal social networks they maintain, because it is her responsibility to take care of her household affairs. She portrays the ecology and phenomenology of the sidewalks with uncanny fidelity and sensitivity, because she has spent years piloting children . . . through these troubled waters, while balancing heavy shopping bags, talking to neighbors and trying to keep hold of her life. Much of her intellectual authority springs from her perfect grasp of the structures and processes of everyday life. She makes her readers feel that women know what it is like to live in cities, street by street, day by day, far better than the men who plan and build them (1988: 322)

For Berman the city in the twentieth century is a place where the temporal and spatial modes of women's lives – neighbourhood, family, home – are being destroyed by the inexorable poundings of what he calls 'the expressway world', represented by the figure of the developer, Robert Moses. Moses is presented by Berman as a powerful, energetic, juggernaut who boasts that '[w]hen you operate in an over-built metropolis, you have to hack your way with a meat ax', an image that evokes a particularly rapacious form of masculinity (Berman 1988: 294). It is not simply nostalgia that drives Berman's celebration of Jacobs' feminised city; her city of small neighbourhoods and local connections is presented as a model for future developers and as a modernist blueprint for a better society:

> her ideal street is full of strangers passing through, of people of many different classes, ethnic groups, ages, beliefs and life-styles; her ideal family is one in which women go out to work, men spend a great deal of time at home, both parents work in small and easily manageable units close to home, so that children can discover and grow into a world where there are two sexes and where work plays a central role in everyday life (Berman 1988: 323)

Thus, the equation between the city and masculinity or between the suburb and femininity, is complex and shifting. Indeed the modernised city of which Berman dreams is a community that draws its values from the domestic and local experiences of women's everyday lives but mixes these with the random transcendence of the modernist city (the street full of strangers for example). Berman's coding of his selective symbols – the expressway, the skyscraper, the dormitory suburb, the street – is undeniably gendered but his recognition that 'women [have] something to tell us about the city' contests some of the classic accounts of modernity in which women only appear as iconographic figures – the prostitute, the actress – 'shoring up nineteenth-century dualistic thought about virtuous and fallen women as well as mythologies of the sexually licentious city' (Berman 1988: 323; Nava 1997: 57). Berman's text is more complicated in its gendering than Felski allows but we are only enabled to see this because of the way in which the city and suburbia have been written and talked about throughout the first half of the twentieth century. In spite of the complexities of Berman's version of modernity it continues to draw on a repertoire of well-established markers of the modern city and its relationship to despised forms of modernisation such as suburbia. It is because of the city's centrality to ideas about modernity that we need to untangle some of the threads that constitute its formation as this paradigmatic symbol and that lay down the iconography that codes the city in certain ways.

For Charles Baudelaire, at the end of the nineteenth century, the *flâneur* (the detached observer or wanderer) is the perfect figure of the modern artist:

The crowd is his element . . . His passion and his profession are to become one flesh with the crowd. For the perfect *flâneur*, for the passionate spectator, it is an immense joy to set up house in the heart of the multitudes, amid the ebb and flow of movement, in the midst of the fugitive and the infinite. To be away from home and yet to feel oneself everywhere at home; to see the world, to be at the centre of the world, and yet to remain hidden from the world. (Baudelaire 1964/1863: 90)

Baudelaire's artist of modern life is anonymous, undomesticated and a spectator rather than a participant. He is also undeniably male. This poses the question does sexual difference produce specific versions of the city and is sexual difference itself produced through the specificity of those versions? As Griselda Pollock has argued, with relation to Paris in the late nineteenth century, visions of the city inscribed certain versions of femininity and masculinity that were linked to the ways in which what could be seen by whom and where were organised around ideas of sexual difference (Pollock 1988). The doctrine of separate spheres which the Victorians mapped onto the conceptual division of public and private produced a particularly bourgeois way of life in which the public sphere, and this would include the geographical and social spaces of the city, became the domain of men. The private realm for men was not only idealised as a haven from the exacting world of commerce and politics but came increasingly to be experienced as a place of constraint (Tosh 1996). The modern city was fashioned for men as a space where the responsibilities of the private sphere could be left behind, as a place of freedom and even immorality. For a man, walking the public streets was a way of losing himself in the crowd, of being 'away from home'. The figure of the *flâneur* not only symbolises the modern artist who observes, describes and categorizes the flux and spectacle of the city streets, but is linked to a certain form of late-nineteenth-century bourgeois masculinity (Benjamin 1973: 36; Wolff 1985/1990; Pollock 1988; Wilson 1992; Parsons 2000). The characteristics of the *flâneur* – his detachment from society, his lack of familial relations, the sense of superiority that underwrites his ability to categorize others – were to a greater or lesser degree characteristics of the forms of 'manliness' promulgated by writers of Empire like H. Rider Haggard and G.W. Henty. They were precisely the characteristics perceived as lacking in those males who immersed themselves in suburban domesticity, men like George Pooter characterised by his creators, George and Weedon Grossmith, as a 'Nobody'. The figure of the *flâneur* has been highly influential in understanding the modern city and the dynamic of modernity but has been much criticised for adopting an uncritical masculine viewpoint (Donald 1999; Frisby 1985; Nava 1997; Parsons 2000; Wolff 1985/1990).

For bourgeois women, to wander the streets was to risk losing one's reputation, to be seen as a 'public' woman or potential prostitute, to be identified as an object of potential purchase or consumption. Rather than allowing them to lose themselves in the crowd, walking the streets for women exposed them to the erotic gaze of men and, for bourgeois women, to the covetous and contemptuous gaze of the proletariat. The public domain was dangerous for it was on the streets that the bourgeois woman risked losing her social identity, an identity defined through the regulating power of femininity. And this should also remind us that class mapped onto gender in the metaphoric and social organisation of the city streets. As Pollock has shown, males and proletarian women frequently inhabited the same spaces – cafes, backstage at the theatre and brothels (Pollock 1988: 73). These spaces were both invisible and unknowable to bourgeois women. The public spaces of the city were imagined as threatening unbridled sexuality and corruption. For example Dante Gabriel Rossetti's painting *Found* depicts a woman being rescued literally and metaphorically from the gutter where she has fallen, by a fresh-faced young drover from the country. The painting deploys all the markers that polarised city and country. The woman, dressed in the kind of tawdry finery associated with prostitution, turns her head away in shame; the man, clothed in the countryman's smock and leggings, helps her to her feet, whilst his cart contains a lamb wrapped in a net; in the distance we see one of the bridges over the Thames, an icon of destitution and despair.[6] Women did, of course, venture out into the public domain in order to shop, to visit, to attend the theatre, to walk or ride in the park and to be on display as objects of style and fashion but the spaces they might occupy were heavily circumscribed. And respectable women of the middle classes did not frequent the city streets unless accompanied by a servant or a male relative. Thus the city that offered freedom and irresponsibility for men was reduced to specific zones for certain classes of women and the differences between bourgeois femininity and proletarian women, thus inscribed, operated to secure concepts of class and gender that worked in men's interests. For men were free to move between the private and public spaces of bourgeois femininity *and* the public spaces in which the bodies of courtesans, actresses, dancers, prostitutes and servants could be observed, commodified and possessed. The proper place of respectable women was the suburban home or the rural village.

However, recent feminist interventions have challenged this narrative and argue that women were not so easily confined to these domestic spaces but were able to move freely around in certain places and in certain roles (Nava 1997; Walkowitz 1992; Wilson 1991). In Britain there were increasing opportunities for women to engage with philanthropic work in some of the most deprived areas of the city. The belief that virtuous women had a moral mission to save their less fortunate sisters allowed middle-class women to visit working-class homes to provide information and advice on cleanliness, childcare, disease prevention and money management. Middle-class women were also involved in charitable organisations and philanthropic schemes to alleviate the sufferings of the poorest sections of urban society. Nava has pointed out that at the end of the nineteenth century in Britain approximately 20,000 women were 'paid officials and an astonishing half million were voluntary workers engaged in philanthropic projects dedicated to improving the life of the urban poor' (Nava 1997: 61). Moreover in the last decades of the nineteenth century the spatial boundaries that marked the acceptable locations for unaccompanied women were changing: art galleries, libraries, tearooms, hotels and department stores all offered facilities for women visitors and in order to access these women took advantage of newly available forms of transport – the suburban railway, the bicycle, the tube as well as walking. 'New Women' chose to live with other single women in the city rather than at home with parents and to work in one of the new employments such as retailing, clerical, secretarial or personal service that were becoming available. In doing so middle-class women encountered, albeit differently, the pleasures and menaces of city life that so fascinated their male counterparts. Nava has suggested that the relative exclusion of women's experiences from accounts of the late-nineteenth-century city and the continued insistence on women's seclusion in the bourgeois home can be understood as 'a form of denial, as a way of attempting to hold back the modern, of resisting – or at the very least regulating – the encroachment of women and the "new woman" in particular' (1997: 46). This attempt to confine women to the private spaces of suburban domesticity which enacts a refusal to see women as agents of modernity requires a constant shoring up of the boundaries between the spaces of masculinity (the city) and femininity (the suburb). From this perspective we can read the constant and insistent denigration of suburbia in terms of attempts to exclude certain groups, notably women and the working class, from the narratives that constitute our understandings of modern times.

'Slums that Stunt the Mind': George Orwell, *Coming Up For Air*

Coming Up for Air, published in 1939, as Britain prepared for war against Germany, was not intended simply as a satiric attack on suburbia. Orwell uses suburban domesticity as a metaphor for, what he believed were, the de-humanising, homogenising and bureaucratic tendencies of twentieth-century life. George Bowling, the narrator, is an insurance salesman who lives in a semi-detached house in the London suburb of West Bletchley with his wife and two young children,

> Do you know the road I live in – Ellesmere Road, West Bletchley? Even if you don't, you know fifty others exactly like it.
>
> You know how these streets fester all over the inner-outer suburbs. Always the same. Long, long rows of little semi-detached houses – the numbers in Ellesmere Road run to 212 and ours is 191 – as much alike as council houses and generally uglier. The stucco front, the creosoted gate, the privet hedge, the green front door. The Laurels, the Myrtles, the Hawthorns, Mon Abri, Mon Repos, Belle Vue . . . what *is* a road like Ellesmere

Road? Just a prison with the cells all in a row. A line of semi-detached torture-chambers where the poor little five-to-ten pound-a-weekers quake and shiver, every one of them with the boss twisting his tail and the wife riding him like the nightmare and the kids sucking his blood like leeches. (Orwell 1939/1987: 13–14)

Orwell's description of Ellesmere Road deploys an established iconography for representing suburbia: rows of semi-detached houses, the privet hedge, the house names (Charles Pooter's house in Holloway was called 'The Laurels'). Depicted as an over-weight, middle-aged man whose life to date has proved disappointing, George Bowling functions both to satirise what Orwell, like others of his class and generation, saw as a suburban mentality and to give voice to warnings of impending doom. George, walking through the streets of London, imagines the streets as peopled with 'sleepwalkers' and 'waxworks', none of whom are aware of what lies ahead, 'like turkeys in November' (Orwell 1939/1987: 28–9). He has a brief prophetic vision in which he sees the streets riddled with bomb-craters and burnt out buildings, he hears 'the air-raid sirens blowing and the loudspeakers bellowing that our glorious troops have taken a hundred thousand prisoners', and he sees 'the posters and the food-queues, and the castor oil and the rubber truncheons and the machine-guns squirting out of bedroom windows' (Orwell 1939/1987: 29–30). George muses: 'Is it going to happen? No knowing. Some days it's impossible to believe it. Some days I say to myself that it's just a scare got up by the newspapers. Some days I know in my bones there's no escaping it' (Orwell 1939/1987: 30). The point is that it could happen and George, the suburban insurance salesman, acts as a prophetic voice warning of the political and militaristic realities that are fomenting beyond the privet hedge and the commuter train. Orwell places his faith for the future in ordinary men like George Bowling, at the same time condemning the moral vacuum created, he believes, by the circumstances of modern life, in which his suburban everyman can later proclaim, '[t]he future! What's the future got to do with chaps like you and me? Holding down our jobs – that's our future' (Orwell 1939/1987: 225). Bernard Crick makes the point that in *Coming Up for Air* Orwell was not simply writing *about* the lower middle class, he was also writing *for* a readership of men like George Bowling in an attempt to challenge their political apathy (Crick 1982: 376). Almost simultaneously with his vision of the future a chance poster triggers George's memory and he is transported in his mind to scenes of his childhood in the small country town of Lower Binfield at the turn of the century. In an attempt to alleviate his anxieties about the future Bowling decides to secretly visit Lower Binfield and to seek there the answers that increasingly elude him in the modern world. Lower Binfield, of course, has been modernised and Bowling's nostalgic return to the rural location of his childhood is ridiculed as much as his suburban life in Ellesmere Road.

At the end of the novel Bowling himself wonders:

Why had I run away like that? Why had I bothered about the future and the past, seeing that the future and the past don't matter? Whatever motives I might have had, I could hardly remember them now. The old life in Lower Binfield, the war and the after, Hitler, Stalin, bombs, machine-guns, food queues, rubber truncheons – it was fading out, all fading out. Nothing remained except a vulgar low-down row in a smell of old mackintoshes. (Orwell 1939/1987: 232)

Unable to explain his reasons for his visit to Lower Binfield to his wife, Hilda, who suspects him of sexual misdemeanours, Bowling sinks into a resigned but despairing passivity:

But what really got me down was the kind of mental squalor, the kind of mental atmosphere in which the real reason why I'd gone to Lower Binfield wouldn't even be conceivable . . . If I spent a week explaining to Hilda *why* I'd been to Lower Binfield, she'd never understand. And who *would* understand, here in Ellesmere Road? . . . Nothing's real in Ellesmere Road except gas-bills, school-fees, boiled cabbage, and the office on Monday. (Orwell 1939/1987: 231)

This bleak ending offers little hope for the future which it is implied will remain unchanged by Bowling's visions or his excursion into the past. Bowling's heroic 'ordinary man's' attempt to understand and resist the implications of bureaucratic, economic and technological modernisation is defeated by the deadening delusions of suburbia, itself a manifestation of the modern. Nor is nostalgia for the Edwardian certainties of his childhood a solution. On the road to Lower Binfield George imagines that all the people who would disapprove of his desire to transcend everyday life are chasing his car. The forces whom he imagines pursuing him include:

all the chaps at the office, and all the poor down-trodden pen-pushers from Ellesmere Road and from all such other roads, some of them wheeling prams and mowing-machines and concrete garden-rollers, some of them chugging along in little Austin Sevens. And all the soul-savers and Nosey Parkers, the people whom you've never seen but who rule your destiny all the same, the Home Secretary, Scotland Yard, the Temperance League, the Bank of England, Lord Beaverbrook, Hitler and Stalin on a tandem bicycle, the bench of Bishops, Mussolini, the Pope . . . (Orwell 1939/1987: 173–4)

Heading this 'huge army' of disapproval are Hilda and his children. Suburban domesticity, symbolised by his family, colludes with the forces of tyranny which are in turn linked to the techno-bureaucratic manifestations of state control that function to 'streamline . . . a chap who thinks he's going to escape!' (Orwell 1939/ 1987: 174). Hilda is a symbolisation of the 'mental squalor' that could never understand 'why a middle-aged man with false teeth should sneak away for a quiet week in the place where he spent his boyhood' (Orwell 1939/1987: 173). 'Mental squalor', suburbia, transcendence, and a loss of masculinity are inextricably intertwined in Orwell's vision.

Throughout the novel fishing acts as a metaphor for a certain kind of manliness. Aged eight George fights with a gang of older boys led by his brother to be allowed to join their fishing expedition; from eight to fifteen he 'chiefly remembers fishing'; at fifteen he chooses sexual gratification over the boyhood joys of fishing; in the First World War the possibility of going fishing represents the pleasures of male camaraderie and a momentary respite from the discomforts and terrors of war; and always there are the enormous, primeval carp that inhabit the deep pool at Binfield House that George dreams of catching one day (Orwell 1939/1987: 66). George confesses 'that after I was sixteen I never fished again' and that 'my active life, if I ever had one, ended when I was sixteen' (Orwell 1939/1987: 31, 80). The end of his childhood and adolescence coincides with the outbreak of the First World War which, as in many novels of the interwar years, is represented as a rupture that irrevocably separates the past from the present and future, and heralds the emergence of the modern world. Light has suggested that a response to the experience of the First World War 'might be an increased attachment to the idea of private life' and that this might constitute a search for a new kind of national identity at a time when the imperialist project of Victorian England no longer appeared tenable (1991: 211). She argues that this new form of conservative Englishness 'could "feminise" the idea of the nation as a whole, giving us a private and retiring people, pipe-smoking "little men" with their quietly competent partners, a nation of gardeners and housewives' (Light 1991: 211). When many years later, on holiday with Hilda and his children in Bournemouth, George mentions fishing and is ridiculed by them as 'a baby' it is impossible not to read this as his 'emasculation' by the 'feminised', domestic world of seaside holidays, family, and a semi-detached house on Ellesmere Road. Suburban domesticity which had proved a refuge and retreat for many men after the horrors of the First World War is savagely attacked by Orwell as a wasteland of disappointed hopes, a dreary space in which petty anxieties about money stifle spontaneity and joy and in which manliness is constantly threatened. It is in this context that we need to try and make sense of his apparently misogynist treatment of female characters in the novel.

Orwell was not alone in linking women with the most despised aspects of suburbia. In the same year that Orwell was writing *Coming Up for Air*, Dr Stephen Taylor, Senior Resident Medical Officer at the Royal Free Hospital in London, published an article in the *Lancet*, entitled 'The Suburban Neurosis'. Based on his work in the outpatient department, Taylor claims that in recent years a new group of 'neurotics' has come to his notice. These are 'less poverty stricken young women with anxiety states, the majority of whom present a definite clinical picture with a uniform background' (Taylor 1938: 759). Taylor's 'suburban neurotics' are from the lower-middle classes: those who, like Hilda and George in *Coming Up for Air*, are the first generation to have bought their own homes in the suburbs. 'Mrs Everyman', as Taylor calls the subject of his composite case study, worries, often justifiably, about money, has few friends and not enough to do or think about. Taylor's description of 'Mrs Everyman' bears a marked resemblance to Orwell's depiction of Hilda:

> Mrs Everyman is 28 or 30 years old. She and her dress are clean but there is a slovenly look about her. She has given up the permanent wave she was so proud of when she was engaged. Her clothes, always respectable and never as smart as those young hussies who work in the biscuit factory, are, like her furniture getting rather shabby. They hang on her rather as a covering than as something to be worn and made the most of. She is pale but not anaemic . . . At school she was not taught to use her brain for her own amusement [and] with time on her hands . . . she starts to think, a process for which she is unadapted. (Taylor 1938: 760)

> Hilda is thirty-nine, and when I first knew her she looked just like a hare. So she does still, but she's got very thin and rather wizened, with a perpetual brooding, worried look in her eyes, and when she's more upset than usual she's got a trick of humping her shoulder and folding her arms across her breast, like an old gypsy woman over her fire . . . What Hilda lacks – I discovered this about a week after we were married – is any kind of joy in life, any kind of interest in things for their own sake . . . sitting there like a lump of pudding. (Orwell 1939/1987: 11, 136, 146)

The lower-middle-class suburban woman, as seen by Taylor and Orwell, is composed from a set of markers that represent her as sexually undesirable and passive, acquisitive and unthinking. While we may find the tone of these writings unpleasant in the twenty-first century, Orwell and Taylor were not unusual in writing of the lower-middle classes, particularly women, in this way. It is also important to note that describing suburban domesticity as stultifying and degrading was not the prerogative of male writers. As Light has pointed out the 'suburban' woman was equally scorned by writers like Jan Struther and feminists like Vera Brittain (Light 1991: 218). Brittain condemned 'the socially irresponsible woman, who does not want to use her mind or to take any part in disinterested service' for using domesticity as 'a way of escape from public obligation similar to that of the "escape into illness" indulged in by the self-centred neurotic' (Berry and Bishop 1985: 143). However, rather than focusing on the obvious dislike of the women thus described it is more fruitful to ask what anxieties about suburbia and femininity are being articulated in these denigrating accounts of suburban wives.

The spread of a suburban lifestyle to the lower-middle and working classes in the first half of the twentieth century was a form of modernity that was not of middle-class making. It represented a threat geographically to the middle-class 'ownership' of the suburbs that had until the late nineteenth and early twentieth century remained largely undisturbed. Socially and culturally it appeared to challenge the social order as, for example, the erstwhile servants of middle-class women might democratically own houses and call themselves 'housewives' along with their ex-employers. It is possible to make sense of Orwell's contempt for the suburban woman once we begin to understand her as typifying a kind of modernity that does not fit the (white, masculine) narratives of modern life. Both *Coming Up for Air* and 'The Suburban Neurosis' work to confine the suburban woman within a network of significations that can only visualise her as 'neurotic', materialistic, a nag or shrew, unable to transcend the tedious routines of everyday life. To represent her as shrewish, acquisitive, unattractive, and lacking any kind of lively intelligence is to assign her a despised place in the canonical narratives of a small group of the (frequently) public-school-educated intelligensia and thus to render her modernity invisible.

While the foregoing may go some way towards unravelling the class tensions in Orwell's text it does not entirely help us to make sense of his use of a *female* figure as a symbol for all that is constraining and stifling about suburban domesticity. To explore this further I want to consider the relationship between mass culture and gender. Andreas Huyssen argues that the 'gender inscriptions in the mass culture debate' that began in the late nineteenth and early twentieth century, positioned woman 'as reader of inferior literature – subjective, emotional and passive – while man . . . emerges as writer of genuine, authentic literature – objective, ironic and in control of his aesthetic means' (1986: 190). Hence, the (male) 'artist-philosopher-hero, the suffering loner who stands in irreconcilable opposition to modern democracy and its inauthentic culture' also stands in opposition to the feminine characteristics ascribed to that 'inauthentic' mass culture (Huyssen, 1986: 194). Furthermore, as Huyssen argues, the identification of femininity with mass culture 'in this age of declining liberalism is always also a fear of woman, a fear of nature out of control, a fear of the unconscious, of sexuality, of the loss of identity and stable ego boundaries in the mass' (1986: 196). George Bowling's vision of being pursued by 'a huge army', headed by Hilda and his children, shouting 'There's a chap who thinks he's going to escape! There's a chap who says he won't be stream-lined!' expresses precisely those fears of being engulfed by the (feminine) mass that Huyssen describes (Orwell 1939/1987: 171). For Orwell, the feminisation of George Bowling in suburbia and his abortive attempts to escape, symbolise a whole culture gone 'soft' and decadent. George Bowling may not be an artist or genius but he is equally in danger of being 'corrupted' by the 'feminised' mass culture of suburbia that, in Orwell's view, is smothering and paralysing. Such views were formed from the classed and gendered subjectivities that constitute the collective psyche that underpins the narrowly conceived modernist aesthetic of a handful of white, usually male artists.[7]

However, as I have noted, George Bowling is not 'the artist-philosopher-hero' standing outside the culture he critiques but is, himself, part of the problem in his tendency towards apathy and passivity. While *Coming Up for Air* draws on auto-biographical elements (Lower Binfield for example is based on Henley-on-Thames where Orwell spent his early childhood), George Bowling's voice is not the voice of George Orwell but the voice of 'mass' man speaking to 'the masses' from whom Orwell hoped revolution would come. Orwell did not perceive himself as 'femin-ised' in the way he believed the 'masses' were but nor did he see himself as part of the literary intelligensia whom, on occasion, he reviled as 'Nancy poets' (Orwell 1937/1986: 31). Throughout his life he forcefully asserted a certain form of masculinity, as manifested in his commitment to a straightforward ('manly') style of writing, in his dislike of effeminacy and in his ambivalent feelings towards women.[8] Orwell, like George Bowling, was of a generation of boys who were young adolescents during the First World War and were thus excluded from active service. As such he grew to adulthood in the years immediately after the war when the heroic masculinity that had sustained dreams of Empire and 'adventure' was seriously compromised by the horrors of trench warfare and the ineptitude, as it was perceived, of the nation's rulers. Neither heroes nor survivors, this generation found itself excluded from an older Victorian masculinity but without a blueprint from which to reformulate 'modern' versions of what it meant to be a man. The heroism of the boys' adventure stories in magazines like *Gem* and *Magnet*, read by the young George Bowling, was less tenable after 1918. As he observes '[n]obody believed the atrocity stories and the gallant little Belgium stuff any longer . . . After that unspeakable idiotic mess you couldn't go on regarding society as something eternal and unquestionable, like a pyramid. You knew it was just a balls-up' (Orwell 1939/1987: 123). One of the things George Bowling is seeking in his return to Lower Binfield is his lost boyhood in which the promise of an achieved masculinity was curtailed by the outbreak of war. *Coming Up for Air* makes visible not only anxieties about femininity but the loss of a certain form of imperialist masculinity that must have sharpened those anxieties.

It is in the ambivalent treatment of Elsie, George Bowling's first love, that fears about femininity surface most forcefully. George tells us that he will always be grateful to Elsie 'because she was the first person who taught me to care about a woman' (Orwell 1939/1987: 103). The atmosphere of the draper's shop where he first meets her is 'peculiarly feminine' and Elsie, leaning against the counter, is 'curiously soft, curiously feminine' (Orwell 1939/1987: 103). But the femininity that attracts George has more to do with the possibility of possession and domin-ance than 'care': '[a]s soon as you saw her you knew that you could take her in your arms and do what you wanted with her. She was really deeply feminine, very gentle, very submissive, the kind that would always do what a man told her, though she wasn't small or weak' (Orwell 1939/1987: 103–4). The scene in the woods when they first make love confirms Elsie's submissive femininity: 'she looked . . . kind of soft, kind of yielding, as though her body was a kind of malleable stuff that you could do what you liked with. She was mine and I could have her, this minute if I wanted to' (Orwell 1939/1987: 105). The relationship with Elsie comes to an abrupt end with the outbreak of war and George does not see her again until he returns to Lower Binfield when 'the girl I'd known, with her milky-white skin and red mouth and kind of dull-gold hair, had turned into this great round-shouldered hag, shambling along on twisted heels' (Orwell 1939/1987: 204). The narrative structure of the novel requires that Elsie, who symbolises, along with the giant carp in Upper Binfield woods, the possibility of combating 'inauthenticity' via a return to a pre-twentieth century rural world of 'natural' impulses, has to disappoint George, but it is hard to see why the transformation of Elsie is so vicious unless we read her as the repository of her creator's ambivalence about femininity. This is borne out by his equally cruel treatment of Hilda, who in her sexual frigidity occupies the opposite position to Elsie's promiscuous sexuality. The text suggests that femininity, like the nostalgia that drew George to Lower Binfield, is an illusion, behind which lies the same ugliness that has touched every aspect of the modern world.

Orwell's essay on his experience of prep school, 'Such, Such Were the Joys', has the following passage,

> At five or six, like many children I had passed through a phase of sexuality. My friends were the plumber's children up the road, and we used sometimes to play games of a vaguely erotic kind. One was called 'playing at doctors', and I remember getting a faint but definitely pleasant thrill from holding a toy trumpet, which was supposed to be a stethoscope, against a little girl's belly. About the same time I fell deeply in love, a far more worshipping kind of love than I have ever felt for anyone since, with a girl named Elsie at the convent school which I attended. She seemed to me grown up, so I suppose she must have been fifteen. After that, as so often happens, all sexual feelings seemed to go out of me for many years. (cited in Crick 1982: 51)

Bernard Crick warns against accepting this essay as factual truth, suggesting that the relationship between fact and fiction in Orwell's autobiographical writings is a complex one (Crick 1982: 40–5). Nevertheless, the 'worshipping kind' of first love and the subsequent turning away from sexual feelings are re-imagined and re-worked in *Coming Up for Air* in ways that suggest Orwell's discomfort with femininity, the 'masses', and modernity. The figure of Elsie invokes a nostalgic desire for an imagined femininity that is linked to an Edenic world of nature and childhood, a femininity that has been distorted by the suburban modernity that has destroyed Lower Binfield and whose representatives are the sexually repressed and mean-spirited Hilda, and the sluttish, worn down adult Elsie. The problem for

Orwell is that while his hopes for the future are pinned on the 'decency of the ordinary man', he, like many intellectuals of his time, despises 'the masses'. As John Carey has persuasively argued, the 'masses' is a construct that served the ideological purposes of a threatened intelligensia, '[t]he mass, that is to say, is a metaphor for the unknowable and invisible' and 'acquires definition through the imposition of imagined attributes' (Carey 1992: 21). For Orwell the 'masses' who inhabit Ellesmere Road and suburbanised Lower Binfield are a disappointment. They prefer consumer pleasures to political action and are motivated by narrow materialistic needs. Orwell's solution in *Coming Up for Air* is to give us the voice of an individuated, ordinary, albeit flawed, man who is thereby rescued from the dehumanised 'mass', while at the same time projecting everything he despises about suburban modernity onto Hilda, Elsie and what he sees as the feminisation of twentieth-century culture.

Space, Place and Time in Women's Experiences of Suburban Domesticity and Everyday Life[9]

I want now to consider the stories of four working-class women and to ask how they experienced everyday modernity, space and time. In doing so I am placing these personal narratives in dialogue with the public representations of suburban and metropolitan space and time that have been discussed earlier in this chapter. Recalling her aspirations as a young woman growing up in the first decades of the twentieth century, Eileen Hutchings said, 'you had to save so hard to get your home together and there was this trend to move from the background and life, not that it wasn't a good one, to something just that little bit better'. Eileen was the daughter of a grocer, her mother was in domestic service and she grew up in a terraced house near the centre of York. After a courtship that lasted seven years, she married a shopkeeper with whom she bought a semi-detached house in the suburbs. While her childhood was not marred by the drunkenness or abject poverty that damaged the lives of many, nevertheless she dreamt of a better life in which 'getting your home together' symbolised the security and belonging that could only infrequently and precariously be achieved in working-class life. And she recognised that the way to achieve this was through prudential marriage:

Interviewer: What did you look for in a husband?

EH: A good deal of stability . . . a decent lad, who you didn't expect to take advantage of you, who was easy on the drink and that sort of thing. He would be of a good stable character . . . not fly-by-nights. You had good lasting relationships which barely touched on sex because you knew very well that one day things would come right and you'd marry and settle down and that was it. And have children.

Eileen's aspirations are the product of the historical moment that she inhabits. Post-First World War reconstruction had as its rallying-cry, 'Homes Fit for Heroes', a slogan that encompassed two underlying assumptions of housing policy in the 1920s and 30s. First, a decent home was just reward for the suffering that had been endured by servicemen, '[t]o let them come home from horrible, water-logged trenches to something little better than a pigsty here would, indeed, be criminal . . . and a negation of all we have said during the war, that we can never repay those men for what they have done for us' (Burnett 1986: 219–20).

Second, the provision of decent homes was seen as the basis of social progress and social harmony and essential if the nation was to rear a stable and healthy citizenry. In 1919 King George V, speaking to representatives of the local authorities, spelt this out with considerable force:

> [I]t is not too much to say that an adequate solution of the housing question is the foundation of all social progress . . . The first point at which the attack must be delivered is the unhealthy, ugly, overcrowded house in the mean street, which all of us know too well. If a healthy race is to be reared, it can be reared only in healthy homes; if drink and crime are to be successfully combated, decent, sanitary houses must be provided; if 'unrest' is to be converted into contentment, the provision of good houses may prove one of the most potent agents in that conversion. (cited in Burnett 1986: 219)

The provision of new houses was not only the result of social conscience. The aftermath of war revealed a housing shortage of 600,000 houses in 1918 and 805,000 by 1921, a shortage that it was felt was beyond the means of private enterprise to supply (Burnett 1986: 220). The solution was a partnership between state and local authority to provide housing for returning servicemen and later for those who lost their homes as a result of slum clearance schemes. Eileen Hutchings may have only been dimly aware of the debates about housing policy but the post-First World War social agenda enabled her to understand herself as belonging to a world in which it was not unreasonable to aspire to an improved standard of material living. The importance of an emerging culture in which millions of women were invited to believe that a decent home was a very real possibility cannot be over-estimated.

The development of English suburbia, whether by private enterprise or local authority schemes, did not simply produce new meanings about home ownership and domesticity; these estates came into being, in part, because of new meanings in the period about home and family, about social responsibility and about citizenship. For example the growth of suburbia after 1918 was no longer simply about providing homes for middle-class families anxious to escape the dirt, overcrowding and crime of the cities but was linked to changing aspirations in the working and lower-middle classes that were themselves constituted in a matrix of factors: improved educational opportunities, new employment prospects, higher wages, the advent of cinema and radio, the broadening of horizons for those who had spent time abroad during the war, increased leisure time and a growth in home-based leisure (Langhamer 2000). It was also connected to the politics of social welfare: a social agenda concerned to alleviate ill health and poverty saw the home as a prime site where this could occur and women as the agents of such improvements. The principle of state intervention in the provision of housing was about this but it was also about the extension of democratic rights to all its citizens. Suburbia after 1918 comprised a number of forms: local authority housing for returning service-men and for those moved out of the inner-city areas; private large semi-detached houses and detached houses for upper-middle-class families who preferred to live away from the city; and smaller, privately built, semi-detacheds for those of the working class and lower-middle classes who could afford them. Suburbanisation offered opportunities to millions of people that would have been unthinkable to previous generations. Suburban modernity for women like Eileen was about the pride of being, at last, worthy of citizenship and was, I would argue, as significant as the vote in enabling people to see themselves as full members of a modern society.

Joyce Storey, a working-class woman from Bristol, writing about life after the Second World War, conveys the excitement of planning a future in her brand new council house:

> I wandered upstairs to view the bedrooms and to stand at the door to look around and imagine all of them carpeted and furnished in different colour schemes. When I came to the bathroom, this to me was the ultimate in luxury. Never in my whole life had I lived in a house with a bathroom. At South Road and at Repton Road, the tin bath was housed on the wall in the back yard and hung on a six inch nail, usually opposite the privy door, which was also outside. No more having to drag it down every week and boil up saucepans of hot water to have a bath. I closed my eyes in sheer ecstasy. Just thinking about it brought a feeling of pride at the thought of owning a bathroom. There was more. There was a toilet upstairs next to the bathroom and another in the garden along with a coalhouse and a shed. No more chamber pots under the bed and the drudgery of having to toil up and down the stairs with slop pails to empty the wretched things. I made my way down the stairs once more and into the kitchen. I opened drawers and cupboards, making little squeals of delight at the discovery of all the light and various up-to-date drawer space. (1992: 164)

For Joyce modernity means a bathroom, an indoor toilet and 'up-to-date drawer space'. These things not only signify a better quality of daily life but they distance her from a past in which she was placed in a subordinate relationship to those who had never had to empty chamber pots or boil up water for baths. Joyce's 'owner-ship' (as a council tenant she only rented the house and its fitments) of a bath is a source of pride and dignity in a world that had until that point granted her, and those like her, little of either. Later, in the early 1960s, she gets the opportunity to buy her council house and recalls her confusion at a friend's response to this. Her friend accuses her of being 'no better than a snob' and a traitor to socialism:

> For a minute or two I stood there feeling confused and uncertain. Yes, I did want a fairer world and equal chances for all, but that surely didn't mean I had to live in poverty all my life myself? I really could see Vi's point of view, but I also wanted all those things which made life comfortable and bearable. I was fed up with bare boards and lino; I wanted all the luxuries of life. I really did. (Storey 1995: 89)

Modernity for Joyce was experienced in the domestic and the suburban spaces in which she lived her everyday life. Like many women, Joyce suffered frustration, depression and constraint in her domestic role; baths and indoor toilets do not solve everything. But, she also sees in the realisation of her material aspirations a sense of self-worth and possibilities for individual creativity that were hitherto unavailable. The provision of well-ventilated, well-lit and hygienic housing for those previously relegated to overcrowded and insanitary living conditions must have been understood by many as a long overdue recognition of their right to the benefits of progress. To be allocated a house by the agencies of the state or offered a mortgage by the financiers of capitalism could be understood as a powerful statement of entry into full citizenship for women like Joyce and Eileen. It is not coincidental that, at the precise moment when ordinary people were able to claim some of the benefits of modernisation as markers of their newly-acquired social status, those most threatened by the increasing democratisation of society and culture began to attack mass culture and suburbia as 'feminine' and, therefore, in their terms, inferior. The discourses of technological and scientific progress offered the idea of a 'better' material life, symbolised in the post-Second World War figure of the housewife in her newly built, labour-saving council house freed from disease and want. But the moment at which the lower-middle or working-class woman gained access to some of the material privileges previously denied her is also the moment at which the desire for commodities is roundly condemned:

> The suburban woman has made a fetish of her home. She is aiming at the kind of lifestyle successfully led by people to whom books, theatres and things of intellect matter. To them, home is a necessary part of life, but only part. To her, because she does not see the rest, the home looks like everything, and she wonders why it does not bring her the happiness it appears to bring them. (Taylor 1938: 237)

While suburban modernity may have offered many women opportunities for a better standard of everyday life and the chance to see themselves as full members of modern society, there were nevertheless losses. Gender and class hierarchies continued to produce deferential, self-denying, envious and angry subjectivities in those who found themselves the objects of masculine and middle-class scrutiny. And all the women I interviewed expressed, in varying degrees, regret for the passing of the older street or rural communities that suburbia replaced although for most this was a price that was willingly paid for the benefits of piped water and indoor toilets. There were other losses too in a world where progress was uneven and where poverty and ill health continued alongside hygienic homes and pleasanter environments.

Jean Slater was born in 1924 in Preston. Jean's mother died when she was nine and a stepmother, who died in 1940 when Jean was sixteen, brought her up. After the death of her stepmother Jean, having just left the local grammar school, took over the care of the family as well as working as a wages clerk in a munitions factory. She describes in some detail the hard work involved in cooking, washing and keeping house for six men – she lived with her father, four brothers and grandfather. After a year of this drudgery Jean collapsed:

> I was not, no I didn't really have much of a teenage, I mean I didn't leave school you see until I was sixteen and then I just had twelve months working in the office of the munitions factory at Exton. I was a wages clerk and then I mean I just collapsed. I was, would be travelling every morning and trying to do the house and everything and I had to give up work and that was my only working experience and then I was just at home you see with my father. It was, it was good, we had a good, a marvellous home life.

Later, she brought her cousin to live with her when she was dying of cancer and nursed her through her last illness. Jean married in 1945. On her honeymoon at Ambleside:

> the very first morning we were married we were walking into Ambleside and he [husband] collapsed and went in a diabetic coma so then we brought, I got the doctor and we brought him round and went back to the hotel and rang home and said we were having a marvellous time, a lovely place, lovely hotel, we're having a lovely time (*laughs*), didn't tell anybody . . . So yes that was the beginning of – as I say we only had twenty years – he died in '66 and we married in '45, twenty years. But eventually it just attacked all the organs of his body, kidney and eyes and everything and as I say he died in '45.

The slip over dates ('he died in '45') suggests the pain and trauma that lie beneath Jean's consistent attempts to deny the magnitude of her losses. After her husband's death Jean ran a tobacconist's shop, worked for the Samaritans, opened a charity shop and became a registrar of births, marriages and deaths. She turned the large house they had bought into flats and worked very hard to make a living for herself and her six children. In recent years she has enjoyed a full life, unmarked by financial worries and closely involved with her children, grandchildren and great-grandchildren. Jean's earlier life was marked by death and loss – first her mother, then her stepmother, followed by her husband, her father, and her cousin. Jean's narrative structures her life around the births, illnesses and deaths of family members. Most notable is the way in which she constantly returns to the death of her mother. Alongside the insistent presence of loss in the story Jean tells there is an equally powerful reiteration that 'they were happy days'. Jean's memory in the context of the interview consistently processes the past as a happy time cut off and separate from her current life. I want to explore this apparent contradiction in the light of ideas about nostalgic desire and the politics of nostalgia as well as in terms of the historical context of loss and death that shaped the cultural landscape of Jean's childhood and young adulthood.

Transience, fragmentation and loss are recurrent motifs in the twentieth-century critique of progress. The optimism characteristic of the mid nineteenth century was severely challenged by the growth of nationalist ideologies and the wars fought in their name, the social disruptions occasioned by the mass migration of people to the new locations of city and suburb, and an increase in bureaucracy and rationalism in the name of 'national efficiency' (O'Shea 1996). Jean's story reminds us that for many people transience and fragmentation were not only occasioned by the public events of twentieth-century history but were also aspects of a daily and local life, structured by the modernising forces of technology, industrialism and urbanism. Two world wars, the high infant and maternal mortality rate, poverty, ill health and disease marked the psyches of all who lived close to such conditions (Alexander 1994: 241; Giles 1995: 34–6). Death was an ever present reality and the untimely loss of a parent, child, friend or relative remained a very real possibility in ways with which those born since 1945 are unfamiliar. After the First World War the emotional worlds inhabited by women included caring for and loving men with dreadful wounds and missing limbs, men who were traumatised and shell-shocked, men who drank to anaesthetise the injuries of war. They also included the possibilities of physical violence and infection from a syphilitic partner.[10] Jean's subjectivity is produced from her sense of the fragility and transience of life, expressed in her litany of death and disease, but also from her struggle, in such circumstances, to believe in a purposeful universe and to deny the magnitude of her losses. One manifestation of this deeply felt conflict is a desire to understand random coincidence and chance encounters as meaningful. For example when asked about the first time she met her husband-to-be she answered:

Well you see there wouldn't be a first time as such because we'd all grown up together, in fact his father and my mother were both in Mount Street Hospital together at the same time and at this stage neither of us knew each other we were both, 'cos as I say my mother died when I was nine and it was when she was in at that time and his father was in and I only learnt this years and years and years later, the nun that was there used to go to his father and say there's a lady in the ladies ward very very poorly, pray for her, she's going, she's very very poorly and she has a lot of children like you, and she used go to my mother and say the same thing, his father recovered, my mother died. Yes, yes, you see his aunt was the Reverend Mother of Mount Street Hospital and of course it all came back afterwards about this, about my mum and his dad being in together.

In this respect Jean's relationship to time is cyclical and repetitive but to characterise this as uncreative and, in De Beauvoir's words, 'only a duplication of the past' is to miss the ways in which the repetitions, coincidences and cycles of everyday life could offer a bulwark against the constant threat of separation and loss. Jean's sense of time is a complex mix of the linear and the cyclical. For example, the birth of her daughter in 1946 is celebrated in her story as the culmination of the cycle of suffering and reproduction that began with her honeymoon and ended with the birth of her child. At the same time Jean recognises the symbolic significance of this birth in historical terms. The film *A Diary for Timothy*, directed by Humphrey Jennings and released in 1946, records the closing stages of the war through a diary that is being kept for a newly born baby. The idea being, of course, that the new baby represents the future, a new world, hopes for a lasting peace, and the film charts the social reconstruction that is required to achieve this. Jean sees the birth of her daughter in a similar way, significant in the linear march of history as well as part of a natural and cyclical process.

Janus-faced, Jean's story looks in two directions. On the one hand her story moves inexorably forward to a future in which modern homes and improved health care render death and illness less prevalent. On the other hand these improvements lead to the dispersal of families and to the break up of those communities that had produced a sense of 'home' and kinship. The creation of a powerful sense of belonging is one of the ways in which subordinate groups may resist denigration, marginalisation and invisibility. Jean's story constantly looks back to a golden past that is remembered in terms of family, community and home and is by definition set in contrast to a less preferred modern present, 'it was a happy time, it was very happy, I had a very very happy home life, it, people say, gosh you know, it must have been hard, maybe I don't know maybe because it was hard that we had such a happy home because we had to pull together'. I want to ask whether the nostalgia evidenced by Jean's story can be seen as simply a desire to escape an intolerable present or whether it has a more active and productive function.[11] Jean's memories of her mother stand as a metaphorical representation of all that she has lost, 'I just remember this lovely person always being there, she was always there when we came home from school . . . I always remember this lovely bubbly chubby lady always being there you know for us when we came in from school.' If, in essentialist accounts, femininity acts as a signifier for a golden age of wholeness and gratification then the figure of the mother offers not only psychic regression to maternal plenitude but also a temporal and spatial return to the secure past of childhood and to the private world of the home. However, in Jean's story Jean not only desires the mother she has lost but *becomes* herself the lost mother for the rest of the family, returning to domesticity and the home, not as the child she once was but as the potential object of the nostalgic dreams of others. Jean's nostalgia for 'the good old days', symbolised by the figure of her lost mother, carries different meanings from those accounts in which the maternal feminine is yearned for as an escape from an intolerable present. Jean constructs her sense of self, and the story she tells about that self, by replacing the lost mother with herself. In this way the desiring subject fuses with the desired object; past and present are linked and integrated: while Jean yearns for the 'happy days' of maternal plenitude these do not exist in some hermetically sealed zone of memory that remains untouched by the present. Jean uses those elements of femininity that she loved in her mother as a way of creating an emotional continuity that links the generations. It is worth noting in this context that Jean's children's memories of childhood also centre on the mother who was there when they came home from school. The values of maternalism and kinship that characterise the past in her memories are appropriated and function to construct a modern present that offers dignity and purpose. For Jean 'home' functions as a signifier of belonging and security but also as a space where the best of both past and present can meet to provide, as she sees it, a 'better' future for her children and grandchildren.

However, it would be a mistake to understand this nostalgia as an uncomplicated site of utopian dreams. Yearning for the past can all too easily ignore or gloss over 'the oppressive dimensions of the past' (Felski 1995: 59). Home, although Jean repeatedly attempts to deny this, was also a place of loss, despair and anxiety, of hard work and tedious drudgery. She comments, 'we are so close, you say, you kick one and they all limp you know, but I think it's because, when you're left like that you have to cling together, you have to bring each other up, you do get close and it makes, yes it's hard, it's hard work but it makes for a happy home'. 'Kick', 'cling', 'limp' suggest a dependency based on injury and fear rather than the stoical solidarity evoked in accounts of working-class life in which tough and canny matriarchs presided over a community bound together by common hopes and aspirations. Social mobility and the dispersal of families and communities throughout the twentieth century has meant that 'home' in all its senses is less easily identifiable and can become more eagerly sought. The sense of solidarity and belonging generated by a social network based on family, kinship and local connections is one of the losses mourned by Jean. Throughout her narrative she remembers the close connections that flourished in her neighbourhood:

> [When I got married] everybody chipped all the coupons in for material for my dresses which I had made. It was made by a friend of the Slater family who was a dressmaker and my old granny lived just round the corner from us and with one of her daughters,

an aunt of mine who was a nurse, my mother's this is my real mother, my own mother's sister and she took, she took me in hand you know and took me out and bought me all my wedding outfits and honeymoon suit and everything, you know, to go away with. And my godmother worked at the Tokyo Café where my dad worked so we did get, the Tokyo Café for our reception which was nice.

As discussed above the break up of local communities as people moved out to the new suburban estates or were re-housed as part of slum clearance schemes was paralleled by a systematic denigration of the new 'homes' acquired by women like Jean. If we understand Jean's yearning for the 'good old days' as both a search for belonging and an attempt to minimise the impact of her many bereavements, it becomes possible to read her nostalgia as one of the ways in which she actively attempts to make herself at home in a world that appears to her to have been dominated by disease and death. Her perception of family and kinship as 'clinging together' in a world of violence and pain expresses a subjectivity formed from loss and separation. In such circumstances yearning for what has been lost may drive the desire to build new forms of 'home' that provide security and plenitude for future generations. Despite the geographical and social mobility of her own children, Jean continues to foster close networks and strong links through family reunions and shared meals and she also makes full use of modern technologies in order to maintain contact with her large and dispersed family. For Jean, the loss of community and loved ones, contingent upon modernisation, is managed through idealised memories, that provide emotional models for the present. In turn these models can be practically enabled through the use of modern communication systems and forms of transport.

Finally, I want to discuss the story told to me by Hannah Armstrong. Hannah was born in a small village on the North Yorkshire moors in 1920. Her father was a stonemason and her mother took in sewing in order to supplement the family's income. Hannah had eight brothers and sisters: the girls went into service and the boys into farming. During the war Hannah joined the Land Army in Kent but returned to North Yorkshire after the war where she married Fred. Fred was ten years older than her and described by her as 'an honourable man'. He worked as a postman until ill health caused his retirement. Fred and Hannah had one child, born when Hannah was thirty-eight. Whilst Hannah enjoyed homemaking and motherhood she does not represent herself as a maternal carer in the way Jean does. Hannah presents herself as a fun-loving young woman who was looking for adventure and new experiences. But beneath the cheerful exterior that is presented as the 'composed' self there are hints of displacement; dislocation from the social milieu in which she grew up and, before and during her marriage, a certain discon-nection from the sexual needs of her body.

After leaving school at fourteen Hannah went to work as a house parlourmaid at the North Yorkshire holiday home of a Harley Street gynaecologist. Just before the outbreak of war she and her sister were recruited to work in the London home of the doctor and his wife. Hannah recalls this move from Yorkshire to London as an adventure, 'so now I'm in London in this posh furnished flat [unintelligible] and me a little lass from Danby right in the middle of London'.[12] For Hannah the move was important because it introduced her to 'the world of the gentry' which she loved. When she and her sister heard Chamberlain's announcement of war on the radio with the doctor and his wife what seems to have most impressed her was the fact that she was 'in good company, we were sort of listening to good conversation'. Hannah was deferential and acutely aware of class differences: her father is described as 'an ordinary little man' and she is 'a little lass from Danby' whilst the doctor is described as 'gentry' and doctor to a relative of royalty. She recalls that she and her sister were 'good material because we more or less didn't mind doing as we were told, we'd rather be told, oh and I loved it'. However, Hannah soon left this employment to join the Land Army where she had a wonderful time free from the constraints of home and service. At the end of the war she returned to North Yorkshire and went to work in the 'mantle department' of a new department store. In 1951 she married and in 1958 gave birth to her son and only child.

Throughout the interview Hannah reminds the interviewer that she is telling a story: 'Aah now, this is how the story evolves actually if you can wait'; 'Well I'll tell you in a minute if you give me long enough, because it's all part of the story.' In telling the story Hannah draws, in part, on 'rags to riches' narratives in which 'a little lass from Danby' finds herself in the metropolitan milieu of wartime London and later in, what she recalls as, the carefree world of the Land Army. Her story is not, however, simply one of mobility and the widening of social horizons, it is also about awakening sexuality. Clothes play an important role as props in the performance that constitutes Hannah's dramatised self. As a housemaid in 'good' service she wears a 'frilly apron'; at the dance where she meets her future husband she is wearing 'a lime green dress with gold embroidery'; in the Land Army she can't wait to throw off her 'khaki drill three-quarter length jacket' at the end of the day and change into her dancing clothes. Even before she left North Yorkshire Hannah loved the glamour and excitement of the dance hall, dressing up to attract 'some nice lad or a scruffy lad or a farmhand. They weren't always, but they were all very friendly and there was no performing, there was no silly business went on, just a giggle.' In telling her story Hannah represents herself in terms of the conventions governing certain forms of femininity in the 1940s. She presents herself as sexually attractive, willing to flirt and cuddle on the backseat at the cinema but always aware of protecting her 'reputation' – heterosexual relationships were not to be taken too seriously and were 'just a giggle'.

In Hannah's narrative sexual awakening and a desire for social status merge. She recalls of her time working for the gynaecologist in Harley Street how, 'I loved him . . . I worshipped him, I thought he was quite wonderful and he was very kind to me, he was, in fact we had so much between us that when we were serving at tables and I was stood at the trolley with my gravy whatever, and he would just look and I'd know what he meant.' The unspoken communion Hannah recalls between herself and her employer draws upon narratives of heterosexual romantic love in which a powerful attraction exists between a wealthy older man and a younger, poorer woman. Hannah was an avid reader of women's magazine fiction and a frequent cinema-goer whose favourite film was *Random Harvest* (1942).[13] Such narratives offered a fantasy space in which young working-class women could imagine a world in which their longings for sexual gratification and material security would be met. However, there was concern in the 1940s that young women, like Hannah, were being offered false aspirations by such popular fictions:[14]

> The air is heavy with the dream-world longings of young people who come from homes where money is hard to come by. Such tales strengthen girls' convictions that they would be bound to have a good time and be happy if only they could be rich . . . The girls know that the world which *Red Star Weekly* presents is quite unlike the real world: but they hope that perhaps some of all this glamour may come their way. It is just possible that the boss's son may ask them to marry him, or a pilot officer may invite them to his father's country mansion next week-end. (Jephcott 1943: 109–110)[15]

The censorious tone of such pronouncements testifies to a deeply-held anxiety on the part of middle-class observers that working-class female sexuality constituted a powerful threat to class boundaries. Sexual liaisons between middle-class men and working-class women were surrounded by eugenic and patrilineal fears but they were also a source of anxiety for middle-class women whose privileged social and domestic position might be weakened if the barriers separating the classes were breached. Hannah may have fostered romantic longings for her employer but she was also acutely aware of her 'place' and the dangers of 'getting a reputation'.

Hannah loved dancing and during her time in the Land Army attended dance halls regularly. She met her future husband at a dance and was still attending dances at the time of the interview when she was seventy-nine. Middle-class observers were as concerned with the effects of dance halls as they were with the influence of cinema and magazines. Pearl Jephcott argued that the dance hall offered, 'a very considerable measure of emotional excitement' and made 'little demand on the dancer's mental capacity' for 'thoughts are nowhere directed to anything apart from the bodily movements of the moment and the person with whom one is in contact. The syncopated music . . . the lowered lights, and the excitement of all the new contacts mean that for many young adolescents, the sex instinct is being over-stimulated at precisely the age when this should be avoided' (1943: 124–5). During the war one of the fears was that British girls would 'take up' with American or Canadian soldiers stationed in Britain and dance halls were seen as one of the prime locations where such liaisons might be encouraged (Jephcott 1943: 123). Hannah recalls dancing and flirting with American and British soldiers but she is always careful to represent these encounters as 'just a giggle' and herself as a 'good' girl who never succumbed to sexual temptation. Nevertheless, her narrative draws on wartime mythologies that represented American soldiers as dangerous, sexual beings in comparison to the safety and familiarity of British men. For Hannah, however, the sexual danger is represented as attractive, rather than threatening, and hints at possibilities that could be exciting to a 'little lass from Danby', 'well I mean they were most attractive during the war, the Americans, the first time I'd seen a fellow's bottom, I don't mean a bare one no, cos their uniforms used to fit the bottom, well all the British soldiers wore baggy things'.

Hannah's narrative divides neatly into two halves, organised around movement between places. The first period includes her time in London and in the Land Army and the second half recounts her return to Yorkshire and her marriage. Working in Harley Street and serving in the Land Army were 'adventures' for Hannah: adventures that extended her knowledge geographically, socially and sexually. When she returned to Yorkshire she felt herself to be something of an outsider, a sense of self that manifested itself in the language she spoke and in her relations to the local men:

> I acquired a slightly silver tongue. I think the young men of Danby were a bit in awe of me . . . I think so. I'm not quite sure but I didn't get many offers (*laughs*) when I came back. Well I'd acquired this slightly different accent cos, only because I didn't want to stand out . . . I thought I was trying to speak the Queen's English to fit in with the southern people, cos there's a terrible gap between Maidstone and Yorkshire.

In due course Hannah met her husband, Fred. He was ten years older and she described him as 'a lovely honourable man, not desperately exciting, he didn't jump over the moon every day but'. The marriage was a reasonably happy one but as Hannah tells it there are hints of loss and alienation after the 'adventures' of her early life. Fred was a dull but good husband and Hannah appears to have found an outlet for her strong feelings in her love for her son who 'was the treasure of my life' and made 'waking up every morning a pleasure'. Sexual mores of the period required that in marrying an 'honourable' man Hannah suppress any expression of those romantic or sexual longings that had been awakened by her earlier 'adventures'. She concludes her story thus,

> yes, well I had this happiness inside me and I used to think to myself if only Fred knew, sometimes he'd take the wrong attitude as men do I think, now if he'd only gone one step the other way I'd have been as happy as can be, but you can't expect other people to know what you're thinking.

Hannah's narrative enacts the psychic splits between sexual longing, awareness of her social position and gender identity that formed her subjectivity. Gender norms and sexual mores dictated that in order to achieve the social respectability and material security she desired Hannah, like many women of her class and generation, was forced to suppress 'the happiness inside me'. Working-class women like Hannah were well aware that allowing free rein to their sexuality might jeopardise the material security that was so important in a world where an unwanted pregnancy or a 'bad reputation' could result in poverty or a failure to make the prudent marriage on which a decent standard of living might depend. In Hannah's story opposing terms like safety/danger, home/away, common-sense/'silliness' are all linked to social position and material security and represented in terms of the geographical places, London and Yorkshire, that in turn encode the oppositions metropolitan/provincial.[16] Hannah left 'the bosom of [her] home' to have 'adventures': her return to North Yorkshire is represented as a settling down into marriage and respectability. As she observes about her return, 'I had stopped being flighty'. However, while the two-part structure of Hannah's story encodes a consciousness split between adventure and security, between transcendence and mundanity, this split is never complete: traces of the 'before ' story surface in the later account of marriage and motherhood. For example witness the following exchange:

HA: I never looked at anybody else after Fred. I daren't (*laughs*).

Interviewer: (*Laughs*) What would he have done?

HA: Well you don't do you.

Interviewer: No.

HA: It isn't a question that arises.

Interviewer: No. There's part of your church upbringing or part of your childhood
            erm . . .

HA: Well it's part of your, what you learn at home isn't it.

Interviewer: About being good.

HA: Well I mean they were most attractive during the war, the Americans, the
            first time I'd seen a fellow's bottom . . .

Thinking about marital fidelity triggers memories for Hannah of her wartime experiences and at this point she continues with a long account of how attractive the American soldiers were in their uniforms. She evades the question of what would have happened if she had 'looked at anybody else' and presents marital fidelity as a moral absolute – 'it isn't a question that arises'. Yet immediately she is reminded of powerful sexual feelings that might undermine fidelity or require strict self-control in order to maintain the respectable self she works hard to 'compose'. For Hannah the move to London involved a social dislocation and a sexual awakening – 'a little lass from Danby in the middle of London'. The return to Yorkshire involved a double dislocation. 'The little lass from Danby' now spoke with a 'silver tongue' and was considered 'posh' by those in her community. Equally in order to marry an 'honourable' man a certain disconnection from the needs and desires of her own sexuality was required.

Young women, who grew up as Hannah did in the 1920s and 1930s, experienced a widening of their cultural horizons that had not been possible for their mothers. As we shall see in Chapter 3, the department store, the cinema, the dance hall and the mass production of newspapers, magazines and cheap books offered a kaleidoscope of images, commodities and experiences, representing a world beyond the family, the home and the locality. Moreover, the growth of public and private transport systems allowed women to extend the geographical boundaries of their worlds. Thus, as we shall see in the next chapter, young women were able to escape the tyranny of domestic service as well as the back-breaking drudgery and limitations of their mothers' lives but they frequently did so via the material aspirations of marriage and a commitment to domesticity and respectability. For this generation of young working-class women found themselves, as we have seen, at a specific historical moment when modernising forces in Britain focused on homes and domesticity. By the 1940s, as others have also noted and as will be discussed further in Chapter 3, the ideal British 'citizen' was no longer the jingoistic imperialist of nineteenth-century rhetoric but home-centred and concerned for family (narrowly defined) with aspirations focused on educational opportunities for children and improved housing (Light 1991: 8–9; Alexander 1994: 232–3). As Light comments, 'the true heroics of the Second [World War] were to be found in the actions of "ordinary people" on "the Home Front"' (1991: 9). The feminisation of culture in this turn towards the home, the domestic and the private, whilst undeniably reasserting women's traditional place, nevertheless, rescued home and femininity from an existence outside the institutional and representational structures of modernity. The home, far from being simply a haven from the demands of modern life or a stifling place from which to escape, became central to the modernity of British life at mid-century. The advent of electricity and labour-saving technologies, the possibility of home-ownership and the trend towards smaller families made full-time housewifery a far more attractive option to women than in the past. Marriage to a home-centred man with a steady income who didn't drink or gamble offered a level of material security and ease that had been missing from many childhoods. Aspiring towards prudential marriage and the provision of a comfortable, hygienic home in which to sustain a male breadwinner and rear healthy children was a rational choice made by many working-class women in a world in which poverty, ill health and exclusion so often pre-dominated (Giles 1995).

It has been suggested to me that women might also understand 'prudential' marriage as one in which they did not experience physical or sexual abuse.[17] For many women modernity may have been understood, not simply as material improvement, but also as emotional and sexual 'betterment'. From the start of the century, and particularly after the First World War, ideas about companionship and pleasurable sex between married couples began to circulate (Gillis 1997: 148–9). Allied to the spread of effective birth control these ideas produced 'modern' concepts of love and courtship. Marriage was no longer simply a matter of convenience but became inextricably linked to romantic love. Books like Edward Griffith's *Modern Marriage and Birth Control*, published by the Left Book Club, proclaimed the importance of spiritual and sexual union as the only basis for a successful marriage (Griffith 1938). While working-class women like Hannah, Joyce, Jean or Eileen would have been unlikely to read such material, changing ideas about marriage and relationships began to construct high expectations of 'love' and partnership. The nineteenth-century belief that women's sexual appetite was far smaller than men's had been challenged by the early twentieth century through the work of Freud and Havelock Ellis. Marriage manuals stressed the importance of both partners achieving satisfactory sex, but alongside this went a new stress on the husband's responsibility for exercising restraint as the means to this end. 'Demanding' or 'inconsiderate' husbands were frequently rebuked in popular self-help manuals:

> If he has little idea of sex technique or thinks that by simply following his own ill-controlled instincts, and insisting upon his 'rights' at all times, all will be well, he may seal his fate for ever . . . There are times and seasons when the woman is attracted or indifferent, or even repelled. Here a young husband must take care to avoid any act which would lead to a habit of unhappy responses being set up. (Edynbury 1938: 196)

For working-class women, growing up in the first half of the century, such ideas could offer a space in which it was acceptable to limit family size in order to aspire to a better quality of life at the same time as making it less acceptable for husbands to physically or sexually abuse their wives. Changing expectations about what constituted the 'proper' relations between men and women allowed millions of women the self-respect and dignity that comes from being seen as worthy of care and consideration. Ellen Holtzmann has suggested that, at least for middle-class women, a shift was taking place in which women were gaining greater sexual authority, a shift which corresponded with the new standards of restraint and consideration being urged on husbands (Holtzmann 1983). This did not, of course, extend to all women, many of whom continued to be cruelly abused. Nevertheless, ideas about what constituted intimate relations between men and women were changing and were being popularised in magazines and manuals, many of which were read by working-class women. One woman interviewed told me that she and her husband decided to have a small family not only because of the economic advantages but also because they wished to have time for companionship. Yet, as Hannah's story suggests, prudential marriage and the stability offered by material betterment might also require a certain amount of sexual repression. They might also engender a yearning for adventure and excitement that is at odds with the mundanity of everyday life. Hannah's story reminds us that the modern longing for transcendence is not confined to the artist-philosopher or modernist writer but may find its own form in the personal narratives of working-class women.

It was not only in the privacy of the bedroom that possibilities for greater consideration and companionship existed. Husbands were often as enthusiastic about the practical benefits of suburban modernity as their wives. The 'homes built for heroes' were offered, as I have discussed above, as a reward for service during both wars and increased domestic comfort was seen as a means of encouraging husbands to become more home-centred. Despite the anxieties of commentators, like Orwell, that suburbia was responsible for the 'feminisation' of men, the spaces of the suburban home were organised to produce gender differences. The interior of the home was the woman's place, one in which, as we shall see in Chapter 3, she was increasingly encouraged to exercise her skills of creative homemaking through her choice of consumer products. Kitchens were represented as her workshop, a space that should be efficient and streamlined. In the 1950s architects began to produce house designs with the kitchen at the front, looking out onto the road and neighbourhood, rather than at the back as in the past (Attfield 1989: 217). This was, in part, a consequence of the demise of domestic service and a valorization of the role of the housewife whose work was no longer invisible – 'at the back' – but represented as part of the social world, albeit still confined behind bricks and glass. By contrast men were encouraged to see the garden as their particular domestic domain. In a 1934 survey of households in Merseyside, it was claimed that three times as many men as women identified gardening as one of their leisure activities (Caradog-Jones 1934: 275). In the 1930s Birmingham City Council ran a Municipal Estates Gardens competition that received considerable publicity in the local press, whilst hammering home the message that gardening made 'respectable' citizens:

> The Lord Mayor who presented the prizes said the two most beautiful things in the world were music and flowers. Many of the municipal gardens in Birmingham were 'colossal' – the tenants producing wonderful results in small room to the delight of themselves and the pleasure of their neighbours . . . But there were a considerable number who did not take a pride in their gardens. A Tenant who allowed weeds to grow rampant was a nuisance to the whole neighbourhood. There were thousands of people who wanted houses and would be only too glad to look after a garden. (*Birmingham Post* 1930)

Gardening was seen as a way of keeping men out of the pub and in the home. In Birmingham and York, there was continued resistance to providing pubs on the estates built for their workers by Cadburys and Rowntrees, local chocolate manufacturers, whose temperance principles influenced housing reform. At the same time funds to encourage gardening on municipal estates were often donated by these benefactors and Birmingham City Council gave free gardening calendars to all its tenants. Although vegetable growing was generally seen as the husband's province (while wives tended the flowerbeds), gardening was often a shared interest that contributed to the family's economy at the same time as enhancing the external appearance of the home.

For Tom Arthurs, who according to his wife, Doris, never went to the pub, his garden was (and is) his pride and joy. When he was younger he belonged to an Allotment Club and grew all the family's vegetables. Similarly, Edith Dickens recalled the fertility of the soil in the garden of their newly built council house, 'we grew some good stuff – it was virgin land you see – lots of potatoes with there being a lot of us, cabbages, sprouts and salad stuff'. In interviews women recall how their husbands grew produce and they would process it through bottling, cooking or baking. Gardens and allotments offered men a space in which they might contribute to the family's domestic well-being without quite the same associations of 'femininity' that attached to cooking or cleaning.[18] Although gardens and allotments are frequently represented as male spaces in which men can escape the demands of the nursery or kitchen, they may also have provided a focus for marital companionship, a shared enterprise whose products were a source of pride. Many of the women interviewed spoke with pleasure of their gardens and the enjoyment these offered. Having spent their childhoods on urban streets, sharing communal toilet facilities and lacking any real privacy, many men and women valued the rural illusion provided by a garden, as well as the privacy afforded by the garden fence which clearly demarcated their 'home' from that of their neighbours. Privacy in the twentieth century was much valued by middle-class women who increasingly believed in their right to interiority and 'a room of their own'. Yet, the emerging symbolic forms of privacy, recognised by working and lower-middle-class men and women, such as the garden fence, were often derided as creating divisions between neighbours: a fatal 'keeping yourself to yourself' that, according to middle-class commentators, separated working people from the communities that had once sustained them.

Aspirations for prudential marriage and a home with garden in the suburbs were an entirely rational response to the drudgery, poverty and ill-treatment that many women had witnessed in the lives of their mothers (Giles 1995). The women who dreamt of a better life running their own homes, with a companionable and caring husband, in a pleasant environment away from the pollution, drunkenness, crime and overcrowding of the city were as 'modern' in their way as the flapper or the Bloomsbury modernist. Such women broke with the traditions of Victorian society that placed working-class women in the homes of their middle-class sisters as servants or positioned them as 'deserving' or 'undeserving' objects of charity. Such women negotiated the kind of marriage that would not result in too many children, violence or sexual abuse, and which would thus facilitate their self-respect. Here were women who, as Light observes, were content with their labour-saving homes and small gardens, and who gained a certain pleasure from the fulfilment of material goals (Light 1991: 218). These women offered a potential challenge to the (middle-class) belief that intellectual pleasures were the only pleasures worth pursuing, for, rather than seeking self-improvement through education, reading or study, 'suburban' women saw 'improvement' in terms of a materially better home life than that experienced by their mothers and grandmothers. A home with a parlour or a bathroom was a visible reminder of the social distance many women had travelled from the bug-ridden, over-crowded homes of their childhood. A reliable, considerate husband was a passport to this sense of self-respect, security and belonging. However while the suburban modernity of such women did not necessarily produce the two-dimensional 'neurotic' acquisitiveness deplored by commentators like Orwell and Taylor, it may have created psyches in which the need for security battled with yearnings for adventure, or in which self-denial and deference hid deeply-felt losses, or envy and resentment produced truculence and hostility. To refuse, as Orwell and Taylor do, such women the complex psychologies that make them fully human is simply the means by which one specific subjectivity (white, educated, and masculine) can be made to stand for 'the modern individual'. And while suburbia undoubtedly offered certain pleasures it was not able ultimately to challenge the gendered and classed nature of the everyday life that it created. Although the new spaces offered by surburban modernity (the garden, the kitchen, and the bathroom) produced new ways of understanding the self, that self continued to be formed by and confined within (albeit changing) divisions of class and gender.

–2–

Help for Housewives: Domestic Service[1]

In her essay 'Character in Fiction' Virginia Woolf used what she saw as the changing behaviour of cooks to illustrate her claim that 'in 1910 human character changed':

> The Victorian cook lived like a leviathan in the lower depths, formidable, silent, obscure, inscrutable; the Georgian cook is a creature of sunshine and fresh air; in and out of the drawing-room, now to borrow the *Daily Herald* now to ask advice about a hat. Do you ask for more solemn instances of the power of the human race to change? (Lee 1997: 239)

Woolf's recognition that changing social patterns could be traced in the relations of mistress and servant was not mere snobbery. It was an astute and accurate perception about the significance of domestic service in the first half of the twentieth century. Most importantly it locates the middle-class home as a key site where class relationships were negotiated. The changing nature of domestic service has rarely been acknowledged in narratives of modernity which, as I have argued, tend to focus on public rather than domestic spaces. Yet, the decline of residential domestic service was at the heart of those changes that transformed domesticity in the first half of the twentieth century and, as such, was a highly significant aspect of the lived experience of millions of women. In her introduction to *Life as We Have Known It* Woolf observes that:

> [o]ne could not be Mrs. Giles of Durham because one's body had never stood at the wash-tub, one's hands had never wrung and scrubbed and chopped up whatever the meat may be that makes a miner's supper. The picture therefore was always letting in irrelevancies. One sat in an armchair or read a book. One saw landscapes and seascapes. (Llewellyn Davies 1931/1977: xxiii)

The enormous gap that Woolf identifies between certain groups of women was understood at a psychic and imaginative level, but it was also experienced materially in the system of domestic service and in the living spaces available to different groups. As we have seen in the previous chapter, the migration of lower-middle and working-class families to the vastly expanding suburbs produced anxiety as they formed an emergent social group with interests and aspirations that rarely imitated the solidly middle-class values of Victorian and Edwardian society. When Mrs Giles of Durham moved to a labour-saving home in the suburbs she may no longer have spent so many hours standing at the wash tub but neither did she sit in an armchair and read books. In this chapter I want to explore the ways in which the changing nature of domestic organisation, represented by the system of domestic service, produced subjectivities that were both gendered and classed. At the end of the chapter I propose that the history of domestic service in the twentieth century suggests a feminine modernity that is striated by very specific class concerns.

Two things are worth noting at this point. First, the cultural significance and legacy of 'servantkeeping' was pervasive: few women born before 1950 remained untouched by the system of class relations manifested in domestic service. The wives and daughters of middle-class men experienced a form of domesticity that assumed it was both natural and right that certain domestic chores be assigned to others. Rose Luttrell, the wife of a prosperous bank manager, recalling her life in the 1920s and 1930s, observes:

> I had a full staff: I had a cook and a kitchenmaid, a housemaid and a parlourmaid, and a nanny and a nurserymaid. I had six servants, you see, so I never did any housework or any domestic work at all. I saw the cook in the morning and ordered the meals for the day and I never went near the kitchen. You didn't go interfering. The cook would have given you notice and left you . . . Of course, it was a great age for letter-writing, everybody wrote a tremendous amount of letters, and then you went out in the garden and you did the flowers. (Humphries and Gordon 1993: 91–2)

And Naomi Mitchison comments on her early-twentieth-century childhood, 'tidying and washing up was just left. In the morning it was done. One was unfamiliar with the process. Dusters, soap, soda? These belonged to another world' (Mitchison 1975: 107). For working-class women domestic service was, until the twentieth century, one of the few 'respectable' occupations open to them. Residential service offered board and lodgings as well as a wage and, for the parents of a large family struggling to subsist on a low income, this was one of the few ways in which they could ensure their daughters were protected from the perceived evils of the factory or the city while contributing to the family budget. Despite winning a scholarship to the local grammar school, Pauline Charles left school in 1937, aged fourteen, and was sent by her mother who was 'very, very strict' to be trained as a house parlourmaid at the local rectory. Doris Arthurs and her sister were both sent into service on leaving school at fourteen in the 1930s. All working-class women knew someone (mother, daughter, sister, aunt, friend) engaged in domestic service or were themselves thus employed.

Second, the demise of residential domestic service was, arguably, the most significant change in the organisation of domestic life in the twentieth century. By

1939 residential domestic service had become a predominantly female occupation, employing 24 per cent of the female labour force in 4.8 per cent of British households (James 1962: 291). While a small number of aristocratic and upper-class families continued to employ relatively large households of servants including male footmen, valets, butlers and gardeners, the predominant pattern established in the years after the First World War was the one or two maid household. There were also regional disparities; the largest concentration of servant-keeping households was in the South and South-East where in 1929 it was estimated there were 447,700 servants. In contrast the same figures show 68,460 servants in the whole of Wales. By 1951 only 11 per cent of women in the labour market were classed as 'indoor domestic' – a drop of 50 per cent in twenty years (Jackson 1991: 344; James 1962: 291). By the 1950s middle-class women were running servantless houses and working-class women were in the process of acquiring their own homes at the same time as benefiting from the variety of jobs open to them. The modernisation of the home that produced suburbia, welfare reforms and, as we shall see in the next chapter, the figure of the consumer housewife was, in large part, a response to, and predicated upon, an end to residential domestic service. The Victorian household, in which distinctions between servants and family were clearly demarcated through its spatial organisation and the social rituals that kept employer and employee at a distance from each other, was breaking down from the turn of the century onwards. 'Moderns', like Woolf, saw in domestic service a symbol of all that was bad about the past: its demise heralded the start of a 'modern' age that would rid itself of Victorian 'stuffiness' and limiting conventions. Yet, as Alison Light points out, 'the schism between women which separated them in the very heart of "private life"' continued to produce tensions and structures of feeling that were classed as well as gendered (1991: 219). Women's sense of themselves as classed subjects was formed as much from their experience in domestic service as from their experience in the workplace.

Although there has been some debate over the precise timing of the demise of residential domestic service there is general agreement that by the 1950s the practice of 'servantkeeping' had all but disappeared except in a few aristocratic households (Horn 1975; Jackson 1991; McBride 1976; Taylor 1979). That this disappearance was inevitable, certainly from 1918 onwards, is assumed, with the interwar period characterised by Pam Taylor as 'the final phase' (Taylor 1978). Explanations for the decline of residential domestic service have emphasised economic factors and the changing occupational structure that accompanied these. For example, the expansion of occupational opportunities for working-class women in retailing, clerical and factory work is frequently cited as a major reason for the increasing shortage of female servants. Working class women were quick to reject domestic service once alternative employment became available although, of course, there were regional disparities.[2] As a result of this shortage, the cost of keeping a servant rose, particularly after 1945, and demand decreased as middle-class households found themselves unable or less willing to incur this expenditure at a time when increasing taxation and a sharp rise in the cost of living were squeezing income (Lewis and Maude 1949: 150–75; Jackson 1991: 330–1). I would not deny the significance of these economic factors but the story of domestic service in the first half of the twentieth century is more uneven than is suggested by such explanations. Many middle-class women continued to expect domestic help and there was considerable debate, before, throughout, and after the Second World War, as to how this could be organised and funded. The *Lady*, a magazine targeted at upper-middle-class women, was still carrying advertisements for live-in maids-of-all-work, cooks and companions in 1950. Out of 131 advertisements for domestic help, only forty-five were for help in institutions – the remainder were for private homes.[3] Certainly, as I shall argue, women, like Violet Markham and Celia Fremlin, who spoke publicly on the subject of domestic help, did not perceive the system as in terminal decline, although they recognised the need for radical reform (Fremlin 1940; Markham and Hancock 1945). Moreover, the economic explanations do not adequately account for the cultural significance of a system so pervasive and taken for granted that, for many, it appeared part of the 'natural' order.

A whole chapter is devoted to domestic service in Roy Lewis and Angus Maude's survey of the middle classes, written in 1949. They point out, 'that the problem of domestic service – or rather the lack of it – is important to the middle classes would hardly be denied by any middle-class person in Britain' and they go on to argue that 'domestic service – albeit somewhat shakily – survives, and is therefore still a matter for discussion' (Lewis and Maude 1949: 204). Lewis and Maude, writing from the standpoint of post-Second World War social democracy, recognise 'anomalies' in the system but their overriding concern is to 'justify the employment of domestic servants by the upper and middle classes' (1949: 205). Their argument is based on the premise that 'the amount of work done within the home by the middle-class housewife is greater than that to be done by the working-class wife with the same number of children' (Lewis and Maude 1949: 206). This claim is based on a belief that the larger size, greater number of possessions, and higher expectations of food and comfort that characterise middle-class domestic life generate too much work and cannot be maintained by one person. The right to 'adequate service' by certain groups is accepted as a self-evident principle of social relations and the task of reformers is to ensure that 'the rich widow and the successful black marketeer' do not secure 'better service' than the 'hard-working professional couple with three children' (Lewis and Maude 1949: 207). Rhetoric, like that used by Lewis and Maude, drew on well-established discourses of domestic service that produced powerful cultural meanings about 'comfort', 'service' and 'place'. Such meanings functioned to naturalise what was, in fact, a specifically middle-class discourse of social relations centred on a belief in the superiority of the middle-class home. Lewis and Maude's concern is to ensure the continuance of 'gracious living' and the kind of 'civilized' life that 'can be lived only with the aid of a modest amount of domestic service' (1949: 213). They see this life as under threat, not only because of the difficulties in getting adequate domestic help, but also as a result of the modernisation of homes and the commercialisation of leisure:

> If [the middle classes] must restrict their families to the size which can be accommodated in a service flat; if they must cut themselves off from leisure activities, however useful, outside the home; if their music and drama are to be purveyed to them only through the radio; if good furniture, good silver and good pictures (all of which need careful maintenance) are to be banished for ever to museums; and if entertaining is to be permanently restricted for all but Cabinet Ministers, then emigration to Eire or South Africa seems the only hope. (Lewis and Maude 1949: 214)

Discussions about how domestic work could be organised were not new. By 1940 there was a long tradition of feminist debate about issues such as domestic service, communal facilities, and the time spent on housework.[4] Government initiatives during the interwar years focused primarily on attempts to increase the supply of servants and interventions by women's groups and servants themselves had centred on the need to improve training, wages and conditions of service.[5] Throughout the 1940s and particularly after 1945, as evidenced by Lewis and Maude's survey, wider questions were raised about who had the right to domestic help and proposals were made for alternative systems of providing this. In the event it was the increasing refusal of working-class women to enter any form of organised domestic service that made many of the proposals unworkable in practice. The post-war decline in 'servantkeeping' was an undoubted threat to the social identity of the middle classes, and of middle-class women in particular. Women's magazines as well as organisations like the Women's Institute saw themselves as having a key role to play in helping women manage their homes without servants. *Good Housekeeping*, for example, ran articles on 'Daily Maids in the Small Town House', 'Running a Home', 'The Housekeeper's Dictionary of Facts', and 'Catering for the Home, What and How to Buy' (Braithwaite et al.: 1986). Such articles were predicated on the need to maintain certain 'standards' despite the shortage of domestic help. The Women's Institute offered housewifery and cookery talks and demonstrations alongside debates on contemporary issues and offered an important forum for middle-class women to voice their concerns about their place in the 'modern' world (Andrews 1997).

The various initiatives around domestic service, that took place throughout the first half of the twentieth century, were a response to the agency of working-class women who increasingly chose not to enter domestic service wherever and whenever there was an alternative. As such the domestic organisation of the middle-class home became the focus for, generally unacknowledged, but nevertheless fierce, struggles around class identities. Discussions were never simply about the shortage of maids; the 'servant problem' became a metaphor for anxieties about class, 'service' and 'deference'. When people discussed the 'servant problem' they were nearly always talking about other things – 'civilized standards', 'comfort', and 'place'. *The English Middle Classes* is one manifestation of this struggle but similar discussions were carried on in Parliament, in national newspapers, in books, in magazines, on the radio and within the civil service, particularly, during the Second World War, in the Ministries of Health and Labour.

The Psychic Economy of Domestic Service

Questions of domestic organisation plagued middle-class women throughout the period. E.M. Delafield's *The Diary of a Provincial Lady*, which was first written for the feminist weekly *Time and Tide*, represents the Provincial Lady as constantly struggling to find, keep and communicate with her servants (Delafield 1930/1984). Vera Brittain wrote articles arguing for co-operative housing and labour-saving homes while employing domestic help to run her household. Brittain was also an advocate of the professionalisation of domestic service in order to encourage recruitment (Brittain 1932/1984: 139–44; Brittain 1928: 31). Molly Hughes, a widowed schools' inspector with three sons, chose to manage without servants because either, 'they are young and you have to look after their health and their morals; or that [*sic*] they are old, faithful and blameless and at last boss you entirely' (Hughes 1940/1979: 59). 'Modern' women like Virginia Woolf, Vera Brittain, Molly Hughes and E.M. Delafield disliked the idea of a relationship rooted in authority and deference. Such relationships smacked of that Victorianism from which such women wished to distance themselves. Yet, at the same time, their sense of the world, and their place in it, was profoundly shaped and mediated by a belief in the superiority of their values and way of life. One of the worst things about the London air raids in the First World War, Woolf said, was having to make conversation with the servants all night and much of Delafield's satire is based on an assumption that the ways of servants are alien and incomprehensible to their employers (Lee 1997: 356; Delafield 1930/1984). Moreover, growing up middle-class brought with it certain rights and responsibilities. A young middle-class woman who married and set up home in the 1920s or 30s did not expect to do very much of her own housework: whatever her views on the 'servant problem' she had no experience of or training in housework. As Naomi Mitchison recalls '[s]o there we were and rooms were clean and tidy, the meals were cooked and served, orders to shops were delivered on time and there were at least three posts a day, all based on our being at the top end of the class structure' (1979: 28). The symbolic as well as the literal function of servants was to keep dirt, chaos and disorder ('the rough') at bay in order to sustain the ideal that middle-class domestic life was ordered, 'civilized' and 'gracious'. A middle-class woman's role in the home was to supervise, teach and guide the invisible hands that kept 'the rough' firmly distinguished from 'the respectable' and 'clean'. To this end she was expected to wield a firm but kindly authority over her servants; as one household manual warned its readers:

> A servant is quick to grasp the fact when her mistress is not versed in the arts of domestic science, and quicker still to take advantage of the ignorance thus displayed. She knows that there is no trained eye to detect flaws in her work; that a room half dusted will seldom evoke a protest; that a table carelessly or slovenly laid will as often as not pass unheeded. The mistress will be made to suffer in many little ways for her ignorance in respect to household duties until by bitter experience she will awaken to the realisation of the fact that knowledge is indeed power, and strive to learn what she should have known when she first began to reign as mistress of her own home. (Jack and Preston c1930: 36)

'To reign as mistress of her own home' was a mark of maturity and a position of power for middle-class women who were still precluded from many public offices.

Moreover, the capacity to 'reign' effectively was a marker of social identity that implicated gender, class and nation for the 'true' Englishwoman of the period was the married woman with children who ran her own home. One of E.M. Delafield's heroines celebrates her marriage as the moment to which her life had hitherto been leading: '[a] home, a husband, a recognized position as a married woman – an occupation. At last, she would have justified her existence. There was no further need to be afraid, or ashamed, or anxious, any more' (Delafield 1930/1984: xi). There may have been no need to be afraid, ashamed or anxious once married but as numerous fictions of the period testify handling servants could give rise to powerful feelings of inadequacy and anxiety. In Daphne du Maurier's novel *Rebecca*, for example, much of the narrator's insecurity comes from her inability to handle the servants and Delafield's Provincial Lady lives in constant fear of being ruled by her servants (Du Maurier 1938/1975; Delafield 1930/1984). The system of domestic service that existed in the first half of the twentieth century was increasingly represented by small households in which one or two maids and possibly a cook or housekeeper carried out the work of the household. Unlike the large establishments that had characterised the Victorian and Edwardian period, these smaller households were conducted on a more personal basis. The distinctions between employer and employee that were easily established in the large Victorian house with its clearly demarcated servants' quarters, protocols and rituals were harder to maintain in the 'modern' houses that were being built from the 1920s onwards. As a result, the relations between maid and mistress became increasingly intimate. Domestic service was never just a matter of paying wages to a grateful employee. For mistresses it involved sharing their homes with women of another class over whom they were supposed to wield authority and, where the servant was young, to stand as moral guardian. For servants it meant the drudgery of cleaning and maintaining someone else's home for low wages, living in someone else's home and, as one domestic servant put it, belonging 'body and soul to the mistress' (Spender 1984: 218). In such circumstances it is not surprising that relations between maids and mistresses produced structures of feeling that involved deeply felt ideas about obligation, privacy, authority, and 'place', and that these might manifest themselves in contempt and belligerence, as well as condescension and deference.

Woolf was never happy with a situation in which some women could 'stroll through the house and say, that cover must go to the wash or those sheets need changing' whilst other women physically undertook the tasks of washing, ironing and cleaning, either in their own home or in the homes of other women (Llewellyn Davies 1931/1977: xxiii). However, like other women of her class and generation, she believed that servants were indispensable. Even when she and her sister, the artist Vanessa Bell, were bemoaning what they felt to be the 'pompous and heavy-footed' atmosphere created by a household of servants, they never seriously imagined living without them (Lee 1997: 238–9). Although Woolf's move from Kensington to Bloomsbury, on the death of her father, Leslie Stephen, precipitated the challenge to Victorian domestic conventions and the determination to seek alternative ways of living that she and her sister advocated, the whole issue of servants and how to relate to them remained difficult. The problem for Woolf, who was always self-consciously aware of living in a modern age, was that she could neither do without servants nor could she be friends with them. The result was that she endured a system that seemed mutually degrading, yet inevitable:

> It is an absurdity, how much time L & I have wasted in talking about servants. And it can never be done with because the fault lies in the system. How can an uneducated woman let herself in, alone, into our lives? What happens is that she becomes a mongrel; & [sic] has no roots anywhere. I could put my theory into practice by getting a daily of a civilised kind, who had her baby in Kentish town; & treated me as an employer, not friend. Here is a fine rubbish heap left by our parents to be swept. (Bell and McNeillie 1977–84: 13 April 1929)

Middle-class women's anxieties about servants centred on what was perceived as a need to exercise authority and the right to certain standards of comfort. But they also focused on the invasion of privacy that employing servants occasioned.

Servants were characterised as rude, resentful, spiteful and likely to spread gossip about their employers. These anxieties deepened as working-class women were increasingly able to reject domestic service or, because of servant shortages and the resulting changes in self-perception, were able to assert themselves in relations with their mistresses. Woolf's eighteen-year relationship with her live-in maid, Nelly Boxall, was 'one of the most stormy and – in a way – intimate of [her] life' (Lee 1997: 355). Nelly complained, amongst other things, about the number of dinner parties given by her employers and the mess made by the Hogarth Press; she gave notice many times and Woolf tried on a number of occasions to give her notice. There were quarrels and scenes with, according to Woolf, Nelly cajoling and apologising, desperate to be kept on. One moment it seems Nelly was dependent and clinging, at another belligerent and threatening. Woolf who valued detachment, self-restraint and reserve found, what she called, Nelly's 'abuse and apology, and hysterics and appeals and maniacal threats' particularly stressful (Nicholson 1979: 285). She once commented that 'a little strain with servants more effectually screws the nerves at the back of my head than any other I am aware of' and, when Nelly finally left in 1934, Woolf likened the relief to the removal of an aching tooth (Bell and McNeillie 1977–84: 41; Nicholson 1979: 285). Although we do not have Nelly's version of events, it is possible, reading between the lines of Woolf's account, to suggest how Nelly's sense of herself may have been shaped by, and a response to, the circumstances of her employment. Nelly was young, single and uneducated when she came to the Woolf household in 1916. She undoubtedly came to see them as family and appears to have become extremely attached to her charismatic mistress. To hand in her notice was to relinquish this surrogate family as well as to lose employment and accommodation. Yet, threatening to leave was Nelly's only way of drawing attention to, not only the dissatisfactions of the job, but her own place in this family which consistently attempted to render her invisible or contemptible. The consciousness that describes Nelly as 'a poor drudge' or 'a mongrel', that sees any discussion of servants and their problems as 'sordid', was formed in a world where servants (and the working class more generally) were perceived as 'other', an incomprehensible and 'foreign race', upon whom could be projected those attributes and behaviours that threatened a certain version of middle-class femininity.

Nelly was accused of emotional manipulation, dependency and lack of control, all 'feminine' qualities that Woolf was at pains to excise in her own writing. This projection of certain, despised, aspects of femininity onto servant figures was not confined to Woolf. Agatha Christie's female servants, for example, are invariably unrestrained, untrustworthy or dependent while her middle-class heroines are robust and unsentimental, and Du Maurier's sinister housekeeper in *Rebecca* is represented as 'neurotic' and obsessive. Middle-class femininity was in the process of reformulation and 'modern' women were anxious to differentiate themselves from the delicate and passive 'lady' of Victorian imaginings. A certain 'masculine' briskness allied to a lack of 'gush' and sentiment characterised the forms of femininity offered in fiction and popular culture. One of the ways of identifying with this image of (middle- class) womanhood was to displace those aspects of femininity that might threaten such identities onto servants who could also be linked with indigenous people in the colonies of the British Empire. In a novel by Lettice Cooper, the heroine, Rhoda, ventures into the 'downstairs world' of the cook and parlourmaid. This world, echoing Freud's description of femininity, imperialist explorers' imagery of Africa, and social investigators' evocation of the urban slums, is described as 'a dark continent, full of unexplored mystery' (Cooper 1936: 82). The problem, however, in constructing servants as middle-class femininity's 'other' was that they did not exist in a faraway country or a different part of town but shared homes, and varying degrees of intimacy, with their mistresses. 'Otherness' required that they be seen as alien and less than human, while the increased intimacy of the 'modern' home made such dehumanisation a constant struggle. Mrs Powell, Rhoda's mother, in *The New House* found it easier than her daughter to see servants as childlike and servile:

> Mrs Powell would be very kind to a servant who was ill or in trouble, but she could never feel that they were independent human beings. It astonished her that they should be unwilling to sacrifice an afternoon out for her convenience. When they had birthdays and were given presents of bath salts, powder-puffs, and coloured beads, she commented on it to Rhoda with surprise. What did they want with things like that? Regarding them at the bottom of her heart as automata, she handled them with assurance and precision, while Rhoda was secretly afraid of asking too much, and got a far more unwilling and inefficient service. (Cooper 1936: 82)

The growing recognition that servants were 'independent human beings' sat uncomfortably with the middle-class need to burden them with, not only the drudgery of washing, scrubbing and polishing, but also specific and historic aspects of a femininity that had by the early twentieth century become despised as old fashioned.

Allied to this was an awareness that the social identity offered to the mistress of servants was increasingly unstable. A household manual published by the Woman's Book Club, advising women on all aspects of homemaking, offers guidance on the legal relationship between husband, wife and servant. The authors of the manual, state:

> As all dealings with servants are mainly conducted by the wife, as superintendent of the domestic side of the home, the mistress is more often than not regarded as having supreme control over them. She it is who engages them, allots their various duties,

provides for their outings and holidays, and dismisses them when their work is unsatis-
factory. This is a typical instance of the wife acting as her husband's agent, for where
husband and wife live together it is the husband who is the legal head of the servants of
a household. (Jack and Preston c1930: 332)

The middle-class wife was the conduit through which middle-class masculinity
wielded authority in the home, in much the same way that the structures of imperialism allowed for the appointment of indigenous agents to act on behalf of white
imperialists in the colonies. While, as we have seen, this role could create anxiety
it also offered opportunities for a measure of power and authority in what had, over
the last century, become the centre of middle-class life and values, the private
home. There are many recorded instances of the unpleasant ways in which this
power manifested itself. Generic names like 'Peggy' or 'Mary Ann' were given to
girls on entering service; a maid-of-all-work could be at the mercy of her mistress's
bell, forced to respond immediately every time it rang; heavy workloads often
made it impossible to take the limited time off allowed; servants were the first to
be suspected or accused when anything went missing; girls in service were not
allowed 'callers' of either sex; and as one mistress is quoted as saying 'I pay my
housemaid her wages, and I shall speak to her as I like' (Spender 1984: 217). Even
where the mistress was benevolent she still controlled the payment of wages and
had the power to give or refuse a reference. Without 'a character' servants were
unlikely to find a similar job elsewhere. The growing willingness of women to
stand up to their mistresses, deplored as 'rudeness', stemmed in part from the
knowledge that there were other jobs available in shops and factories that did not
require references. The gradual erosion of middle-class woman's supervisory role
in the home left her increasingly bereft of that power and control which had
defined her 'place' in the bourgeois home.

Finally, at a practical level, domestic service made possible the entry of some
middle-class women into the professions, and, for many others, it allowed them to
participate in voluntary or charitable work, to sit on committees locally and
nationally. While the enforced intimacy of sharing a home with servants could be
unpleasant, it did offer women opportunities to sit in an armchair and read, to 'see
landscapes and seascapes', to visit friends, to go shopping in the new department
stores, to arrange flowers or to write letters, and to engage in certain kinds of public
work. The example of Violet Markham, who produced the *Report on the Post-War
Organization of Private Domestic Employment* in 1945, is illustrative. Born in
1872, Markham was the granddaughter of Joseph Paxton, her father was Managing
Director of the Stavely Coal and Iron Company in Chesterfield and she spent her
childhood surrounded by domestic servants, some of whom provided the easy
affection that appears to have been missing in her relationship with her mother
(Markham 1953: 18–43). She received little formal education, apart from during

a brief period in her teens, and, while she enjoyed a companionable marriage, she never had children. From 1914 onwards Markham sat on numerous committees, corresponded with a wide range of notable public figures and, although she never entered parliament or had a paid job, was an influential figure in national and local politics until her death in 1959. Markham's success as a public figure was helped considerably by her ability to employ domestic help. For Markham, as for Woolf, actually doing housework was unthinkable and her wartime letters to her sister-in-law bemoan the shortage of domestic help, '[t]here is something badly wrong with the whole organisation of society which lands housewives into the dreadful mess which afflicts women both in England and America', and complain that the 'strains are quite intolerable at the moment' (Jones 1994: 180). After the war, she goes on to assert, 'the problem must be tackled if women are to have *any* peace and leisure' (Jones 1994: 180). For Woolf and Markham housework is the antithesis of creativity, useful work, leisure and intellectual thought. Both women were aware that their own identities as public figures and private individuals rested on a division of labour in which some women 'read a book' or 'saw landscapes and seascapes' whilst others 'stood at the washtub'.

'Servantkeeping' dwindled as a marker of middle-class status as it became harder to find and keep servants. If the system was to be reformed and maintained it was important that it could be justified and increasingly the debates in the first half of the twentieth century address this. Over and over again the reasons why middle-class women require help in the home are couched in terms of their need for 'peace' or space for themselves if they are to make a full contribution to 'modern' society. Markham is insistent in her Report and elsewhere, as we shall see, that women will refuse to undertake childbearing and rearing if they have no domestic help and, from the beginning of the century, feminists had been insisting that the problems of childcare and housework must be addressed if women were to enter public life (Dyhouse 1989: 111–23). Brittain, who advocated communal laundries and day nurseries rather than servants, insisted that '[t]he woman who washes dishes, knits woollies and makes junkets when she might be leading a local education committee . . . is as much an example of national waste as a brilliant playwright condemned to darn stockings' (1932/1984: 141). Freedom from domestic chores was not seen as a license for the kinds of leisured lives many people believed had been the experience of the Victorian 'lady'. In the early twentieth century the figures of the rich widow or the hedonistic socialite appear in fictions and articles, always to be condemned for their 'parasitism'. The 'modern' middle-class woman, freed from the expectations of nineteenth-century conventions, was to lead a 'useful' life as a fully participating member of the society to which she belonged. This could, if she was single and childless, involve paid work outside the home. Otherwise she might make her contribution via motherhood, as well as through philanthropic and voluntary initiatives. In order to do so she required domestic help (in the form of servants or communal facilities) not only so that she could engage in work of 'national importance' but also so that she might enjoy the right to leisure and privacy that had always been accorded to men. Charlotte Perkins Gilman, writing in 1910, insisted that the home, so often sentimentalised as a haven of privacy, afforded educated women neither the time nor the space to concentrate on creative or worthwhile work.

> From parlour to kitchen, from cellar to garret, she is at the mercy of children, servants, tradesmen and callers. So chased and trodden is she that the very idea of privacy is lost to her mind; she never had any, she doesn't know what it is, and she cannot understand why her husband should wish to have any 'reserves', any place or time, any thought or feeling, with which she may not make free. (Dyhouse 1989: 115)

Brittain, writing in 1953, listed as one of the achievements of women's emancipation, the right to leisure: 'the past fifty years have brought relative security, and the acknowledged right to leisure' (1953: 8).

'Peace' and privacy figure again and again, not only as matters of physical space and actual time, but also as spatial and temporal metaphors for an inner privacy that manifested itself in a certain detachment and reserve in public situations and personal relations. Images of private space abound in women's writing of the period as well as in popular culture. Woolf's *A Room of One's Own* is, of course, the most well-known example but household manuals and women's magazines also recognised (middle-class) women's need for privacy (Woolf 1929). For example, in *My Home* for January 1950, a feature on a country home in the Cotswolds shows a bedroom in which there is no sign of a dressing table, that symbol of femininity as spectacle and masquerade, but instead 'the mistress of the house finds a desk in her bedroom a boon and a blessing for quiet moments "away from it all"' (1950: 8). And *The Book of Good Housekeeping*, published in 1944, suggests that it is possible 'even in quite small houses . . . for man and wife to have separate bedrooms, each bedroom furnished as a "bed-sitting-room"' (*The Book of Good Housekeeping* 1944: 92). The desire for domestic privacy, however, was double-edged. The need for space and time in which, as Woolf put it, one could be 'private, secret, as anonymous and submerged as possible' required the freedom from domestic tasks that servants provided (Woolf cited in Gordon 1984: 5). At the same time, the presence of servants in the home could be experienced as a constant invasion of that privacy. It is perhaps for this reason that some evocations of domestic interiors render invisible the hands that have created the comfort and privacy that is being extolled. Jan Struther's description of Mrs Miniver's return to her London home is a particularly telling example:

> She rearranged the fire a little, mostly for the pleasure of handling the fluted steel poker, and then sat down by it. Tea was already laid: there were honey sandwiches, brandy-

snaps, and small ratafia biscuits; and there would, she knew, be crumpets. Three new library books lay virginally on the fender-stool, their bright paper wrappers unsullied by subscriber's hand. The clock on the mantlepiece chimed, very softly and precisely, five times. A tug hooted from the river. A sudden breeze brought the sharp tang of a bonfire in at the window. The jig-saw was almost complete, but, here was still one piece missing. And then, from the other end of the square, came the familiar sound of the Wednesday barrel-organ, playing, with a hundred apocryphal trills and arpeggios, the 'Blue Danube' waltz. And Mrs Miniver, with a little sigh of contentment, rang for tea. (1939/1991: 2–3)

This scene of domestic contentment is not unlike a stage set in which the various props have been assembled in order to produce the comfort and safety conjured up by the idea of 'coming home'. Struther, the writer, creates the scene for her (middle-class) readers in the same way that the invisible hands of Mrs Miniver's servants ensured that the fire was lit, tea was laid and crumpets would be served. This passage provides a temporary and imaginary world in which (middle-class) women's desire for privacy, comfort and ease without the obtrusive presence of servants can be fantasised through the leisured activity of reading.

If middle-class women's subjectivities were shaped by the system of domestic service, so too were those of working-class women although in very different ways. Entering residential domestic service required young women to live in another woman's home and to encounter a more affluent and privileged lifestyle than that of their own families. They were expected to behave in certain ways and to inhabit certain spaces of the house. For example, maids could not initiate conversations with their employers but had to wait to be spoken to; it was an accepted convention that, in order to exclude servants from what was being said, employers would often speak to each other in French; and maids were not allowed in the family's living areas unless they were cleaning, serving at table, answering the door or bringing in the morning tea. The maids' quarters were separate from the rooms used by the family and were frequently small, tucked away in the attics, and sparsely furnished. *The Woman's Book* provides plans for a modern 'house of moderate price' located in the suburbs. It insists on the provision of 'a comfortably-furnished sitting-room for the maids' in accordance with contemporary thinking about the amenities required to attract domestic servants while continuing the practice of spatial segregation (Jack and Preston c1930: 4–7). Hence, even the spatial arrangements of moderately affluent middle-class homes continued to inscribe the social relations that should exist between maid and mistress. Material privilege, expected behaviours and spatial organisation all spoke the 'place' of servants in the middle-class home. Servants, like the indigenous peoples of the colonies, were encouraged to see themselves as grateful, deferential and willing to learn and imitate middle-class ways. They were also seen as potentially dishonest and disobedient if not kept under constant surveillance. *The Book of Good House-keeping* advises its readers 'if you suspect that your servant is guilty of theft, you should not give your servant into custody or search her boxes' but follow certain formal procedures and *The Home Counsellor* urges similar caution, 'if you suspect that Jane has stolen your handkerchiefs or your silk stockings but have no definite proof, you will be acting very rashly if you tell her to "pack her box"' (*The Book of Good Housekeeping* 1944: 429; *The Home Counsellor* 1936: 229).[6] There must also have been persistent anxieties, on both sides, that middle-class fathers and sons would engage in sexual relations with the servants. As we saw in Chapter 1, Hannah negotiated the potential dangers of a sexual liaison with her employer by casting his attraction as unrequited romantic love. The ever-present anxiety that a 'bad' servant might steal from her mistress or engage in sexual relations with the males of the family undoubtedly bred an atmosphere of mutual suspicion and hostility. As an ex-housemaid explained in *Time and Tide*, 'the whole atmosphere is so awful; the way one is spoken to is so insulting, and so often what one says is disbelieved. Surely a servant coming from a good home, brought up to be truthful and honest, would find it very difficult to remain so under these circumstances' (Spender 1984: 217).

There were a number of strategies adopted by servants. First, there were maids who refused what they saw as the 'slavery' of domestic service and actively rebelled against it. Fourteen-year-old Joyce Storey, forced to wash the coal cellar floor, before beginning her afternoon off, fuelled with righteous rage, at what she, correctly, perceived as her mistress's game-playing, vowed, 'God or the Devil . . . this is the last time in my entire bloody life I will ever do anyone's housework. Never again will I be on my knees with my nose to the ground, for I belong up there with my eyes to the light and walking upright and tall' (Storey 1987: 104). She finished washing the floor and with her 'coal-black face', torn stockings and dishevelled hair confronted her employer who:

> opened her mouth to say something when she saw the state I was in, but took a step backward when she also saw the wild glint in my eyes that held the clear message that our paths would never meet again. She held out my five shillings to me as though I were a leper that she had no intention of touching. I passed her without a word. (Storey 1987: 105)

Joyce never went back into service. Instead she found employment in factories and warehouses until she married in 1939. She had not disliked the work which involved preparing meals, washing-up, cleaning the house and looking after her employer's daughter. What she did rebel against was the way in which her mistress exploited the power relationship between them. Joyce's assertion that she belonged 'up there with my eyes to the light and walking upright and tall' was the kind of response that mistresses dreaded. Joyce's anger found its expression in many other instances where she perceived injustices due to class and privilege and was one of the ways in which she sustained a sense of self-worth and dignity. However, for every Joyce there were many more who, living in an atmosphere of suspicion and hostility, adopted the characteristics attributed to them in order to cope with the myriad exploitations and injustices of service. 'Walking upright and tall' was made difficult by the knowledge that middle-class culture had already set the terms in which servants were invited to see themselves: deferential, loyal, celibate or deceitful, dishonest, lazy, and always childlike, in need of guidance, protection and discipline.

If open anger was one response to the injustices of domestic service, covert resistance was another. Winifred Foley's account of her first job as a fourteen-year-old represents the relationship between her and her ninety-year-old employer as one that was characterised by duplicity and deception. Winifred took considerable pleasure and pride in hoodwinking what she called the 'cantankerous old tartar', altering the clocks, for example, in order to get more time in bed (Foley 1986: 132–9). Pauline Charles became adept at pretending to be dusting or scrubbing when she had, in fact, been reading and, during the Second World War, when her mistress removed all the light bulbs and expected the servants to operate in the dark, she managed on occasions to subvert this. Pauline remembers that she would also use the threat of leaving to get what she wanted. And on one occasion when the housekeeper insisted that she go to church, that this was expected of 'all the girls that come into this house', Pauline countered by placing herself in a position of moral authority that undermined the rule about church attendance, 'I go to church to worship God, not to please my employer or anyone else, so I'm not going.' The result was that, unlike the other servants in the house, Pauline did not attend church for six months. Eventually, she chose the moment when she was most needed in the kitchen to announce that she was going to church, secure in the knowledge that she was too good a worker to be dismissed and anyway, as she'd been told, 'girls from this house always go to church'. Domestic service could become an emotional war zone in which numerous battles of attrition and manipulation were fought between suspicious mistresses and resentful maids. Servants, like Winifred and Pauline, believed that the privileged circumstances in which their mistresses lived and the injustices heaped upon them as servants, justified minor deceptions. Satisfaction was expressed at successful attempts to outwit their employers and stories about these small victories were narrated with relish. However, while some working-class women responded to the exploitative conditions of domestic service with belligerence and resentment, contemptuous of their employers whom they saw as legitimate targets for covert acts of hostility and disdain, the subjectivities of others were formed via the deference and self-effacement that mistresses desired. Yet, of course, it is rarely the deferential maid whose story has been recorded. Those accounts of servant life that we do have, found their way into the public domain precisely because their authors resisted and rebelled against the system of 'servantkeeping'. In what follows, therefore, I am drawing on the perceptions of residential service analysed by a middle-class woman interested in the psychology of deference and service.

Fremlin's *The Seven Chars of Chelsea* is intended as a survey of domestic service with the purpose of alerting mistresses to the reasons why they could not get the servants they wanted. Fremlin is probably better known as a writer of psychological thrillers – a precursor of Ruth Rendell – and the author of *War Factory*, a Mass Observation study of morale among the female workers in a rurally located factory established as part of the war effort (Fremlin 1943/1987). The daughter of a Hertfordshire doctor, turned bacteriologist, she graduated from Oxford in 1936 with a classics degree and little idea about what she wanted to do next. In the late 1930s, disguising herself as a maid of all work, Fremlin took a number of jobs in different establishments in order to examine 'the peculiarities of the class structure of our society . . . from the angle of domestic service' (Fremlin 1940: 7). She not only observed and participated in the daily life of maids-of-all-work, 'chars', cooks and parlourmaids but also received 211 responses to a questionnaire sent to mistresses, 160 of whom employed a single maid. Her intention, like those social explorers of late-Victorian London who visited the East End, was to reveal to the upper and middle classes the lives, experiences and attitudes of the poorer classes in the hope of activating reform (Keating 1976: 65–6). Fremlin believed that people like herself could 'act to some slight extent as messengers and interpreters between the two worlds' (1940: 2).

The book's central chapter entitled 'The Seven Chars of Chelsea' is a comic account of Fremlin's time as a cleaner in a hospital. The 'chars' are represented as stoical, phlegmatic, 'salt of the earth' characters, apparently indifferent to the appalling conditions of their lives and reacting to events with humour and fatalism. They act and move in chorus and they bicker good-heartedly throughout the day. The depiction of the 'chars' draws on a certain middle-class myth of working-class vigour and phlegm that has its masculine counterpart in the figure of the British Tommy. This vitality which characterises the 'chars' (and the waitresses that are described in a later chapter) is in sharp contrast to the repression and waste that Fremlin claims is the lot of the residential servant. And this is the stated point of the book, 'the point I wanted to make a lot was that these girls [residential servants] were not getting married . . . the work itself was not unpleasant at all compared with a lot of work' (Interview Stanley 1981). The ideal of residential service, represented by the figure of the faithful retainer, devoted, deferential and celibate, is critiqued by Fremlin for its potentially damaging effects on a femininity defined in terms of wifehood and motherhood. When the text turns to examining residential service there is a shift in register and idiom: the comic mode used to present the daily cleaners and waitresses gives way to something approaching Gothic intensity. A whole chapter is devoted to residential domestic service in which Fremlin evokes what she sees as the psychology of deference. The residential household is described

as a 'nightmare boarding-school, full of children slowly growing grey' in which the
female servants are represented as occupying a psychosexual landscape of suppressed desire and wasted potential (Fremlin 1940: 148). Trapped in the structures
of deference and duty, intimacy and isolation, doomed not to marry, these servants
live, according to Fremlin, sterile and purposeless lives in which an obsessive
devotion to cleanliness and order has replaced the 'natural' outlets for female
desire. Her description of a visit to Agnes, a retired family servant, is illustrative:

> She [Agnes] lived in a little house deep in the woods . . . Inside the garden, shut off by
> the garden fence from the wilderness of leaves and scents and sounds, her geraniums
> were doing very well, row upon row of them, without a single weed.
>
> Inside the house was silent. No wasps were ever heard buzzing after Agnes's jam; no
> flies hummed hopefully round her larder door. The wire netting on her windows was
> completely effective. The last mouse had been trapped years ago, and now the whole
> house stood trim and silent. Its barricades against the surge of life were impregnable.
>
> We knocked on the brass knocker, and Agnes came to the door. She was tall and erect,
> and her face was clammily white, with few wrinkles for her seventy years. She wore an
> old-fashioned black dress of very good material, a tight lace front and choker, and her
> hair was grey and wisp-like. You could not tell what colour it had once been. (Fremlin
> 1940: 151)

Agnes displays a sensuous and possessive pleasure in commodities and furnishings. She shows her visitors the material from which she intends to make new
curtains, 'stroking it with strange relish, letting her thin fingers slide across its
folds' and describes a damaging mark on her furniture thus,

> 'I don't know how it is with my furniture, I can feel everything that touches it, just as if
> it was my own flesh. But I got some oil and put it on, straight away, and rubbed it, ever
> so gentle, you know, not to rough the polish. I rub it several minutes every day, and it's
> getting better, I know it's getting better' Her voice had grown soft, and she stooped and
> felt the injured patch with all the pent-up tenderness of seventy years. (Fremlin 1940:
> 156)

Fremlin treats Agnes with gentle pathos using her as an example of the psychological damage occasioned by a life in residential service. Agnes who lives 'deep
in the woods' has lost the power to bewitch and can only measure out her days by
cleaning and polishing her treasured pieces of furniture which come to symbolise
the material privilege and social status of the family of which she was once a part.

Another servant, Lydia, has been in service for fifteen years and while, according to Fremlin, she dreams of love and romance, she has become resigned to living
a shadowy half-life in what she regards as 'a good place' with 'real gentry, too, you
don't get put upon here' (Fremlin 1940: 30). Lydia, like Woolf's maid Nelly,

spends her afternoons off with her sister who works as a parlourmaid in the same London square.[7] Fremlin describes these visits:

> If you hadn't got a sister of your own working in the Square you popped round to see somebody else's. We seemed to form almost a closed community, the servants working in this Square; we knew practically no one but each other and talked about practically nothing outside its confines. Almost every afternoon one or other of my colleagues' sisters or friends would drop in, and we would sit talking endlessly and aimlessly about the other servants in our respective establishments. Sometimes the gossip was extended to our respective gentry too. But it was very mild and usually rather admiring gossip; nothing like what is popularly supposed to go on below stairs. There was a certain amount of chatter about which kitchen-maids were 'soft' on which cooks and head housemaids; which led me to suppose that the atmosphere of congealed adolescence in our household was not quite peculiar to it. (Fremlin 1940: 41–2)

However, Lydia, who is in awe of her mistress, who would never leave this 'good' place, and who seems happy enough to spend her leisure time in another servants' hall, suffers with her 'nerves' and 'feels the cold'. She watches the comings and goings of the parties and dances held in the Square and remarks that 'it's ever so nice' before, according to the story Fremlin tells, sobbing herself to sleep (Fremlin 1940: 48–9).

Agnes' obsessive behaviour and Lydia's suppressed sexuality and envy are represented as pathological and thus slightly sinister. In this Fremlin draws on contemporary discourses of spinsterhood. A.M. Ludovici's attitude, drawing on a popularised version of Freudian theory, was extreme but his perception of celibacy as 'unnatural' was not:

> spinsters . . . who are not leading natural lives, and whose fundamental instincts are able to find no normal expression or satisfaction . . . the influence of this body of spinsters on the life of the nation to which they belong, must be abnormal, and therefore contrary to the normal needs and the natural development of the nation. (1923: 231)

Sex was celebrated amongst certain groups in the 1920s and 30s as 'one of the fundamental elements of life, and without it no life is simple or normal'(Clephane, 1935: 212). Victorian attitudes to sex were seen as outdated and repressive, but nonetheless sexual relationships outside marriage remained confined to a small 'emancipated' minority. Hence, to lead a 'natural' life required marriage and those women who, through circumstance or choice, did not marry, were at best pitied and at worst condemned as pathologically abnormal. In Agnes and Lydia thwarted sexuality has manifested itself as passivity and an obsession with cleanliness and detail: both women are represented as 'hysterical'. The structures of authority and deference that organise residential domestic service produce women who, according to Fremlin, are 'well-cared for school-children . . . contented poodles eternally on leads' living a 'congealed adolescence' (1940: 38). Fremlin admires one of the maids, Irene, because 'she was fighting like a drowning man for life' and her 'angry normality' finds an outlet in heterosexual flirtation and heavy make-up (1940: 40).[8]

The rhetoric of *The Seven Chars of Chelsea* sets up an opposition between the traditional and the modern that is experienced as a particular form of class relations between women. The qualities asked of residential servants (deference, loyalty and celibacy) are pathologised as the cause of a 'neurotic' and 'hysterical' femininity that harks back to what is perceived as an outdated mode of service and repressive sexuality. A 'modern' form of working-class femininity, epitomised by non-residential 'chars' and waitresses, is represented as robust and independent. The residential woman servant, according to Fremlin, is a legacy of the past who 'may remain safe and secure all her life long, out of hearing of the battles and storms that the rest of the working-class are facing . . . she will be living in the world of feudalism, whose battles are long past; while the others of her class are living in the fighting, struggling world of capitalism' (1940: 150). It is difficult not to see these residential servant figures, at least in part, as projections of their creator's fears and anxieties about traditional femininity. Fremlin rejected the conventional life of a middle-class daughter, choosing instead to live and work as a single woman in London. 'Modern', urban working-class women are seen by her as active agents in the rapidly changing world of modern capitalism and in many ways she identifies with these urban waitresses and 'chars' rather than the suburban mistresses and residential servants with whom she works.

The psychic economy of domestic service formed the classed subjectivities of women in the first half of the twentieth century in particular ways. But Victorian practices of 'servantkeeping' were increasingly seen as outmoded. The 'modern' home was envisioned as servantless, labour-saving and run according to the principles of rational efficiency. This might involve daily non-residential help that would be organised as paid labour thus avoiding the worst manifestations of enforced intimacy. Few, however, envisaged a world in which middle-class women would do their own housework. Fremlin's *The Seven Chars of Chelsea* was an attempt to propose a modernised version of service in line with progressive thinking on social relations and for this reason it requires more detailed examination.

The Seven Chars of Chelsea (1940)

The methods Fremlin used for collecting material for her study of domestic service were influenced by the political allegiance to social realism and documentary that characterised much writing and filmmaking of the late 1930s.[9] George Orwell,

Walter Greenwood, Mass Observation, and documentary filmmakers such as John Grierson were all concerned to represent and document the lives of the working-class in attempts to generate more egalitarian and social democratic attitudes in Britain (Orwell 1937/1986; Greenwood 1933/1993).[10] The significance of Fremlin's study of domestic service lies in her appropriation of the rhetoric of social realism and documentary to an institution that was of particular relevance to women. In addressing the wider questions of class through the lens of domestic service, she not only links class and gender but demonstrates very precisely how these relations were experienced in specific ways by women. It is made clear at the start that the readership being addressed is those women who employ domestic help of whatever kind:

> you would have no idea how to set about finding out from your charwoman what it feels like to live and work as she does. You would not know what questions to ask her, and she would not know how to answer them, not even what you were getting at. Deadlock would be reached in the second sentence.
>
> The trouble is that the two of you speak different languages; you think different thoughts; you live in different worlds. In a word, you belong to different classes in this British society of ours. (Fremlin 1940: 2)

Fremlin was not unaware of the tensions and strains that underpinned the relation-ships of domestic service and her survey was, at least in part, an attempt to dispel some of the fear and hostility that attended middle-class women's relations with their servants. The first half of *The Seven Chars of Chelsea* is written in the form of a series of quasi fictional case studies, highlighting the kindliness, humour, and friendship that Fremlin encountered in her work as a maid. The three case studies involve an upper-class household with many residential servants, a working-class boarding house and working as a cleaner in a hospital. Employment in the board-ing house and the hospital are represented more positively than the maid's job in the upper-class household, which, as we have seen, is shown to be 'a shadowy, feudal' life (Fremlin 1940: 150). The second half of the book analyses the issues raised by the case studies and discusses solutions to the problems that have been raised. The first step Fremlin advocated was supporting the Domestic Workers' Union established to regulate and standardise the conditions of domestic workers (see note 5). Beyond that, however, her stated aim was to work for,

> a state of society in which maid and mistress are of the same class, with the same cultural background and the same education. The day they can work and laugh and struggle together – perhaps for two hours a day – perhaps for eighteen. Neither will bother to count, because both will be too much interested in the job for its own sake. Such a state of affairs can be realized almost within a generation. But it can be realized only by attacking the root and origin of class antagonism, not merely its symptoms. (Fremlin 1940: 177)

Fremlin's utopian vision was a woman-centred one but depended crucially on the removal of 'class antagonism'. For her the symbol of an egalitarian society was the classless maid and mistress working together in domestic harmony. In order to achieve this, Fremlin argued, it would be necessary to 'work for an economic system in which all girls *are* your own class' – to 'do away with the form of society which . . . forces even the best of employers to behave like a slave-driver; even the most willing of workmen to behave like an obstinate saboteur' (1940: 174–8).

However, until the day when 'class equality based on a genuine identity of interests becomes a reality in this country' *The Seven Chars of Chelsea* urged mistresses to support the Domestic Union (Fremlin 1940: 175–6). In offering solutions to the problems of domestic service Fremlin was at pains to distance herself from militant industrial action, perhaps recognising, rightly, that too fervent an advocacy of trade unionism would alienate those women of her own class. Despite the detailing of injustice and exploitation, *The Seven Chars of Chelsea* was ultimately concerned to persuade those women who employed domestic help that treating their employees in a 'business-like' manner was the most realistic solution to the current problems (Fremlin 1940: 161). This, Fremlin claimed, was the only way to ensure that 'the mistress [will] be able to secure competent and willing service' (Fremlin 1940: 161). *The Seven Chars of Chelsea* does not let mistresses off lightly: they are condemned for the snobbery and prejudice with which they treat their servants. Yet, the overall intention of the survey was to persuade middle-class women that treating their servants in a humane and decent way with proper conditions of service was in their own interests. Fremlin believed that once domestic service was set on a professional footing working-class women would willingly enter a profession that offered regulated hours and reasonable wages and middle-class women would receive the help they were entitled to. Moreover, Fremlin, whilst concerned for the well-being of domestic servants, never questions the sexual division of labour within the home nor the right of some women to employ other women to carry out domestic work. She believed that women should work together to share domestic tasks and that the conditions under which domestic help was provided should be better but her focus on dismantling 'class antagonism' took precedence over any analysis of the gendered nature of domesticity.

The Seven Chars of Chelsea was written in 1940 when many believed that the 'people's war' heralded the prospect of a 'people's peace' in which the barriers of class and prejudice would be dismantled finally. Fremlin's achievement was to appropriate the language and ideals of social egalitarianism in order to make visible the class inequalities that were reproduced daily, not in the public spaces of work, politics, leisure and education, but at the very heart of private (and feminised) life – the middle-class home. Ultimately, however, her commitment to improving the relationships between middle and working-class women is undermined by her inability to imagine a world without domestic help. Fremlin ends her book by spelling out clearly the options available to middle-class women,

You don't like the idea of the Union. You don't want to see the spirit of hostile Trade Unionism introduced permanently into your home. Very well. You have three alternatives clearly before you.

You can employ girls of your own class. You will have to search long and hard for them.

You can work for an economic system in which all girls *are* of your own class.

You can put up with your servants as they are.

These are the alternatives. You can take your choice. (1940: 177–8)

What Fremlin's rhetoric failed to grasp was the fact that whatever the conditions of service and however kindly the mistress, helping another woman with her housework for wages involved an unequal relationship. Working-class women, however, grasped this point very well and were increasingly able to reject what, for many, would always be 'servitude'. It was not only the opportunities for alternative employment that enabled working-class women to refuse any form of organised private domestic work but a growing sense of their own worth as workers and housewives. As we shall see in the next chapter this was accelerated by the importance of women of all classes to the 'home front' during the Second World War but also by changes that positioned women as central to economic production and consumption. Fremlin's rhetoric of maid and mistress working alongside each other as equals expresses a specifically liberal middle-class dream despite the quasi socialist analysis of her case studies. Drawing on the rhetoric of liberalism Fremlin's utopia is one in which 'all girls are of your own class'. Working-class women had different aspirations. Many working-class women, as we saw in Chapter 1, dreamed of a home of their own, or opportunities for part-time, rather than full-time, employment, and the dignity that comes from performing socially useful work (Giles 1995: 64–95). In the 1940s, and particularly in the post-war years, these aspirations appeared to be becoming material realities.

Help for Housewives: Post-war Debates on Domestic Service

In January 1943 Ernest Bevin, then Minister of Labour and National Service, wrote to Ernest Brown at the Ministry of Health proposing that a committee be established to 'investigate the extent to which necessary domestic help is not available for private households and hospitals and institutions and to propose methods for making such help available during the war and in the transitional period at the end of the war'. Bevin's proposal that ways should be found of making domestic help available during and after the war was not a new one. As early as 1941 the Ministry of Labour had initiated discussions on the possibility of setting up a National Service Orderly Corps to provide domestic help for various institutions such as hospitals, nursing homes and nurseries as well as for private households. The aim was to establish a quasi-military Corps akin to the women's services that could conscript a ready supply of domestic labour and appeal to women who wished to undertake some form of war work. Although the idea was perceived as fraught with difficulties, not least over whether members of such a Corps should wear a uniform, it was felt that:

> the formation of a Corps would raise the status of domestic work in national services and might improve recruitment by attracting women who at the moment were not subject to any form of compulsion from the Ministry of Labour and National Service (such as women with young children) and might also encourage women who registered to opt for domestic work. (Ministry of Health 1942)

However, in 1943 pressure from the Ministry of Health and the Women's Consultative Committee caused Bevin to conclude that the needs of hospitals for domestic workers should take precedence over the needs of private households. As a result it was decided that priority should be given to establishing 'a uniformed corps from which at a later stage help might be obtained for the private household when hardship arises from lack of domestic help in periods of sickness or confinement' (Bevin, Proposal 1943). In June 1943 Violet Markham, ex chair of the Central Committee on Women's Training and Employment (see note 5) and the only woman to sit on the Home Office Aliens Committee, wrote to Bevin urging him to do something to alleviate 'the hardships to certain classes of private persons, e.g. the old, the young, the sick and women engaged on essential war duties, owing to the shortage of domestic help' (Jones 1994: 173). As a result, although the National Service Orderly Corps was never established, Markham was charged by Bevin with conducting a survey and producing a report on the future of private domestic employment.

Markham was in her seventies when she produced the *Report on the Post-War Organization of Private Domestic Employment*. Reading the Report's recommendations is to become aware of the ways in which her attempts to engage with the 'changed and more egalitarian outlook of the present day' were brought into tension with a subjectivity formed in the context of Victorian and Edwardian social practices and middle-class beliefs. The Report contextualises the present situation in terms of a traditional model of middle-class family life, rooted in the kind of Victorian homes that were soon to be improved by developments in household technology and replaced by the modern labour-saving homes built in the 1950s and 60s:

> [f]amily life among the middle and upper classes in this country has for generations rested largely on the assumption of domestic help of some kind being available. Unlike the US where that assumption only affects a very small minority of the population, most houses in this country have not been specially designed with mechanised devices to deal with a permanent shortage. The single-handed care of an old-fashioned house with stone passages, coal fires and an antiquated range has proved a heavy task during the war for

a mistress bereft of her maids. There is much evidence of strain and consequent ill-health. (Markham and Hancock 1945: 7)

Although the Report recognises that 'the burdens of working-class women have for generations been notorious' and that some provision should be made to 'lighten the load of the working-class mother', it is difficult to see how the final recommend-ations would have achieved this (Markham and Hancock 1945: 7). The Report's main concern remains the needs of 'the woman who can afford to pay for regular service' and while such women must be encouraged to offer better conditions and wages, the refusal of working-class women to enter domestic service is perceived, in large part, as a response to media caricatures of servants and the stigmatisation of service by other workers, rather than as a rational response to intolerable conditions of work (Markham and Hancock 1945: 7). Like Fremlin, Markham believed that the solution should be 'a new and determined effort to regularise and popularise a form of employment which under rational conditions is both honour-able to the worker and essential to the well being of the community' (Markham and Hancock 1945: 8).

Bevin's original concern about help for private households and the Report that followed need to be seen in the wider context of the challenges presented by the mobilisation of women for the war effort from 1941 onwards. The conscription of women into the services and into industry which had begun with the National Services (No 2) Act in 1941 introduced the category of 'mobile' women to identify women free of domestic responsibilities who could be moved from their homes to areas of need if required. Penny Summerfield has argued that 19 per cent of women transferred, under this Act, to 'essential' work were 'labourers and domestic servants' but opportunities for war work and increased mobility undoubtedly enabled countless others to escape the servitude of service (Summerfield 1993b: 68). Women, like Pauline Charles, whose mistress attempted to keep her by arguing that domestic drudgery to a demanding mistress for low wages was an honourable way of serving her country, felt that the war offered them the means of escape from a job they hated. While, the government was committed to the increas-ing mobilisation of women as a necessary prelude to winning the war, this co-existed and, at times, conflicted with traditional beliefs about women's 'natural' sphere (Summerfield 1996: 35–52). Anxieties about the potential disruptions to family life caused by wartime circumstances manifested themselves in concerns about the effects on home life of women's war work, female mobility, and the lack of domestic help for middle-class women. Bevin believed the provision of domestic help to be 'one of our most difficult problems' and one which was exacerbated by the increas-ing mobilisation of women for the war effort, 'our mobilisation of woman-power has reached a pitch where I fear we are inflicting undue hardship on individual households particularly where there are sick people and children' (Bevin to Brown

1943). The fear that the encouragement, indeed compulsion, of women to become 'mobile' might prise women away from, even shatter, their traditional links with and obligations to domesticity, be it as wives and mothers or domestic servants, lay behind the anxieties about domestic help. The *Report on the Post-War Organiz-ation of Private Domestic Employment* was informed by these concerns and, in important ways, contributed to the formations of femininity and class that emerged in the post-war period. The rhetoric of post-war pronatalism and concerns for the stability of the family, beset by the upheavals of war, maps onto both gender and class and can be traced in the Report.[11] For example, while it was acknowledged that men should be encouraged to take responsibility for household tasks and 'home duties', there was no allusion to this aspect of domesticity in the final summary of recommendations (Markham and Hancock 1945: 17). At the same time the rationale for the Report's recommendations makes it very clear that the problem is about middle-class women and their role in post-war society, 'behind domestic problems stands the greater issue of the birth rate and our menaced existence as a great nation' (Markham and Hancock 1945: 18). (Middle-class) women who cannot share their husband's leisure or be a companion because of excessive domestic duties 'will not undertake the burden of childbearing' (Markham and Hancock 1945: 18).

Women were perceived as both the problem and the solution: as 'mobile' workers they were essential to the economy *and* threatened the stability of the home. As mothers in the home (and it is important to note how worker and mother were always kept separate in the conceptual vocabulary of the period), women reproduced the next generation but, it was believed, required practical help if they were to be persuaded to undertake this task. Because it was believed that 'most of the nation's brains, leadership and organizing ability' were to be found in the middle classes, it was middle-class families who must be persuaded to have children (Lewis and Maude 1949: subtitle). Hence it was assumed that waged domestic workers on at least a daily basis would be required for middle-class homes. Implicit in the debates of this period was the assumption that the provision of help for middle-class mothers should be a priority. At the same time, it was argued, local authority provided, means-tested Home Helps should be made available for those working-class mothers who, because of sickness or other emergencies, were temporarily unable to fulfil their domestic duties (Markham and Hancock 1945: 7). In order to ensure a continuing supply of domestic help for middle-class households, the Report recommended that a National Institute of Homeworkers be established to provide a six-month training for women and girls in local centres (with maintenance allowances) after which they would be placed in approved households. The Report also recommended that in order to offset the high cost of employing trained workers which would put domestic help beyond the reach of most middle-class families, the wages of domestic workers should be deductible from the employer's income prior to tax levels being assessed. The post-war Labour Government adopted the Report's recommendation to establish a National Institute of Homeworkers. In the event this was never fully established due to difficulties over finding suitable premises. More significant, in the long term, the recommended tax allowances were never implemented. As a result the high cost of employing trained domestic help allied to the continuing refusal of women to consider domestic work as a full-time occupation resulted in a pattern whereby those who could afford it increasingly employed cheaper non-residential part-time help.

In April 1946 the BBC Home Service broadcast a round table discussion on domestic help, chaired by Markham. This programme was undoubtedly orchestrated in order to publicise and popularise the ideas that underpinned the Government's intention to establish a National Institute of Homeworkers. Markham concluded the broadcast with a rallying cry to women:

> This [domestic help] is really a problem for women. Because it is a field where women have exploited women in the past. And if the difficulty of getting the housework done is not solved, women will not be able to make their contribution in the world. This is the test today: can women share the work of the home, no longer on any basis of cond-escension or rank, but on terms of justice and mutual respect and independence? So that 'service' will cease to be considered a badge of inferiority but will find its true place as a princely motive for the enrichment of life. Above all we want family life with its loyalties and affections to be made safe, and *home* – not an apartment house or a residential hotel – the centre of it. (*Listener* 1946: 466)

Women's 'contribution in the world' is here represented as securing home and family life rather than participating in public affairs or employment. The selection of participants and the topics debated reinforced this underlying message: in the post-war world citizenship for women would focus on their role in the family.

The discussion involved four women categorised in the transcript of the broadcast as 'middle-class housewives', two women categorised as 'working-class house-wives', three women categorised as 'domestic workers', and a representative of the National Union of Domestic Workers. All those with children are identified as 'housewives' and, as far as it is possible to tell from the transcript, none of these worked outside the home either part or full-time. Yet, figures of the period show that approximately 5,710,000 women were working either full or part-time in 1946 (Riley 1983: 146). Markham herself, whilst never a salaried employee, influenced national and local politics, sitting on numerous committees, lecturing in France and Germany after the war and working in a voluntary capacity for women's organis-ations. Nevertheless the middle-class women in the discussion are represented as full-time housewives in need of domestic help in order to cope with the demands of motherhood:

> *Mrs Smith* [middle-class housewife]: I've four children, three of school age, but they can't stay to lunch at school, so I have lunch for four children and dinner again at night for my husband. I can't even get daily help. I've only got Nanny after about a three months' wait, costing about £20, from Ireland. She wants to leave but doesn't want to leave me stranded. (*Listener* 1946: 464)

In the context of this debate the issue of domestic help is linked to the needs of women identified as mothers in the home rather than to their needs as workers. Moreover, the middle-class women selected for the discussion are models of pronatalist rhetoric. Mrs Smith has four children and Mrs Serpell uses the language of pronatalist thought to justify her need for domestic help:

> *Mrs Serpell* [middle-class housewife]: I've got two small children. When you are trying to cope with two toddlers, trying to bring them up to become more or less *rational citizens*, it's almost impossible to cope with all the housework yourself . . . I personally feel I don't want to have more than two in my family unless I'm sure of getting somebody to help. (my emphasis) (*Listener* 1946: 464)

Mrs Proctor, on the other hand, is also categorised as a 'housewife' but defines herself as a 'different' kind of housewife – a 'working-man's wife' with two children,

> *Mrs Proctor* [working-class housewife]: I'm just a working-man's wife and I'm on seven or eight different committees, social welfare, chairman of schools [sic], and so on. I've two children – I'll admit there's twelve years between them – but it never dawned on me that I wanted help. I always managed, and I think I can face up with any one round this table for sixty-nine years of age. (*Listener* 1946: 464)

Throughout the discussion Mrs Proctor only speaks four times and when she does it is to ask what help is envisaged for working-class women, a question to which she never receives an adequate reply. Mrs Silver, the other 'working-class house-wife', speaks three times and her remarks suggest that she herself was once a domestic servant thus blurring the boundaries the programme attempts to establish between working-class housewives and domestic workers.

The greater part of the discussion is carried on between the 'middle-class housewives' and the 'domestic workers', and covers wages, time off, uniforms, living-in and the difficulties of negotiating what is 'a very close and often very difficult personal relationship' between mistress and maid (*Listener* 1946: 465). The structure of the discussion appears to be to hear and acknowledge the complaints of domestic servants and then to reveal, via Markham as chair, the proposals for ameliorating these. In the process, the pleasures of housework and running a home are extolled by the domestic workers and reiterated by Mrs Silver,

Dunkley [domestic worker]: As a domestic worker – not servant, please, ladies – you do develop a sense of responsibility. It is not like repetition work in a factory. Domestic work is creative. You can see something growing under your fingers: the well-polished floor, the beautiful brass, the well-kept china and all those hundred-and-one details which go to make the home not merely a house or a domestic museum . . .

Mrs Silver [working-class housewife]: Yes, there is always something going on that you really would not get in a factory, especially where there are children. You get a wonderful variety.

Ayris [domestic worker]: I would not wish to do anything else . . . I do not think there is anything more marvellous than running a house and cooking a meal. (*Listener* 1946: 465–6)[12]

Mrs Smith (middle-class housewife) responds '[t]hat sounds better. Surely we women can co-operate to help each other'. Mrs Smith's words function at this point to reassure any middle-class housewives listening to the programme whose dislike of and anxiety about servants may have been confirmed by the earlier 'militancy' of the domestic workers. The intended message is that maid and mistress *can* work together despite their differences in a spirit of tolerance and fair play. Yet, this apparent egalitarianism is achieved only at the point at which the domestic workers and a working-class housewife confess their love of domestic work thus 'proving' that the 'lower classes' are 'naturally' suited to undertake housework. Mrs Proctor contributes to this assumption when she insists that *she* had never felt the need for help with housework. Whereas, as Mrs Serpell (middle-class housewife) points out,

[i]t's very hard when women have at last come into their own and realise they have got a brain and there are things they can do other than domestic work, if they never have time to sit down and read a book. I don't want sherry parties or to play bridge, but your brain just becomes stagnant when you do nothing but housework. (*Listener* 1946: 465)

In the light of the foregoing discussion, when Markham concludes by claiming that 'if the difficulty of getting the housework done is not solved, women will not be able to make their contribution in the world', it is very clear, if not explicitly stated, who will be doing the housework and who will be making a 'contribution in the world' (*Listener* 1946: 466). Markham's notes for the programme reveal that, despite her genuine concern for greater opportunities for working-class women, she remains wedded to a traditional hierarchy in which '[n]o [working-class] girl can be better employed than in helping another woman to bring up her children & [sic] make home comfortable for the breadwinner' (Jones 1994: 189). The fact that Mrs Proctor served on numerous committees and ran a home without any domestic help is ignored. Indeed I suspect the representation of working-class housewives by the highly competent figure of Mrs Proctor is intended to demonstrate that working-class women do not really require daily help in the home.

Markham's proposals for providing more domestic help met with a degree of scepticism and anxiety from the middle-class housewives. One concern was the cost: trained domestic workers would command a rate similar to that paid to women in factory work. Another concern was that of 'overtraining'. Mrs Smith pointed out that 'not all housework is skilled work. Cooking undoubtedly is, but is making a bed? Isn't there a great deal of help we get from the girls of an unskilled type?' (*Listener* 1946: 466). This is in direct opposition to Miss Dunkley who, earlier in the discussion, insisted that '[d]omestic work is creative' and continued by extolling the pleasures of polishing and cleaning furniture, china and brass. These distinctions formed the conceptual framework within which the practices of housework were given value and meaning. Those tasks that required physical 'brawn' – scrubbing, washing, polishing – were distinguished in middle-class consciousness from those that might involve thought and artistry – cooking, decorating, sewing. It should not be surprising therefore given the homology middle class: working class/mind: body that those tasks defined as physical were the very tasks for which middle-class women continued to demand help. The discussion reveals the irreconcilable tensions around the meanings of housework which were variously understood as creative (the domestic workers), unskilled (the middle-class housewives), or practical necessity (Mrs Proctor). Working-class women were making an entirely rational choice when they rejected a form of employment that not only deprived them of their independence but continued to value the tasks involved on terms not of their choosing. Markham was right to recognise that any scheme for recruiting domestic workers required a re-valuing of domestic work. However, neither Markham nor the middle-class housewives taking part in the 'Help for Housewives' debate could or would willingly choose to think beyond the structures of middle-class subjectivity that understood the daily routines of housework as alien and 'other'. Markham's final words in which she hopes that '"service" will cease to be considered a badge of inferiority but will find its true place as a princely motive for the enrichment of life' were little more than the rhetorical flourish of a system struggling to survive (*Listener* 1946: 466).

Domestic Service and Modernity

The anxieties about domestic service that surfaced again and again throughout the first half of the century reached a peak in the late 1940s. There are a number of reasons why the debates, which were the public manifestations of these anxieties, repay careful attention. First, the discussions around domestic help demonstrate very clearly that many of the markers of class identity that distinguished women from each other were structured around home and service. In 1901 B.S. Rowntree had identified 'servantkeeping' as 'marking the division between the working classes and those of a higher social scale' (Rowntree 1901: 14). In 1946 this was a distinction that was becoming difficult to sustain, as fewer households were able to employ servants. However, class differences far from being dissolved, as the egalitarian rhetoric of the period implied, were in the process of being reformulated and domestic organisation was a key factor in this process. The increased economic and social independence of working-class women during the war allied to their continuing refusal to enter domestic service was a source of anxiety to middle-class observers (Jephcott 1943). For domestic service had not only provided help with housework, it had also kept working-class women dependent and, at least, on the surface, deferential. The system by which young women had left their homes to work in the houses of their 'betters' meant that not only were they subject to the moral authority of their employers but also that they were exposed to the 'civilising' values of middle-class domesticity. Commentators perceived, in the refusal of working-class women to enter domestic service, a worrying hedonism and lack of responsibility amongst young working-class women that, they believed, had the potential to disrupt not only traditional gender ideologies but also the hierarchies of class.

The account of domestic service that I have outlined draws attention to the cultural assumptions on which the middle-class home was predicated. The middle classes assumed the right to a superior level of domestic comfort. They took warmth, good food and comfortable surroundings for granted in ways that working-class families could never do, and saw these as rights rather than privileges. For middle-class women home meant certain standards of privacy, leisure, comfort and ease. For working-class women home often meant the opposite: overcrowding and drudgery, allied to a struggle to provide basic food, clothing and warmth. When working-class women demanded opportunities to housekeep their own home in the suburbs they were asserting their right to that comfort and ease that had for too long been denied them. The constant discussion of 'the servant problem' expresses a (middle-class) preoccupation with the perceived threat to the right of middle-class families to certain standards of domestic comfort. Without domestic help it would prove impossible to maintain the standards of 'gracious living' and ease that had characterised domestic life. Indeed 'the servant problem', that plagued the middle classes during the first half of the twentieth century, made visible the fragility and instability of these rights and revealed them as privileges that could all too easily be eroded or dismantled. Moreover, it was the collective agency of those working-class women who refused to go into service that created a situation over which the middle classes had little control. For middle-class women this must have been particularly difficult. On the one hand to be rid of servants was to make the home a more private place in which intimacy and companionship between family members could be more easily expressed and in which the, sometimes crippling, expectations of authority were removed. On the other hand, the price extracted was to take on the daily burdens of routine housework and childcare, making it, potentially, harder to engage in any kind of sustained creative, voluntary or paid work. At the same time, middle-class women must have been aware that those women who would once have been their maids and cooks, were now forming autonomous cultures of domesticity that may or may not have imitated middle-class standards of comfort. The loss of servants meant a reconstruction of the identity of the married middle-class woman. No longer 'mistress' of the household with all the associated connotations of power and control, she was invited to see herself as the more socially egalitarian 'housewife'. As we shall see in the next chapter, there were determined attempts to represent this identity as a professional one, but it must have produced considerable confusion and a sense of loss for young middle-class women whose understanding of domesticity had been learned from an earlier generation of mothers secure and confident in their role as middle-class mistresses.

Moreover, the representation of the housewife, as is evident from the BBC discussion above, was never as classless as its creators would have us believe. Beneath the rhetoric of egalitarianism and social democracy it is possible to detect a fierce struggle on the part of middle-class women to reformulate a set of distinguishing markers that would continue to assert their difference from and superiority to 'the wives of working-men'. The home continued to be the central locus of this struggle but the meanings attributed to housework, rather than 'servantkeeping' itself, became key signifiers of social identity. The legacy of domestic service meant that working-class women remained linked in the minds of middle-class women with deference and with the drudgery of housework. Thus those tasks that could be conceptualised as creative homemaking – cooking, sewing, decorating – became acceptable ways of spending time while 'the rough' (scrubbing, washing, polishing) continued to be seen as 'wasted time' (Gavron 1966: 132). In saying this I am not trying to deny the drudgery and tedium that can accompany housework. What I am concerned to do is to demonstrate the ways in which 'homemaking' and 'housework' came to be understood differently and the ways in which those understandings were (and continue to be) linked with ideas about class and status. It is possible to see the first fifty years of the century, with its, often heated, discussions of the so-called 'servant problem', as a transitional phase in the modernisation of private and domestic life that was to find its completion in the 1950s. On the one hand the refusal of women to enter domestic service as alternative occupations became available threatened the collapse of a social system based on deference, servility, authority and breeding. On the other hand, middle-class women, who encountered the loosening of social hierarchies that accompanied many people's experience of the years after 1914, were aware that 'modern' relations between servant and employer required recognition of equal status and an equal humanity. Caught between the (?guilty) desire to maintain a known social system that offered certain forms of power and control, and an equally fraught anxiety about how to democratise what was self-evidently hierarchical, many middle-class women must have felt themselves to be inadequate and reluctant midwives to the birth of modern forms of domesticity. And if one of the paradigmatic experiences of modernity is the tension between the desire for individual fulfilment, growth and development, and the equally powerful drive for democracy, community and collectivity, then in the struggles of bourgeois women to solve 'the servant problem' we can see a feminine version of this conflict.

The debates over domestic service reveal the very real tensions for liberal-minded middle-class women as they attempted to reconcile their commitment to egalitarianism and social reform with an equally powerful need to maintain social markers and boundaries. In her autobiography written in 1953, Markham, who was a lifelong member of the Liberal Party with a particular interest in education and training for working-class women, wrote '[t]here is an unresolved conflict taking place in many minds today between a desire for greater social equality and the half-reluctant recognition of the need for an *élite*' (Markham 1953: 33). As I have argued above, for middle-class women, this 'need for an *élite*' could find expression in the discourses of home and housework. However, discussions about how domestic work was to be organised and who was to do it were part of a wider debate about the role and place of women in post-war society: '[w]omen in large measure fail to recognize how much their own future as independent beings turns on finding some solution of [sic] the problem of domestic help' (Markham 1953: 33). In relation to her own personal life, Markham recognised that the struggle for equality for women in the public world of politics and the professions was inextricably linked to their perceived duties and obligations in the domestic world of home and family. Nevertheless, in the Report and in the Home Service debate, Markham was at pains to stress the importance of women's role in maintaining family life. Born in the 1870s Markham's life and career straddled two worlds. Strongly influenced, as a young woman, by her mother's traditional beliefs, Markham always had one foot in Victorianism. Yet the social changes of the twentieth century developed in her a lifelong commitment to educational reforms to enable middle-class women to take up new job opportunities. At the same time she advocated traditional occupations, particularly domestic service, for working-class women but on a regularised and skilled basis. The uneven mixture of conservative, feminist and liberal thought in her concern for and ambivalence about domestic reorganisation is testament not only to the varied sources from which she drew her political beliefs but also to the confusions around gender, class and domesticity that constituted her experience of modernity.

Neither *The Seven Chars of Chelsea* nor the Report question the assumption that 'home duties' are women's responsibility nor the right of some women to employ other women to help maintain their homes and family life. Privately Markham viewed the employment of working-class women as domestic servants as a means by which middle-class women like herself might be enabled to take up professional careers and public work. Despite her socialist leanings, Fremlin also assumes that middle-class women will wish and need to continue employing servants after the war. However, there are generational differences. Fremlin benefited from the educational reforms won by women in the late nineteenth century. She was educated at a girls' secondary school and, from 1933 to 1936, at Somerville College, Oxford where she read 'Greats'. Markham, born in 1872, received one year's formal education in her late teens but, like most women of her generation, was expected to devote herself to the limiting life of the Victorian and Edwardian 'lady'. Fremlin believed that the injustices of domestic service were allied to the oppressions of capitalism and could only be remedied by attacking what she called 'class antagonism'. While at Oxford she was a member of the Communist Party but soon came to believe that her friends in the Party talked 'what sounded like rubbish about working-class life' (Fremlin 1980).[13] As a result she decided to 'find out what it really is like' by taking jobs in domestic service (Fremlin 1980). Such ideas would not have found favour with Markham who believed in a world based on the structures of deference and dependence that Fremlin attacks in *The Seven Chars of Chelsea*. Fremlin's ideal domestic worker is the independently minded 'char' working on a daily basis; Markham's ideal is the residential but skilled maid who takes pride in cleaning someone else's belongings. However, the difficulty of imagining a world without domestic help was common to both Fremlin and Markham. For both women the question was how domestic help should be organised in the 'modern' world. As a result neither was able to address adequately the causes and obstacles that made it problematic for *all* women 'to make their contribution in the world'. Instead both women drew on what had become by the 1940s a well-established rhetoric of optimism that represented the problems that existed between mistresses and maids as ones that could be solved by greater co-operation between classes. Such co-operation, it was believed, would evolve from the 'common sufferings and tribulations shared by all alike during the war' and the result would be a reformed form of egalitarian domestic service. (Markham and Hancock 1945: 21)

Throughout the immediate post-war period numerous schemes were floated for alleviating the burden on the housewife. The National Federation of Women's Institutes recommended that married ex-dairymaids be recruited to work for farmers' wives; the Ministry of Health attempted to recruit part-time 'home helps' from amongst married women at home in the wake of doctors' reports of an increase in 'nervous troubles' amongst mothers of young families; and under the European Volunteer Workers' Scheme domestic agencies might recruit migrant female labour to help in private households, particularly those of doctors, clergymen, dentists and farmers, as well as in hospitals and hostels.[14] And, of course, in the post-war period immigration from the crumbling British Empire provided a renewed pool of labour for domestic work, particularly in schools, hospitals and other institutions (Webster 1998). Yet, despite Government initiatives and official enthusiasm for the continuance of domestic service in some form, usually envisaged as part-time and non-residential, there was a continued reluctance on the part of working-class women to take up such work. The circumstances of full employment from the late 1940s onwards and the expansion of part-time opportunities enabled many women to move up the occupational ladder into office, factory and shop work and away from domestic service. Miriam Glucksmann has argued that the first half of the twentieth century witnessed a movement of working-class women out of domestic employment and into the production of commodities and services for purchase. At the same time, she claims, middle-class consumption of commodities and services was stimulated and the 'greater relative purchasing power of the middle class' became one of the markers of class identity rather than 'servant-keeping' (Glucksmann 1990: 254). These changes focus on women who were perceived as the new consumers of modern capitalism and, in patriarchal discourse, the guardians of the home where such consumption would increasingly occur. As such, working-class women played a key part in the social relations contingent upon such changes. As workers in factory production they produced the vacuum cleaners, fridges and washing machines that enabled their erstwhile employers to run 'servantless' houses, and, as newly constituted housewives with homes of their own, they began, particularly after 1945, to purchase these commodities for themselves.

The tensions between renewal and destruction, between the traditional and the modern that characterise modernity are particularly visible in the story of domestic service in the twentieth century. Middle-class women like Woolf, Markham and Fremlin were, in their different ways, concerned to modernise the ways in which domestic help was organised. They saw in the nineteenth-century middle-class home, structures and conventions that they believed to be outmoded and the enemy of 'modern' living; at the same time they remained wedded to the privileges and advantages that such traditionalism fostered. Perhaps the real 'moderns' were those working-class women who chose not to enter an occupation they despised but found work elsewhere. Sometimes this work was in jobs that echoed the demands of domestic service: hairdressing, waitressing, 'charring' in institutions, working as a shop assistant and cooking for restaurants and cafés.[15] These jobs demanded many of the skills and qualities that had once been required by domestic servants and continued to offer low wages, few opportunities for promotion and low status. Nevertheless, in one particular they differed significantly. Such work enabled working-class women to inhabit the same public spaces as middle-class women, albeit not on the same terms, but certainly on ones that did not 'own them body and soul' as had been the case with residential domestic service. It would not do to be too optimistic here. Working-class women have continued in domestic occupations such as cleaning and catering and such occupations have remained invisible and exploitative. In the early 1980s I worked as a part-time dinner lady in a boys' public school and was regularly referred to as 'the maid'. Yet, for better or worse, after the Second World War, the relationship between middle and working-class women was less likely to take place behind the closed doors of the middle-class home. Instead it was acted out in the institutions, shops, offices and factories that constituted the public world. As such, class relations between women became a more publicly visible aspect of the modern urban and suburban experience and the consumer culture that increasingly defined this.

−3−

Getting and Spending, Identity and Consumption

The expansion of suburbia and the decline of domestic service were two significant aspects of women's experience of domestic modernity. The third was the shift to a consumer-oriented economy that began in the late nineteenth century but finally established itself in the years between 1900 and 1960. In this chapter I consider some of the ways in which this shift had an impact on the domestic identities offered to women with specific reference to domestic commodities and to women's magazines. Women were positioned at the forefront of this economic shift and the 'modern' home, run by a 'professional' housewife, was the place where the practices of getting and spending found their most potent expression.

In his *The Romantic Ethic and the Spirit of Modern Consumerism* Colin Campbell notes that, '[t]he cultural logic of modernity is not merely that of rationality as expressed in the activities of calculation and experiment; it is also that of passion, and the creative dreaming born of longing' (1987: 227). As we saw in the introduction and in Chapter 1, one of the tensions of modern life is the contradictory pull of conflicting discourses. On the one hand the discourse of rationality and betterment offers the promise of order and stability, on the other hand the discourse of romantic transcendence invites us to leave behind the mundanity of everyday life that is the price for this security. In the twentieth century dreams of transcendence have increasingly found expression in the consumption of commodities and leisure: advertising, the cinema, and other forms of popular culture have all expressed 'the creative dreaming born of longing'. To examine twentieth-century life through the lens of such consumption is to situate femininity at the centre of modernity and to re-assign women a key place in the cultural transitions of the twentieth century (Felski 1995: 62–3). For, from the late nineteenth century onwards, the consumer was generally figured as a (middle-class) woman: the new department stores, the provincial chain stores, and the proliferation of advertising and magazines urged her to consume, not only an increasing range of products but also, the identities, dreams and longings inscribed in these. As Felski observes '[t]he emergence of a culture of consumption helped to shape new forms of subjectivity for women, whose intimate needs, desires, and perceptions of self were mediated by public representations of commodities and the gratifications that they promised' (1995: 62). There are two points to make here. First, the forms of subjectivity that were shaped by an emerging culture of consumption were, for the most part, centred on the home and increasingly focused on the reformulation of the role of housewife. Second, as Felski points out, the linking of femininity and consumption has led to certain narratives of modernity in which 'the idea of the modern becomes aligned with a pessimistic vision of an unpredictable yet curiously passive femininity seduced by the glittering phantasmagoria of an emerging consumer culture' (1995: 62). Women, who, in these narratives, come to signify the duped and exploited 'masses', are impelled by irrational desire into an ever-spiralling cycle of consumption, squandering money on the acquisition of more and more products that are neither useful nor necessary. It is not my intention to argue, in defence of consumption, that it is an unproblematic and celebratory space from which the female consumer can mount meaningful resistances and sub-versions. The dangers of such a position have been remarked by a number of feminist critics who, while wishing to problematise the production/consumption dichotomy and to rescue the female consumer from persistent accusations of irrationality and passivity, remain aware that consumption is not a series of free choices but is shaped by racial, economic and geographical constraints (Felski 1995; Nava 1992; Williams 1991). In what follows it will become clear that early-twentieth-century representations of the white female consumer in Britain were differentiated according to class and that access to commodities (and the dreams and identities linked to these) was limited to those with some degree of relative affluence. Nevertheless, a growing culture of consumption did offer some women opportunities to redefine themselves in ways that counter the dystopian perspective of feminist theorists who have, until recently, tended to adopt the Frankfurt School tradition of seeing consumers as passive victims of ideologies that serve only the interests of capitalism. As Erica Carter observes, women 'participate in the regul-ation and organization of market processes. The machine itself, if vast and apparently all-embracing, is never intrinsically monstrous; it is both manipulative and manip-ulated' (Carter 1984/1993: 107).

Until recently theorists have tended to see consumption as subordinate to production. Consumption is seen as frivolous, passive, even decadent, while production, understood as work, is perceived as noble, dignifying and a source of pride. Such distinctions, of course, have gender implications: passivity and frivolity are congruent with the passivity and narcissism culturally attributed to women. One of the consequences of thinking about consumption and production in this way has been to privilege the world of work over the home, seeing production as taking place in the workplace and consumption as an activity closely related to the home. As we have seen in earlier chapters, the domestic arena has been largely ignored in narratives of modernity or where it has appeared it has been seen as either a refuge from modernity or a stifling, outdated place from which to escape into a freer, modern world. More recently consumption has been seen as an active process through which people can forge identities and participate as citizens, and the home a key site for the working out of this process. In Britain the identity 'housewife' and the consumption of domestic commodities became inextricably linked in the first half of the twentieth century, finding their apotheosis in the Second World War when the housewife became a national icon and an essential worker in the victory over fascism (Lury 1997; Mackay 1997: 3–5).

One of the relatively unremarked phenomena of the twentieth century has been a shift in the identities offered to wives and mothers. At the end of the nineteenth century the middle-class wife and mother was talked about as 'mistress of the house'. As we have seen this role included the supervision of servants and the management of the home as a signifier of the family's status. Working-class wives were largely ignored until the Boer and First World War revealed the dreadful ill health of huge numbers of conscripts and 'national efficiency' demanded that working-class mothers be educated in hygienic childcare and housewifery (Davin 1989). Sixty years later, with the virtual disappearance of domestic service and the emergence of a home-centred culture, the cultural identities of middle-class mistress and 'working man's' wife had been substituted in public discourse by 'the housewife', an apparently classless figure, whose earlier functions had been replaced with a new and 'modern' role as 'Mrs Consumer'. Mark Abrams talked about these changes on a BBC Third Programme broadcast in 1959:

> So long as the main activities of the bread-winner and the main expenditure of his money was outside the home, his wife was primarily his housekeeper. If the home has now become his centre of activity, and if most of his earnings are spent on his home or in his home, his wife becomes the chooser and the spender, and gains a new status and control – her taste forms his life. (1959: 915)[1]

One of the most important aspects of this shift was the housewife's role as purchaser of commodities that would create the 'modern' home, a place that 'is warm, comfortable and able to provide its own fireside entertainment' (Abrams 1959: 915). Equally important was the significance of 'taste'. As we shall see, the middle classes continued to assert their position as arbiters of style and taste, and women, in their role as consumers, became increasingly central to this project.

The socio-economic shift to a more home-centred, consumer-oriented society that took place in the first half of the twentieth century, produced extensive advertising and publications targeted at women in their domestic role. Publications that aimed to provide women with information, advice and guidance on creating 'ideal homes' were not new. In the nineteenth century, bourgeois women in France, for example, were being exhorted to devote themselves to the purchase of commodities that would enhance the family's social position. Leora Auslander suggests that,

The new institutions of distribution were supported and sustained by an expansion in the media of advice. By this period [1820–1914], a model of domesticity, with the woman/wife as consumer, was already becoming quite apparent in the developing genres of women's magazines, etiquette books, marriage manuals and furnishings guides – genres largely, although not entirely, controlled by men. This literature was dominated by discussions of fashion, style, society news, and women's responsibilities. Primary among those responsibilities was buying the right goods for the family's social position, a topic discussed in great detail. (1996: 84)

This 'media of advice', which increased dramatically after 1914, was crucial in constructing the figure of the 'modern housewife'. From the 1920s onwards magazines, household manuals, and the women's pages of national newspapers offered guidance on a whole range of activities associated with homemaking as well as offering health, beauty and fashion advice. Abrams sees the 'modern housewife' as wielding a 'new status and control' (1959: 915). It is the purpose of this chapter to explore how far the proffered identity of 'modern' housewife offered women 'status and control'. At the same time it is important to remain aware that domestic modernity, despite the pleasures it offered, continued to tie women to what was seen as their appropriate place, and was understood and experienced differently by women of different classes.

Shopping and the 'Ideal Home'

With relation to nineteenth-century France, Auslander has noted that as early as the 1820s women '[w]ere already facing a more diversified and expanded network of retailers, and new conventions of shopping were emerging. The first stores with fixed (as opposed to negotiated) prices opened in this period; displays of goods became more important and shops more comfortable' (1996: 86). It is estimated that today women make at least 80 per cent of decisions about consumption, that is they select and purchase goods for use in the home and with the family, as well as for their own self-fashioning. Shopping, as one form of consumption, is generally understood as women's work and advertisers have long recognised that 'the role of consumer is constructed as a feminine one' (Lury 1997: 121). The spectacular new department stores that sprung up in Paris towards the end of the nineteenth century were described by Emile Zola as a 'triumph of modern activity' and the Daily Mail Home Exhibition, that ran annually from 1908 to 1951 in Britain, encouraged women to consume the products of science and technology (household appliances, interior decoration, house designs) and to use these products to create 'ideal' homes (Nava 1997: 46; Ryan 1995). Indeed Nava has suggested that it was 'in the exploding culture of consumption and spectacle', symbolised by the department store and the exhibition, that the daily lives of ordinary women were most touched by the processes of modernity. Yet, as Nava has also noted, women's experiences of 'consumption and spectacle' have received little attention from historians and this aspect of modernity has remained relatively undocumented.[2]

By the end of the nineteenth century department stores were established in major cities in Europe and America. These vast emporia modernised retailing by offering mass-produced commodities and fashion items, by utilising economies of scale, rationalising the use of space, and by displaying goods in ways that enabled consumers (usually women) to look and examine with no obligation to purchase. Department stores were among the first public buildings to use electric light to create spectacular effects thus making shopping into a pleasurable, visual exper-ience as well as a pragmatic necessity. Orchestras in the restaurants and tearooms, fashion shows, exotic pageants and a range of facilities, including toilets, writing rooms, children's areas, roof gardens, hairdressers and delivery services made shopping an enjoyable and multi-faceted activity. Women could meet friends, have their hair done, window-shop and make purchases under the same roof. Depart-ment stores were envisaged as social spaces that were safe and pleasurable for women. As the publicity material for Selfridges proclaimed 'This is not a shop – it's a community centre' and a souvenir booklet for Debenhams, produced for visitors to the Franco-British Exhibition in 1908, described in detail the facilities available,

> You may visit the various departments, then, if you wish, have lunch or tea at very moderate charges in the quiet, elegant Restaurant, to which a Smoking-room and Gentlemen's Cloakroom are attached. The Ladies' Club Room, which adjoins a luxur-iously appointed suite of Dressing and Retiring Rooms, is open to lady visitors, who may there read the papers and magazines, telephone, write letters, or meet their friends. Parcels and letters may be addressed in the Cloak Room. (Benson 1994: 188)

The use of the term 'lady' suggests precisely who was being invited to use the facilities. Working-class women had neither the time nor the money to visit metropolitan department stores although, as I outline below, they were able to make use of the chain stores that opened in most provincial towns during the interwar years. Where the large department stores were beneficial for working-class women was in providing alternative forms of employment to domestic service. The attributes that made a 'good' personal maid were precisely those required of sales assistants – deference, tact and an interest in someone else's clothes, make-up and furnishings.

Stores like Selfridges and Debenhams not only encouraged (middle-class) women to browse, to look, and to construct a subjectivity that was both voyeuristic and narcissistic but also enabled them to practise skills of financial management and expertise as they compared prices and judged the quality of the goods on display. Nava insists that department stores must be 'recognized as one of the main contexts in which women developed a new consciousness of the possibilities and entitlements that modern life was able to offer.' Certainly at the time, entrepreneurs like Gordon Selfridge were reputedly quick to foster links between women's emancipation and their stores, 'I came along just when they [women] wanted to step out on their own. They came to the store and realized some of their dreams' (Nava 1997: 64–73).[3] No doubt store owners, like Gordon Selfridge, saw marketing and advertising opportunities in the rhetoric and discourses of women's emancipation and, for many women shopping could be arduous, time-consuming and frequently anxiety-provoking. Nevertheless, the spectacular displays of furnishings, ornaments, and clothes that were offered for purchase in the new department stores offered opportunities for many women to envisage a world in which they could enhance their status in the home through their expertise as consumers at the same time as finding visual signifiers that might serve to carry profounder yearnings for those inexpressible desires, outlawed by socially acceptable norms of femininity.

There is a scene in Du Maurier's novel *Rebecca*, a scene that is made much of in the Alfred Hitchcock film of 1940, in which the narrator visits the forbidden west wing of Manderley which has remained undisturbed since Rebecca's death. The sinister housekeeper, Mrs Danvers, in a voice 'ingratiating and sweet as honey, horrible, false . . . low and intimate' guides her round Rebecca's bedroom and seductively displays Rebecca's lavish clothes and possessions. The bed with its golden cover, the wardrobe of clothes, the scent bottles, the hairbrushes, the slippers, the monogrammed nightdress case and, of course, the flimsy, see-through nightdress all function as markers of Rebecca's modern femininity, a femininity that refuses the Victorian attributes of passivity and modesty. They also work as signifiers of a particular wealth and social position. Manderley is a place of conspicuous consumption with its valuable furnishings, paintings and ornaments, large household of servants and, in particular, this erotically charged bedroom, 'the most beautiful room in the house' (Du Maurier 1938/1975: 174). And it is the socially inferior housekeeper with her 'skull's face' who performs the role of Mephistopheles, tempting both narrator and reader to consume the erotic and aesthetic symbolisations she offers. Rebecca's bedroom is an excessively commodified stage set that itself performs the imagined persona of the absent Rebecca, 'the room had more the appearance of a setting on the stage. The scene set between performances. The curtain having fallen for the night, the evening over, and the first act set for tomorrow's matinée' (Du Maurier 1938/1975: 173–4). This remarkable scene articulates a complex subjectivity in which longings for social and sexual power are displaced onto a range of expensive and luxury commodities that come to signify a femininity that is recognised as a masquerade available for 'purchase'. At the same time, the narrator fears her seduction by the (socially inferior) 'seller' and struggles to resist the voice that is as 'sweet as honey', refusing to be tempted by the promises inscribed in Rebecca's modern femininity. The language of theatre and seduction inextricably links performance, sexuality and commodification to suggest the anxieties as well as the pleasures that accompanied consumption for middle-class women.

Mrs Danvers not only acts as a Mephistophelian actor-director who brings the stage to light; who offers the narrator a glimpse of what might be socially and sexually. She also has the attributes of the sales personnel who guided customers through the theatrical phantasmagoria of the department store. Sales assistants in the new department stores were increasingly those who, like Mrs Danvers, might once have entered domestic service. Deferential and astute, female shop assistants could, it was believed, 'understand so much more readily what other women want. They can fathom the agony of despair as to the arrangement of colours, the alternative trimmings, the duration of a fashion and the depth of a woman's purse' (Nava 1997: 68). Moreover, a 'skilled professional salesperson will tactfully, delicately, but determinedly, ferret out [women shoppers'] needs and satisfy them' (Lury 1997: 131). Department stores offered new forms of employment to lower-middle and working-class women that brought them into *public* contact with their middle-class sisters. As we saw in Chapter 1 the spaces of the nineteenth-century city were classed as well as gendered and 'respectable' women rarely occupied the spaces inhabited by the working classes. For most bourgeois women, contact with the 'lower' classes took place in the private home, mediated by the rituals and forms of domestic service. Increasingly, as retailing was modernised, this contact took place in a public and, less mediated, space. Shopping offered numerous pleasures – looking, dreaming and the exercise of budgeting skills – but it could also be a source of anxiety. Shop assistants, who longed for the commodities they were forced to display and sell, might be rude or contemptuous, overtly deferential but covertly hostile. The relationship between buyer and seller was less easily controlled than the employer/employee relationship between mistress and servant, and a sales assistant, with the attributes of a Mrs Danvers, could strike terror in the heart of a young middle-class woman, as she determinedly 'ferreted out' the private dreams of her customer and attempted to 'seduce' her into purchasing commodities.

For many 'respectable' women there must have been anxieties about overspending, not only because extravagance could lead to debt and poverty, but also because ideas about financial extravagance were linked in the minds of many to fears about unrestrained female sexuality. Economic and sexual profligacy went hand in hand. Zola's description of the courtesan, Nana, exemplifies this association,

She rose higher than ever on the horizon of vice, dominating the city with her insolent display of luxury, and that contempt for money which made her openly squander fortunes. Her house had become a sort of glowing forge, where her continual desires burned fiercely and the slightest breath from her lips changed gold into fine ash which the wind swept away every hour. Nobody had ever seen such a passion for spending. The house seemed to have been built over an abyss in which men were swallowed up – their possessions, their bodies, their names – without leaving even a trace of dust behind them. (1972: 409–10)

The linking of sex, money, spending and luxury was not confined to fiction. Fears about feminine irrationality over spending were always close to the surface and, although women were encouraged to purchase commodities, the boundaries separating what was seen as excess from what was seen as acceptable were constantly policed. As Elizabeth Wilson has pointed out, the new crime of shoplifting emerged with modern forms of retailing and medical science was quick to transform this into the 'disease' of kleptomania thus pathologising those women who were unable to operate within the acceptable boundaries of consumption (1985: 152). Shopping, Wilson observes, 'was almost sexualised, fetishistically, as women who had "fallen" spoke of the irresistible touch of silk and satin, the visual seduction of displays, and their thirst for possession' (1985: 152). Anxieties about acquisitiveness and excessive materialism were, as we saw in Chapter 1, also linked to condemnation of a supposed 'suburban mentality', mass culture and the alienation and estrangement that, it was believed, accompanied these.

In his study of York, undertaken in the mid 1930s, Seebohm Rowntree described the impact of the newly established chain stores:

> There are three large chain stores in York: Woolworth's, Marks and Spencer, and British Home Stores. They affect the lives of the workers in two different ways.
>
> First they place within the reach of people of limited means a range of foods far wider than was available to them before, and sold in many cases at prices noticeably lower than those charged elsewhere . . . [Commodities such as] tinned foods, confectionery, biscuits, clothing, crockery, glass-ware, toilet articles, tools, stationery and hundreds of other miscellaneous goods which people of limited means buy.
>
> A second way in which these stores affect the lives of the workers is that they provide a form of entertainment! There is no doubt that thousands of people enter the stores just for the fun of having a look round. They see a vast assortment of goods displayed which they may examine at their leisure without being asked to buy. (1941: 218–19)

Although Rowntree refers to chain store customers as 'workers', it was the wives of the 'workers' who frequented the shops like Marks and Spencer, Woolworth's and Home and Colonial that were mushrooming throughout the 1920s and 1930s on the high streets of many provincial towns. The small independent retailers that had previously served working-class wives were gradually superseded by high-street chain stores and co-operatives: it has been estimated that the proportion of retail trade done by independents reduced from 82 per cent in 1915 to 65 per cent by 1939, and to 31 per cent in 1980/81 (Pollard 1983: 111, 303). Co-operative retail societies, of which the Co-op is the most well known, took 11 per cent of the retail trade in 1939 and were very popular with working-class housewives who were able to accrue dividends on their purchases. The years between 1918 and 1939 witnessed not only an expansion in chain store and co-operative retailing but also an increase in the amount people spent on household goods: in 1937 22 per cent of consumer expenditure went on food, 6 per cent on household furnishings and 10 per cent on clothing (Benson 1994: 63). Much of this household expenditure was managed by women who shopped in the newly established chain stores buying the family's clothing and shoes, bed and table linen, soft furnishings, cleaning materials, toothpaste, men's razor blades and shaving products. Like the metropolitan department stores but unlike the small independent retailers, high street shops offered consumers the opportunity to browse and to look without any obligation to buy. As one woman, the wife of a cabinet-maker, told Mass Observation in 1949, 'I just go to Timothy Whites [chain store chemist] and have a look round sometimes. It's more or less like a departmental store, you can go and have a look without being worried to buy and I think that's a very good thing' (Benson 1994: 189). The impact on women of being able to look cannot be overestimated. Conventionally the object of (male) scrutiny and surveillance, 'just looking' enabled women to position themselves as both subject and object as they gazed, for example, upon displays of clothing and cosmetics that might enhance their femininity at the same time as weighing the cost of these against the cost of a labour-saving cleaner that could make more time available for self-fashioning. These complex calculations were not simply financial; they involved, as we shall see, active decisions about self-worth and identity.

If the early department stores targeted middle-class women as their customers, the Daily Mail Ideal Home Exhibition catered mainly for the emerging lower-middle class, those for whom home ownership was becoming a very real possibility and who, it was believed, required guidance in the purchase of labour-saving domestic appliances and the creation of a home. In 1908, when the first exhibition was held, one of the aims of the Exhibition was to teach housewives how to live without servants. In particular the *Daily Mail* was concerned to woo the emerging lower-middle class who offered a lucrative market for advertisers, manufacturers and retailers. It has been estimated that in 1911–13 the average earnings of male clerks was about £142, a figure that had more than doubled by 1935 to £368, and had risen to £1040 in 1960 (Benson 1994: 25–6). It was believed that the theme of the 'ideal home' would appeal to the consumer aspirations of this section of society anxious to consolidate its emerging identity as part of the middle classes. The Daily Mail Home Exhibition contributed to the formation of a *commercial* culture of home-making, and lower-middle-class women were specifically targeted as consumers of this culture. Lord Northcliffe, owner of the *Daily Mail*, believed the best way to attract women as readers of his newspaper and the advertising that supported it, was by addressing them in terms of gender difference. Concerned about competition from the rival *Daily Express*, Northcliffe wrote 'I notice that while the *Express* . . . is trying to take away our women readers, one of our main sources of strength for advertising, the *Daily Mail* magazine page is less and less feminine . . . it ought to be almost entirely feminine. It ought, I think, to be a women's page, without saying so' (Ryan 1995: 69).[4] The *Mail* assumed that this female readership was 'the relatively affluent consumer of the 1930s, filling her mortgaged house with the essential labour-saving devices made necessary by the absence of domestic servants' and addressed her supposed needs through edit-orials, advertising, and pages on beauty, fashion and home-making, as well as through the annual Ideal Home Exhibitions which aimed to bring the latest in modern household design to the attention of its millions of women visitors (Jeffrey and McClelland 1987: 50; Ryan 1995).[5]

The Exhibition also has to be seen in the context of an increasing emphasis on visual display and spectacle that is characteristic of modernity. After the Great Exhibition of 1851 there was a proliferation of exhibitions in Britain and the rest of Europe. In 1908, the first year in which the Ideal Home Exhibition was held, London hosted, among others, the following exhibitions: the Franco-British Exhibition at White City, the Hungarian Exhibition at Earl's Court, the Heavy Motor Exhibition at Olympia, the 'What to do with our girls' Exhibition, the Mexican Exhibition at Crystal Palace, the 'Orient in London' Exhibition at the Royal Agricultural Hall, and the Home Arts and Industries Exhibition at the Horticultural Hall. Retail exhibitions were seen not only as venues to promote 'the retail sale to the general public of novel and popular commodities' but also as opportunities to display, often spectacularly, the products of science and tech-nology as well as educating the general public in the cultures of other countries, particularly those belonging to the British Empire (Ryan 1995: 33). While exhibitions fostered imperialist values and can be seen as an instrument of state propaganda, they were equally shaped by the commercial possibilities offered by an expanding market in retail commodities. Like the department and chain stores, exhibitions offered opportunities to look and be looked at, to sample or dream of new ident-ities, and to escape a dreary present in settings that spoke of luxury, exotic other worlds and glamour. As one visitor to the Ideal Home Exhibition in 1910 com-mented, 'if you cannot have everything you want in the world, you can imagine yourself having it, and there are so many things here that you do want, or would want if you dared to, that you must have some of them some day, if not all of them at once' (Ryan 1995: 81). Exhibitions, in all their theatricality and spectacle, constituted social spaces in which dreams and longings found visual expression for those who visited them and who, frequently, were women. As such they enabled women to understand themselves as consumers in ways that neither pathologised them nor saw them as passive victims of irrational impulse.

The Daily Mail Home Exhibition with its focus on the aim of the 'ideal home' inscribed modernity's dilemmas with particular acuity. As one commentator on the Exhibition observed:

> Since the Ideal Home Exhibition opened its doors in 1908 the progress of home-making has greatly accelerated. Woman's striving for more freedom, for self-expression, has probably been the greatest factor in this speeding up of the march towards the Ideal Home, and nothing has done more to bring the perfect home nearer than woman's determination to be freed from the thraldom of domestic duties carried out in archaic and inefficient ways. (Ryan 1995)

Women are here constructed as agents of modernity, seeking self-expression through their homes; a need that, it is believed, is impelled by the desire to escape the drudgery that previously accompanied housework. Such pronouncements invited women to see their place in the modern world, not in the workplace, politics or commerce, but as 'modern' housewives in the modernised home, financed through their increased control of household funds. However, technology and commerce under capitalism require that each new labour-saving device or fashion be replaced as soon as it becomes familiar, making 'the ideal' always unachievable and tantalisingly out of reach. Inscribed in the idea of the 'ideal home' was always the promise of new and advanced technology to reduce the time and energy spent on household tasks as well as the necessity of keeping pace with the changing fashions of interior design. This is an example of what Marshall Berman has called the 'maelstrom of perpetual disintegration and renewal' that constitutes modern life, an example that demonstrates the centrality of domesticity to women's experience of modernity (Berman 1988: 15). The Daily Mail Home Exhibition, like department and chain stores, made home, housekeeping and consumerism public as well as private experiences. Women visited the stores and exhibitions, purchased or simply looked at the products on offer, which were then taken back to the home and consumed or used to produce clothing, meals, room settings and an attractive appearance. In this way women consumers not only crossed the spatial boundaries between public and private more easily than is often imagined but also blurred the conceptual distinctions between consumption (seen as leisure) and production (seen as worthwhile work). Shopping was work that required financial acumen and a measure of restraint, skills increasingly recognised in the rhetoric of the 'modern' housewife. At the same time the goods purchased often needed creative work, in the form of sewing, cooking, decorating or arranging, to transform them into the aestheticised products of the 'ideal home'. The 'modern' housewife addressed by advertisers and manufacturers was skilled in budgeting but was equally adept at domestic creativity. So, did women adopt or appropriate these new identities? How did they understand the concept of the 'ideal home'? And what pleasures or social status did such understandings bring?

Sue Bowden and Avner Offer have argued that diffusion rates for electrical household appliances were much slower in Britain (and in Europe generally) than in America and that this cannot be explained simply in terms of incomes and prices but is related to the meanings attributed to leisure, housework and women's time (Bowden and Offer 1996: 247). As we have seen with regard to the Daily Mail Home Exhibition middle-class women were urged to purchase new technology such as irons, vacuum cleaners and refrigerators as a solution to the shortage of servants after the First World War. Such technology also promised to alleviate the drudgery of household work, particularly the less skilled tasks of manual labour such as washing, cleaning, preparing fires and ironing, leaving housewives freer to concentrate on 'management' tasks such as menu planning and financial budgeting, and the more creative tasks of meal preparation, childcare and interior design. Yet, as Bowden and Offer demonstrate, the take-up of electrical appliances was slow: 'irons and refrigerators took over two decades to enter the majority of households, while the water heater, washing machine, and vacuum cleaner reached only a 20 per cent ownership level in the same time' (1996: 247). In contrast, they argue, radios and televisions diffused more rapidly: radios introduced into households in 1923 had reached an 80 per cent ownership level by 1939 and televisions first introduced in 1949 had reached 50 per cent by 1958. Moreover, the ownership of electrical appliances was differentiated by class and region. In the 1930s middle-class households in the South were more likely to purchase appliances than those in the depressed North, while working-class women did not really begin to acquire these items until after the Second World War. The cost of installing an electric lighting system was between £5 and £6 in the 1930s and appliances cost between £1 for a standard electric fire and £35 for a refrigerator (Bowden and Offer 1996: 254–5). At a time when approximately three-quarters of all households were in receipt of an income of less than £5 per week, such outlay was prohibitive even where hire purchase terms were offered and taking into account the running costs of such items. Alternatives to the new electrical devices in the form of gas and solid fuel for cooking, lighting and heating were considered to be cheaper and more efficient and other claims on family income took priority (Bowden and Offer 1996: 256). Furniture, clothing and leisure commodities such as radios were the preferred purchases of many women. For example, expenditure on household textiles, in the form of sheets, pillow cases, blankets, towels, net curtains and curtain material, grew from £14 million in 1924 to £18.2 million in 1937. In 1938 £567 million was spent on clothing, double the amount spent on furniture and household equipment. Middle-class women, as might be expected, spent more, both in actual terms and in proportion to their incomes, on all these items than working-class women (Bowden and Offer 1996: 257–8).

These statistics suggest that it was not only the price of electrical appliances that made them less attractive to women consumers but a preference for spending money on display, luxuries and leisure rather than on reducing the time spent on household tasks. Radios, for example, were frequently listened to in the evenings when housewives sewed or knitted and were perceived as luxury items that made housework more tolerable. Curtains, furniture and wallpaper functioned to signify the pride a woman took in her skills as a housewife and in this sense the display was about a 'modern' identity based on hard work in contrast to the Victorian ideal of the ornamental, leisured lady. From the 1920s the bridge-playing, 'parasitical' lady of leisure was a figure much derided in women's magazines both in Britain and America. As one interviewee from Judy Attfield's study of women living in the new town of Harlow in the 1950s commented, 'We were the homeworkers . . . We had to get on and make the best of everything that we could. That was taking pride in what you'd got. Everything was polished' (1995: 226). Doris Arthurs who had been a housemaid in the household of the Lord Mayor of Birmingham recalled the suite she acquired on her marriage in 1932:

> We saw this beautiful brocade seven-piece suite. It was beautiful, covered in green with pale pink, all pale green little like forget-me-nots all over, it was lovely, and it had one wing chair for the gentleman and another sort of tub chair and the corner of the settee was like a tub but the other was a bolster effort, and we thought it was lovely.

For women like these the pleasure gained from the purchase of furnishings and non-functional household items for display was inextricably linked to a sense of pride both in the work carried out to make a comfortable home and in ownership of those commodities that previously had belonged only to the affluent.

Middle-class women who might have been expected to purchase the new labour-saving equipment were, as Bowden and Offer argue, slow to do so. Like their working-class counterparts, they were more likely to spend spare money on radios and entertainment than on the purchase, for example, of a washing machine. And, despite the shortage of 'live-in' servants, middle-class families continued to employ part-time domestic help. It is estimated that even a family with an income of between £250 and £350 in 1939 spent 1.3 per cent of its weekly income on domestic help, 1.5 per cent on entertainment and 2.4 per cent on furniture (Bowden and Offer 1996: 261–5).[6] Washing machines are a good example of the complex motivations, desires and satisfactions that surrounded the acquisition of labour-saving devices. Middle-class housewives expressed a preference for having the weekly wash done at home rather than using laundries.[7] Yet, they did not rush to purchase the new electric washing machines that became available in the 1930s, preferring instead to employ part-time (or, where possible, full-time) help with laundry even where this meant sending it out to a washerwoman (Zmroczek 1994:

13). Electric washing machines, which could have saved time and energy, were regarded with some suspicion as unhygienic because it was believed things could not be boiled in them (Mass Observation 1939a; Zmroczek 1994). There was a general consensus amongst women of all classes that the only way to ensure cleanliness, and the whiteness that signified this, was by boiling. When the soap powder Persil advertised itself as labour-saving because it only required a two-minutes soak and a two-minutes boil, many women were disdainful, insisting that the wash must be boiled for twenty to thirty minutes if it is to 'get them a nice white and all sort of sterilizing them. When you boil things, you sterilize them. The whiteness is the important part' (Mass Observation 1939a). This emphasis on cleanliness and whiteness was linked to an investment in hard work: women whose washing was grey were perceived as lazy, 'they should be ashamed, they should change the water more often' (Mass Observation 1939a).

As I have argued above, pride in their housewifely abilities was an important aspect of working-class women's expenditure choices. Pride and self-esteem were important also to middle-class women but in slightly different ways. An unpublished 1930s Mass Observation report on the psychology of housework claims that the majority of complaints about the drudgery of housework came from middle-class women, complaints that had not been alleviated by the availability of labour-saving devices or the continued employment of domestic help. The report concludes condescendingly that:

> Since these women's trouble is not really overwork but anxiety to prove to themselves their indispensability, then the only effect of increased labour-saving mechanisms, unaccompanied by other drastic social changes, will be to intensify the situation just described. Faced by yet further curtailment of useful work in the home, the more spirited will be even more willing to abandon their homes, and the weaker will be driven to even more neurotic symptoms in the effort to convince themselves that their job at home is a full-time one. (Mass Observation, 1939b)

This anxiety about the role of the middle-class housewife was fuelled by a fear that, freed from household tasks, women might abandon their domestic obligations either by leaving the home or by a retreat into 'neuroticism'. It is easy for us today to condemn the thinking that underpins these assertions but we need to be aware that, at a time when career opportunities for women were limited and generally required a woman to remain childless, if not single, many middle-class women believed that identity and satisfaction could be gained from their roles as wife, mother, and mistress of a home. Modernity, in the form of science and technology, could threaten that identity, at the same time as it promised to remove the burden of drudgery, a burden that it should be noted was never as pressing for the middle-class woman with servants as it was for her working-class counterpart.

In an unpublished manuscript written in 1944, Fremlin attempts to untangle the complex psychology that she believes constitutes middle-class femininity at this specific historical moment, drawing on the wartime diaries she collected as a member of the Mass Observation team (Fremlin 1944).[8] Fremlin argues that the work of the middle-class wife has become redundant: restaurants provide good food, laundries can do the washing, clothes are produced by chain stores and tailors, the loss of servants means the role of mistress is no longer necessary, and labour-saving devices have reduced the work involved in the running of a small, 'modern' home. She concludes that the middle-class woman's 'natural job has been taken from her by the triumphs of modern science and modern organisation' and that 'she is left in the most terrifying of all situations . . . that of being virtually unnecessary to the society to which . . . she irrevocably belongs' (Fremlin 1944: 5– 6). The point that Fremlin goes on to argue is that the experiences and circum- stances of war might further exacerbate this sense of redundancy. Not only was the middle-class woman's home broken up or threatened by the departure of husbands and the evacuation of children, but the standards of comfort and good food that it had always been her job to maintain no longer earned the approval of society. Working-class housewives, Fremlin goes on, did not find themselves in this position as they were not affluent enough to send clothes to the laundry or to purchase labour-saving homes and appliances. Fremlin was not advocating a return to the traditional homes of Victorian Britain: elsewhere, as we have seen, she proposed the modernisation of domestic service. Middle-class housewives *were* likely to be anxious about maintaining their class status at a time when, as we saw in the previous chapters, this was perceived as under threat from a newly emerging suburban culture and the loss of servants. According to Lewis and Maude the middle-class housewife:

> normally insists upon a rather higher standard of feeding than – at any rate – the urban working-class wife. She may not spend more money on food; she tends to expend more time and care on buying; to prepare and cook more food at home; to produce, with the aid of a stock-pot, more soups and stews, as well as making more jam, bottling more fruit, and so forth. The house or flat which the middle-class housewife has to run is normally larger, and contains more belongings. Often special rooms must be looked after, such as a husband's study, studio, or consulting room, and generally a nursery. (Lewis and Maude 1949: 206)

The emphasis on cooking and preparing food is telling. As John Carey has shown, eating tinned food was one of the attributes ascribed to 'the masses' by modernist writers. E.M. Forster's lower-middle-class Leonard Bast 'eats tinned food, a practice that is meant to tell us something significant about Leonard and not to his advantage' and Orwell lists tinned food as one of the evils of modern life (Carey

1992: 21; Orwell 1939/1987: 17). The use of convenience foods was seen as a lower-middle and working-class habit while preparing and cooking fresh foods was a signifier of a certain 'cultural capital' even though such work had more often than not been performed by a cook or general servant.

Middle-class women may have been pulled in two directions. While they recognised the potential to save time offered by new household appliances, they may have been aware simultaneously of the 'cultural capital' attributed to their use of time (Bourdieu 1984). Time invested in cooking, sewing, bottling fruit and jam was, as Lewis and Maude suggest, a marker of social status. Lewis and Maude also distinguish between 'deserving' and 'undeserving' members of the middle-class: 'the hard-working professional couple with three children' are the former while the 'rich widow and the successful black marketeer' are the latter. Contempt for those who led a 'leisured' and 'idle' life and the concomitant emphasis on the values of efficiency and hard work made it difficult for middle-class housewives to admit to having any spare time. Thus, as Fremlin's diarists illustrated, 'to confess to having any ease or leisure . . . was . . . tantamount to an admission of inefficiency' and many of the middle-class women whose diaries Fremlin read prided themselves on having no time and feeling overworked. The saving and spending of time were not simply pragmatic considerations, they were symbolic activities that signified in complex ways. Equally, the consumption of furnishings, curtains and domestic help was a means by which middle-class housewives could assert, through public displays of their managerial efficiency and hard work, their continued status as *the* arbiters of taste, fashion, good food and comfort.

While there is evidence to suggest that middle-class women may have felt some collective 'crisis' of identity in the 1930s and 1940s this was neither uniform nor complete: some undoubtedly did suffer profound anxieties, many found new opportunities in the circumstances of war, and others had probably always sought their sense of self from alternative satisfactions. I consider the figure of the wartime housewife more fully below but for now the point I want to make is that the demise of residential domestic service in the first half of the twentieth century did not seamlessly give way to the labour-saving 'modern' home, ruled over by the middle-class consumer housewife, beloved of advertisers and commentators. The reality was more complicated. Although there were staunch defenders of the traditional home who feared its break-up, there were others, like Fremlin, who recognised that domestic modernity brought gains and losses, and there were those, like the organisers of the Daily Mail Home Exhibition, retailers and advertisers, who saw commercial opportunities in the reformulation of women's role in the home. Middle-class women's subjectivities were constructed from a variety of discourses on consumption and domesticity and their responses, like those of their working-class sisters, expressed the full range of these tensions. In the next section I turn to the ways in which some of the ideas discussed above were articulated in the women's magazine industry that expanded dramatically in the first sixty years of the century.

Discourses of Femininity and Consumption in Advertising and Women's Magazines

One of the most resonant discourses of the early twentieth century was that of 'efficiency'. The initial principles of Frederick Winslow Taylor's 'scientific management' were appropriated for industrial production by Henry Ford. His introduction of the assembly line in 1914 enormously increased production and profit and was considered a major example of the values of efficiency. The rhetoric of scientific management and industrial rationalisation advocated by Taylor and Ford was quickly adapted to discussing women's work within the home and now-here more vigorously than in the proliferating women's magazines of the period. 'National efficiency' demanded that the private sphere of motherhood and house-work be reconstructed as being as important to the survival of the nation as advances in war technology or industrial production. However, there were fund-amental contradictions in this discourse of 'domestic efficiency'. Unlike industrial production, housework is not done for wages and increased production does not make 'profits' that can be ploughed back into higher wages or modernised mach-inery. Instead, stimulating higher standards of housework benefits those who manufacture household products and appliances that can be marketed as helping to produce these standards. Hence, if there are no wage incentives to housework, it becomes necessary to construct other incentives that will ensure women continue to take pride in their role as housewife (and continue to purchase new machinery and products). The most pervasive were the ideas that housework is a labour of creative love and motherhood and a service to the nation; discourses that effect-ively prevented any examination of the contradictions concealed beneath the rhetoric of 'domestic efficiency'. The ideal of the 'professional' housewife, promoted by women's magazines and advice manuals, bears further examination, emerging as it did at a moment when middle-class women's autonomy and mana-gerial status in the home was in decline, and working-class women were acquiring 'homes of their own' to maintain.

An advertisement in *Good Housekeeping* (1927) for Sunlight Soap combines the 'labour of love' discourse with the discourse of rational efficiency. The text reads,

> When it comes to highly-skilled washing, a man can't keep pace with his wife. With her washing is not a job – it's an art. Breakfast things are washed up – Bedrooms are tidied – Dinner is prepared – Children's needs are seen to – *and all the time it's Wash-day*. Truly a good wife brings Sunlight into the home.

> In Sunlight Soap there is everything to help the good wife and nothing to hinder her. Sunlight represents a scientific combination of nature's finest cleansing oils and fats. The best materials are selected – the most efficient methods of manufacture are rigidly adhered to – every boiling has to pass an analytical test for purity. (Braithwaite, Walsh and Davies 1986: 70, original emphasis)

The housewife's 'art' which consists of bringing 'sunlight into the home' is underpinned by the 'scientific', 'analytical' and 'efficient' methods that go into the manufacture of Sunlight Soap. In this way 'efficiency' is an element of the 'art' of housewifery that brings love into the home. The illustration accompanying the text shows a traditional English village street scene in which a man and a woman carry out traditional roles. Thus, the modernity, suggested by the emphasis on science, technology and efficiency, is (temporarily) linked with traditional ideas of gender, marital relationships and Englishness. The advertisement mobilises ideas about 'domestic efficiency' in the context of traditional values thus evading the contradictions that are thus inscribed. Another advertisement – this time for gas – avoids the implications of labour-saving devices. The advert depicts a gas salesman demonstrating the advantages of gas to a middle-class woman and her maid. The strapline reads 'That's good-bye to unnecessary drudgery' and goes on 'goodbye to all the work and trouble of fire-making, cleaning grates, and removing ashes'. Good-bye too, we might surmise, to the maid who has previously carried out these tasks and good-bye to the middle-class woman's managerial role as mistress of servants. However, this potential disruption to traditional ways of running a home is avoided by the strategy of representing the salesman in terms that signify deference and service. He is called punningly, Mr G.A. Service and he wears a black suit, is slightly stooped and has all the attributes of a butler in a well-placed household. The middle-class woman is positioned between her maid and this butler-like figure both of whom gesture deferentially towards her. It is made clear that modern efficiency, in the form of gas appliances, does not threaten the traditional structures that organise class relationships within the home: deference and service, albeit in different forms, are still available in the 'ideal home' celebrated by the advertisement. Wilson suggests that department stores mimicked the social relations of aristocratic and upper-middle-class homes thus creating 'an ambience of service rather than commerce'. This illusion, that a dying way of life can be continued, is equally implicit in the advertisment I have just described. Both department stores and advertising invested in creating visual spectacles and performances that allowed traditional forms of class relationships to exist alongside the new and 'modern' (Wilson 1985: 152).

These advertisements remind us of the complex nexus of needs and desires that were being addressed by those who marketed new machinery and products at the newly constructed figure of the 'professional' housewife. However, advertisers tapped into aspirations and anxieties that already existed: dreams, fantasies, needs were not simply created by marketing specialists but produced from a heady mix that included ideas about tradition, modernity and efficiency in society at large, and in the home in particular. Like department stores, women's magazines and the advertising that financed them were a *visual* experience, a new form of modern mass communication that was to become increasingly popular throughout the century. Sally Stein in her case study of the American magazine *Ladies Home Journal* makes the point that 'the women's magazine in the twentieth century, though continuing to include lengthy literary texts, was becoming a predominantly visual experience, constructing an audience of spectators and, by extension, consumers' and she argues that this 'trained the female viewer for the distinctive flow of messages delivered by the predominant cultural institution of the postwar era: tv' (1985: 8, 16). The idea of modern life as a visual spectacle in which we participate as both spectators and performers is central to many of the canonical narratives of modernity. For example, as we have seen, Baudelaire's modern painter, who merges with the crowd and visually records the spectacle that he observes, is a key figure in late-nineteenth-century accounts of modernity. I am arguing that women's magazines, as well as the Daily Mail Home Exhibition and department stores, offered visual spectacles and performances that related to the private world of the home rather than the public world of the city street. In doing so, these new forms of popular culture mediated the public/private divide, making homemaking, beauty and personal relationships visible and public while at the same time demonstrating that these 'private' areas of life were inextricably enmeshed in the social and economic changes that constituted modern life.

Although the beginnings of the women's magazine industry are discernible in the publications produced from the mid nineteenth century onwards, it was in the twentieth century that magazines took on the characteristics that make it possible to see them as a modern form of mass communication (White 1970; Winship 1987). By the beginning of the twentieth century the number of titles available had doubled and the market for magazines was increasingly class differentiated. Upper-class magazines carried items on society and high fashion, middle-class, and increasingly lower-middle-class, magazines offered a service to their readers, providing advice and information, while working-class magazines offered romantic fiction with an emphasis on melodrama and sensation (Winship 1987: 27). Magazines like *Good Housekeeping*, *Woman's Own*, *Woman and Home* and *Woman's Sphere* (the magazines studied here) juxtaposed visual images with written text, advertisements with editorial material, monochrome with colour to produce a reading experience that was very different from that required of traditional literatures. Stein quotes an Indiana housewife on this reading practice: 'I just read magazines in my scraps of time. I should so like to do more consecutive reading but I don't know of any reading course or how to make one out' (1985: 7). Stein goes on to argue that although readers believe that they are negotiating a freely chosen and personal path through the visual diversity of the modern magazine, the magazine's internal organisation functions 'to sustain the reader's interest *and* to draw the reader closer to the marketplace' (1985: 8). This is achieved, Stein demonstrates, by the ways in which new graphic techniques such as colour and photography are used to create internal links, a welcome familiarity, and distinctions between weighty instructive material and pleasurable visual experiences. Advertisements frequently deployed modernist aesthetics, using geometric lines and highly stylised images, were increasingly pictorial, and occasionally in colour. Instructive features were mostly monochrome written text. Women's magazines, like the shop windows of department stores, displayed a range of products but interspersed these with features and fiction that together demonstrated what a 'commodified modernised domestic world' and a modern (professional, efficient) femininity could look like (Stein 1985: 16).

Magazines like *Good Housekeeping*, *Woman's Own*, *Woman's Sphere* and *Woman and Home* addressed their women readers as professional homemakers, interested in the latest technology and concerned about housework, childcare and appearance. *Good Housekeeping* (along with *Ideal Home*) was the most expensive of these 'service' magazines and was close in price to the so-called 'quality' magazines such as *Homes and Gardens* (three shillings), *Woman's Home Journal* (three shillings and sixpence) and *Queen* (four shillings).[9] However, it was not only price that differentiated *Good Housekeeping* from cheaper magazines like *Woman and Home* and *Woman's Sphere* but also the cultural identities offered. The opening editorial of *Good Housekeeping*, first published in 1922 and targeted at middle-class women, states very clearly its aims:

> Any keen observer of the times cannot have failed to notice that we are on the threshold of a great feminine awakening. Apathy and levity are alike giving place to a wholesome and intelligent interest in the affairs of life, and above all in the home. We believe that time is ripe for a great new magazine which shall worthily meet the needs of the homekeeping woman of to-day. (Braithwaite et al. 1986: 11)

It goes on 'there should be no drudgery in the house' but 'time to think, to read, to enjoy life'. The housewife, suffering from servant shortages, it is asserted, 'does not always know the best ways to lessen her burdens' but in order to help her 'household management will be a feature of *Good Housekeeping*, and every new invention that is practical and economical in use will be brought to her notice after careful examination month by month' (Braithwaite et al. 1986: 11). Even 'home cookery' will be subject to the kinds of standardisation increasingly found in post-Fordist industrial production, the housekeeper has no time to test new dishes and has a certain suspicion of the *untested* recipe. Well, in the offices of *Good Housekeeping*, a modern and properly equipped kitchen has been installed, and there every recipe before being printed will be tested, and only those recipes which have passed the test of a widely known practical cookery expert, skilled in the knowledge of what a family welcomes, will be given. (Braithwaite et al. 1986: 11)

Good Housekeeping is insistent that the 'modern' housewife will not be totally preoccupied with her domestic tasks; she will be encouraged to read 'articles by women who can lead women, and who are fearless, frank, and outspoken' on 'the burning questions of the day' (Braithwaite et al. 1986: 11). The time released by her use of more efficient methods of housekeeping will enable her to take 'a wholesome and intelligent interest in the affairs of life' *but* always and primarily from her position as homemaker (Braithwaite et al. 1986: 11). *Good Housekeeping* throughout the 1920s and 1930s offered a mix of household advice *and* articles on a wide range of subjects from established writers. A small selection illustrates the point: Rose Macaulay on 'Problems for the Citizen'; 'Should Married Women Work?' by Mrs Alfred Sidgwick; 'Should Wives Have Wages?' by Violet Bonham Carter; 'To Marry or Not to Marry' by Leonora Eyles in the 1920s; 'Why Are We Failing the Dead?' by Godfrey Winn; a pessimistic account of the present condition of society entitled 'A Study in Black' by Beverley Nichols; 'A Second Queen Elizabeth' by Margaret Irwin; and a sketch of Oxford Street by Virginia Woolf in the 1930s. Such articles are set alongside features on 'Daily Maids in the Small Town House', 'Running a Home', and 'Budgeting the Income' that address house-wives as skilled managers and supervisors.

The ideal reader constructed in the pages of *Good Housekeeping* cultivates an understated modest style in appearance and dress, is intelligent, cheerful, and above all efficient. She is someone who recognises 'quality', whether in clothes, household furnishings or the arts. Her attributes are remarkably similar to those of Jan Struther's fictional character Mrs Miniver. Created at the request of the *Times* editor Peter Fleming, to brighten up the Court Page, Mrs Miniver's journal of a respectable housewife, married to a professional man, in late 1930s England delighted readers of the paper. Mrs Miniver has no job but is content as mistress of a small household, employing a nanny, maid and cook, and Struther's sketches celebrate her enjoyment of this particular form of domesticity. The first piece makes clear that this is no self-deprecating, inept and dissatisfied 'provincial lady' in the tradition of E.M. Delafield's *Diary of a Provincial Lady*. Instead Mrs Miniver is self-possessed and at ease in her role as middle-class wife, mother and mistress, '[h]er normal life pleased her so well that she was half afraid to step out of its frame in case one day she should find herself unable to get back' (Struther 1939/1989: 1). There are no anxieties about 'being ruled by one's servants' and a brisk common sense is Mrs Miniver's response to the vicissitudes of running a home:

> As a rule she managed to keep household matters in what she considered their proper place. They should be no more, she felt, than a low, unobtrusive humming in the background of consciousness: the mechanics of life should never be allowed to interfere with living. But every now and then some impish poltergeist seemed to throw a spanner into the works. Everything went wrong at once: chimneys smoked, pipes burst, vacuum-cleaners fused, china and glass fell to pieces, net curtains disintegrated in the wash. Nannie sprained her ankle, the cook got tonsillitis, the house-parlourmaid left to be married, and the butterfly nut off the mincing-machine was nowhere to be found. (Struther 1939/1989: 92–3)

As Light has observed, such an acute awareness of the 'mechanics' of running a home 'would have ill-befitted the Victorian or Edwardian lady' who would have neither known about, nor thought it appropriate to discuss, such matters as smoking chimneys or burst pipes (1991: 138). Moreover, the use of industrial metaphor in which the home is imagined, not as an organic whole, but as a giant machine, draws from a technological discourse of modernisation that approved the use of machinery to create efficiency. The consciousness expressed here is a particular manifestation of the changes in domesticity and their representation that were taking place in the interwar years. New technology and consumer markets for domestic products, debates about how homes could and should be run, the decline in domestic service and the growing emphasis on housing, household finances, and family hygiene and nutrition evidenced by government surveys and political debate, created a cultural space in which the materiality and efficient running of homes were foregrounded. Light draws attention to the 'increased consciousness of the materiality of domestic life, of home as the place of things, as well as of social relations, of things which need buying, cleaning, moving, maintaining' to be found in fiction by women in the 1920s and 1930s (1991: 137).

The reader addressed by *Good Housekeeping* is not only efficient, self-confident, an arbiter of middlebrow and middle-class taste, but also a woman, like Mrs Miniver, who is aware of the materiality of the home and the demands its paraphernalia can make on her. As with Mrs Miniver, an ability to control the potentially wayward 'mechanics' of a home is linked in *Good Housekeeping* to the capacity for self-restraint in social and personal relations, and a rational, balanced approach to the arts and politics: 'all sides and phases of women's interest – art, music, and the drama, and the social side of life – will find a place on our platform, and both sides of every open question will be given a hearing, though partisan politics and parties will be rigorously excluded' (Braithwaite et al. 1986: 11). *Good Housekeeping*, in fulfilling its aim of giving women access to the 'burning issues of the day', tackled Freudian theories of sexuality on at least one occasion. A writer for the magazine in 1938 suggested that:

Freud, whether right or wrong, did succeed in convincing [women] that they had sex desires and that these desires were not wicked . . . The result of such a violent fracture has been bad as well as good. Instead of the terrifying repression of the old maid, we have the complete repudiation of any kind of self-control as a danger to her sanity, or at least to the normal and free development of her age. It was perhaps an inevitable reaction from the false belief that the physical side of marriage meant nothing to a woman, to the obsession with sex which has prevailed now for some years. (White 1970: 107–8)

The idea of 'rational balance' and self-discipline are as important in the area of sexual relations as in the appropriate approach towards the arts, and are represented as the hallmark of a modern (middle-class) femininity. Yet, the same magazine offered its women readers a plethora of commodities for purchase through its advertising and service articles. Beauty products, cosmetics, cars, houses, home medicines, fashion and household appliances are all displayed for consumption, either by 'just looking' or by later purchase. On the one hand *Good Housekeeping* preaches self-control and moderation, on the other hand it urges consumption. Nevertheless, in ways that are different from the two magazines I examine below, *Good Housekeeping* works to sustain a distinction between the rational world of advice, debate, and information, and the world of spectacle and display inscribed in the advertising it carries. It offered its middle-class women readers a version of femininity in which 'common sense' and robust reason were highlighted rather than the promiscuous passivity inscribed in the figure of the irrational female consumer or the 'neuroticism' of the suburban wife.

Good Housekeeping sees itself as providing a forum for women in which rational debate about issues of public concern is carried out alongside the provision of domestic advice and information. In this sense the magazine locates itself firmly in the public realm, identified by Jurgen Habermas, that ideally exists between individual and state interests and was associated with the rise of the European bourgeoisie in the seventeenth and eighteenth century, and which, according to Habermas, ensured, through rational discussion, the public good (Habermas 1989). Whether such a sphere is possible given the competing interests of increasingly fractionalised groups in the twentieth century is not the issue I want to discuss here. However, I would point out, as Nancy Fraser and Lynn Spigel have done, that Habermas's 'public' sphere has historically always been a space reserved for certain privileged sections of society (Fraser 1992; Spigel 2001). As Spigel comments '[w]omen, the working-class, and people of colour in general were not typically included in the ideal public sphere of Habermas's imagination' (Spigel 2001: 6). The women addressed by *Good Housekeeping* were assumed to be white and middle-class; housewives managing a home with one or no servants but used to 'good food without monotony and good service without jangled tempers': Mrs Minivers to a tee (Braithwaite et al. 1986: 11). *Good Housekeeping* offers a new identity to its readers that includes the possibility of their participation in a public forum for rational debate. In so doing it blurs the distinctions between the private and the public realms of experience, suggesting that the 'modern' woman, unlike her Victorian counterpart, should take the opportunities, conferred by education and labour-saving efficiency, to look up from her household tasks and outwards to the public sphere of rational discourse, politics and work. However, although the issues chosen for discussion do occasionally touch on careers or paid work, they only deal with political issues such as rearmament, the rise of totalitarianism, or the General Strike in very generalised terms.[10] Nevertheless, that women like Virginia Woolf, Leonara Eyles and Rose Macaulay should choose to write for a mass publication suggests a certain instability around the dividing line between mass and high culture, between 'housewives' and 'educated women', that *Good Housekeeping* was able to exploit in order to create a sense of a public forum for the 'modern' housewife.

While the magazine makes clear that a woman's place is first and foremost in the home, it does not construct the suburban housewife as unintelligent or apathetic, 'neurotic' or passive. On the contrary, she is addressed as someone who is a quietly competent manager of her home, capable of reading and debating controversial issues, and a discerning consumer. Many of the advertisements in *Good Housekeeping* emphasise value for money and labour-saving qualities, and the articles on beauty and fashion suggest sewing patterns and cosmetics to meet a range of budgets. *Good Housekeeping* takes the problems of homemaking and femininity seriously, addressing its readers as sensible, efficient equals. Above all it celebrates, as do Jan Struther's sketches, the values of restraint and control whether this be in running the home, applying make-up, buying commodities, or in personal and social relationships. Modern femininity, as represented by *Good Housekeeping*, has all the attributes of (masculine) rational efficiency and none of the excesses of the irrational (feminine) mass, despite its inscription, in magazine form, in a, frequently despised, commercially mass-produced culture.

Woman and Home, unlike *Good Housekeeping*, is less obviously concerned to construct a 'typical' reader identity. *Woman and Home* was directed at lower-middle-class women, the group seen by advertisers and media as presenting new opportunities for commercial marketing, the group whom Lord Northcliffe tried to woo in the *Daily Mail* and the Ideal Home Exhibition. It is made up of fiction, occasional sewing or knitting features, and a large amount of advertising. The edition for May 1929 has eight pages of advertisements at the front and much of the space around the stories is taken up by advertising. The magazine announces itself as 'A Magazine of Delightful Suggestions'. Most of these are made by advertisers. There is only one feature on crocheting and the rest of the magazine is fiction. The practice, used increasingly by magazines, of breaking up the page continuity of stories and articles in order to ensure the reader moves backwards and forwards across the whole magazine, makes it difficult in *Woman and Home* to distinguish between advertisement and feature. Both are offered in monochrome except for the front and back cover advertisements which are in colour. Thus, although there is no direct editorial address, the mass of advertising and its organisation in the magazine suggest that it is the housewife as consumer who is assumed to be the reader. This is reinforced by the magazine's title, for the home aspects of the magazine are almost entirely to be found in the advertising which promotes foodstuffs, furniture, household appliances, clothing, beauty items, home medicines and cleaning products. *Woman and Home* implies a link between woman, home and consumption that is nowhere explicitly stated but nevertheless links the pleasures of window-shopping with the reading of (romantic) fiction to provide an experience that avoids the more directly instructive mode characteristic of *Good Housekeeping*.

One of the magazine's stories, entitled 'The Opportunist', illuminates the way in which advertising and fiction work together to produce a reader position that foregrounds woman as consumer. The story is about a young, lower-middle-class woman, Jennifer, who meets and falls in love with an upper-class man, Dana Corinth. The plot hinges on Jennifer's uncertainty about the ethics of linking herself to a man wealthier and more socially elevated than herself. She is anxious that she cannot fit into his social world and that, in aspiring to do so, she is guilty of 'opportunism' and 'gold-digging'. In the end she realises that love transcends these qualms of conscience and she sinks happily into Dana's arms. What is interesting for the argument I am developing here is the story's 'message' (money is unimportant when you encounter 'true love') and the devices that are used to carry this which suggest an alternative (and contradictory) subtext about women, money and commodities. The story begins with Jennifer returning home to the flat she shares with another woman to discover that a friend, Larry, has sent her a fur coat. Jennifer and her friend, Marian, are represented as 'modern', but impoverished, young women, sharing a flat, living and working in London. On occasions Jennifer helps Larry to entertain business clients at restaurants and night clubs 'where the cover charge alone was enough to pay her weekly grocery bill' (*Woman and Home* 1929: 22). Jennifer returns the fur coat on the grounds that to accept would be to compromise her integrity. The reader is intended to approve this decision which is questioned by Marian who is given 'silk stockings, gloves, all the little luxuries of life . . . Flowers, boxes of chocolates, books, magazines' by her young, stockbroker friends (*Woman and Home* 1929: 22). Jennifer suggests that Marian may be a little bit of a 'gold-digger' but the story does not condemn Marian for this. What it does suggest is how difficult it is for women with little money not to be 'seduced' by such gifts.

When Jennifer meets Dana Corinth she finds herself in a world of glamour and money. Dana's flat is a phantasmagoria of erotic wealth and luxury, 'women in lovely gowns – the bed, in the spare room where they had left their coats, was a mound of luscious furs. Pearls, misty white, close against women's throats, the clear lights of diamonds gleaming from white fingers' (*Woman and Home* 1929: 24). Later in their relationship, after a road accident in which Jennifer's only evening dress is ruined, Dana takes her shopping for new clothes. Jennifer's thoughts as she watches the models who display a selection of dresses are narrated from within her consciousness:

> Jade velvet – slender, long-fingered hands, one holding a cigarette, the other resting possessively upon the back of her chair. Yellow taffeta – his profile surprised her; it was at once handsomer and more mature than his front face, grave, almost placid. Flame-coloured chiffon – he turned and smiled at her and she smiled back tremulously. (*Woman and Home* 1929: 64)

The gifts Dana might buy for her become mixed up with her growing sexual desire for him and 'she tried to feel ashamed of herself and didn't' (*Woman and Home* 1929: 64). Whether it is sexual desire or the pleasures of consumerism about which she feels she should be ashamed is not made clear and this ambiguity suggests the links between sex, commodities and women that the story's resolution attempts to deny. The reader is intended to share Jennifer's lack of shame and, at the end of the story, to endorse her love for Dana as having transcended the material realities of wealth and status. At one level the story suggests that women, like Jennifer, cannot be bought with money and commodities. The only genuine currency is 'true love'. At another level, however, it does not condemn women for wanting luxury goods nor does it wish to deny them the pleasures of looking and consuming, and in linking this pleasure to sexual desire it also represents female sexuality as acceptable and a source of pleasure. Alone in her room with the purchases Dana has made for her, Jennifer indulges in a pleasurable moment of looking:

> She lifted the golden dress from its wrappings and hung it on a hanger, not in the cupboard but on the wall, where she could see it. She unwrapped the golden slippers and set them beneath it, little Cinderella-like slippers with buckles as fragile and exquisite as spider webs, flecked with rhinestones. Like a shred of mist before the sun she let the stockings fall in a little heap beside them. (*Woman and Home* 1929: 64)

The reference to the Cinderella 'rags to riches' narrative functions to remove Jennifer's story from the economic realities of her position, in which she earns five pounds a week as a publisher's assistant and accepts meals at restaurants in payment for entertaining business clients, to the realm of romantic fairy-tale in which these realities only surface in the gaps and on the margins of the narrative.

The story's subtext suggests that both sexual and consumer seduction are something the 'modern' woman can learn to negotiate in order to maximise pleasure and minimise shame. The placing of the story between and amongst advertisements that tempt the reader with a cornucopia of products links the consumerism of the story with an extra-textual reality in which the reader herself negotiates the consumer market-place that is the magazine. In the story it is the men who lavish goods on Jennifer in attempts to buy, seduce and reward her. In the magazine world outside the story it is the reader/consumer who is doing the buying. *Woman and Home* invites the reader, as she moves backwards and forwards from story to adverts, to think about Jennifer's dilemma in the context of a social world of increasing consumerism in which sexuality and commodities are inextricably linked with gender identities. The story offers one resolution – love transcends material reality – but the eroticised descriptions of commodities and Jennifer's internal reveries insist on an alternative version in which sexual desire, money and the purchase of objects cannot be separated so easily. The magazine's organisation, as well as its content, invites its readers to see themselves as active agents, positioned and addressed as consumer rather than consumed, as a negotiator of ethical dilemmas as well as commodity transactions. In doing so it may have offered a space in which women could learn to withstand the blandishments of advertisers and seducers, and to negotiate their own pleasure in looking and buying with regard to both material objects and sexual desire.

Woman's Sphere (December 1936), a magazine similar in style and organisation to *Woman and Home*, carries a story entitled 'Fifty Pounds Reward!' in which the heroine is a shop assistant in the toy department of a large store. Claire lives by herself in a London bedsit but longs for wealth and romance. As she prepares for Christmas alone she muses on the fact that 'she had not managed, in the three years since she left home, to make her fortune!' and wryly observes that 'there are too many girls in London . . . Far too many of them, and not enough work, let alone romance to go round' (*Woman's Sphere* 1936: 12–13). On Christmas Eve Claire sees an elderly lady shoplifting and chooses not to report her. Soon afterwards, by a convoluted plot device, Claire meets an impoverished young artist who falls in love with her and paints her portrait. Brian's integrity as an artist is, however, in danger of being compromised by a breakfast food manufacturer who wants to purchase an earlier painting of the toy department. The elderly lady turns out to be a duchess and, as a reward for not reporting her, she gives Claire fifty pounds thus removing the necessity of selling Brian's paintings to the 'breakfast food man' who 'had a little paunch, and a beady eye, and . . . knew real value when he saw it' (*Woman's Sphere* 1936: 76). Once again consumption is highlighted, this time by setting up a dichotomy between the garish commercial world of the toy department, represented in Brian's paintings, and Claire's femininity and integrity (she poses for him darning and mending his pyjamas!). The reader is meant to endorse Brian's refusal to sell to the breakfast food manufacturer and Claire's decision not to report the duchess for shoplifting as exemplifying an ethic that places artistic integrity and compassion beyond any money nexus. Yet, this constructed dichotomy is ultimately destabilised by the information that Brian's picture of Claire causes 'a sensation' and is 'sold in America for . . . a comfortable sum' (*Woman's Sphere* 1936: 15). Nor is the elderly shoplifter romanticised as a poverty-stricken grandmother intent on acquiring presents for her grandchildren at Christmas. Instead she is represented as cunning, bad-tempered and imperious: no rationale is given for her shoplifting other than her own pleasure ('Her Grace, in her spare moments, did a spot of shop-lifting') thus rendering Claire's compassion slightly misplaced while, at the same time, drawing attention to the pleasures of acquiring and possessing material objects (*Woman's Sphere* 1936: 76).

Both stories make use of modern urban spaces in which to inscribe the ethical dilemmas and values of their lower-middle-class heroines. Jennifer and Claire live as single women in London bedsits; Jennifer spends her leisure time in restaurants, night clubs and cinemas; Claire works in a large department store. These spaces would have resonated with symbolic meaning for their female readerships, suggesting a 'modern' femininity far removed from the conventions of respectable Victorian and Edwardian society, that would see, in the living arrangements of these young women, the decadence that was frequently attributed to single women working in and moving freely around the city. It seems paradoxical that while the heroines of such stories invited reader identification, narrated as they are through the consciousness of the female protagonist, magazines like *Woman and Home* and *Woman's Sphere* were consumed, in the main, by married housewives living in the suburbs rather than by single women working in large cities like London or Manchester.[11] I suggest that this lack of fit between proffered identity and reader, which is considerably less characteristic of *Good Housekeeping*, produces a space in which female readers might 'try on' and shop for identities other than that of professional housewife thus practising their skills as 'consumers' of fiction as well as advertising. In interviews, lower-middle and working-class women have consistently reported that they bought magazines for the knitting and sewing patterns, the recipes or the advice on health and childcare. In other words the ostensible purpose of magazine consumption was to acquire information and advice. It was the service aspects that were recalled as prompting purchase rather than the 'dream worlds' of magazine fiction and advertising, although, of course, such recall may have been aligned to what was expected rather than what was. Certainly, the insistence of these women that magazines were consumed for instruction rather than pleasure asserts a subjectivity that prioritises hard work and household production over what was seen as wasteful dreaming and consumption. This takes us back to the earlier discussion on the purchase of labour-saving appliances and suggests that, for many women, the 'right' expenditure of time was seen as crucial to self-definition. Yet, as Stein has argued, twentieth-century magazines organised a new mode of reading that was not straightforwardly linear but in certain ways mimicked the experience of modern (American) highway driving, a 'form of mobility [that] allows us to achieve specific destinations while constantly recharging our desire for less immediately attainable ends. The car encloses us, the road directs us, and these conditions make ads especially welcome as points of reference and as emblems of our long-term goals' (Stein 1985: 7). In the context of women's magazines we might add romantic fiction to the advertisements that act as 'points of reference' and 'emblems of our long-term goals'. Fictions, such as 'The Opportunist' and 'Fifty Pounds Reward!' may have allowed female readers to look beyond the 'specific destination' of the recipe and the knitting pattern, and to rehearse, at least in imagination, the ethical dilemmas and moral values, consequent upon living in a growing culture of consumerism. Nor is it insignificant that the heroines of these stories are never solidly middle or upper-middle-class. Both Jennifer and Claire occupy a social position that denies them the privileges of affluence but places them in modern environments in which the dilemmas and values associated with the longing for material comfort are treated sympathetically. Unlike *Good Housekeeping* or the advertisements discussed above, these magazine stories do not create 'an ambience of service rather than commerce' but deliberately foreground the cash nexus around which social and personal relationships were so often organised and experienced.

In this section I have concentrated on the discourses articulated in a number of women's magazines and have suggested that these were differentiated along class lines. *Good Housekeeping*, I suggested, constructs a specific version of the (middle-class) housewife for its readers, a version which spoke to a continued desire for deference and service and a sense of confidence as the arbiters of taste and 'culture' in the home. *Woman and Home* and *Woman's Sphere* are less concerned to construct an 'ideal' reader. Instead they concentrate on fiction and advertising with far fewer features, recipes, and patterns and in so doing they overtly link pleasure and desire with the consumption of material objects.[12] In consequence these magazines produced cultural spaces that were potentially more fluid than those offered by *Good Housekeeping*. However, it would not do to overstate the case for these magazines as 'progressive'. Like *Good Housekeeping* they continued to represent women's place as primarily in the home. That they did so within the context of a growing culture of consumption, may have offered imaginary spaces to those class fractions who, rather than imitating middle-class culture, wished to develop their own forms.

The Housewife and National Identity

During the Dunkirk crisis of 1940 the BBC invited the writer and playwright, J.B. Priestley to broadcast a series of short 'Postscripts' to the nine o'clock Sunday night *News*. These 'Postscripts' would explain national events in a way that avoided 'exaggerated propaganda' and overblown rhetoric, 'a personal, independent comment that it was hoped would have a rallying, encouraging quality, without ever smacking of official propaganda' (Priestley 1967: xv). Priestley was brought in because the BBC believed that his Bradford background and, in particular, his Yorkshire vowels would offer 'a contrast in voice, upbringing and outlook' to the 'posh' received pronounciation voices that dominated the airwaves. Priestley gave nineteen broadcasts between June and October 1940 and was listened to by an average of 31 per cent of the population (Briggs 1970: 210–11; Calder 1991: 196–202). Lilian Duff recalls the 'overwhelming response of the public to the "Postscripts". They became essential listening on a Sunday evening' and BBC audience research showed that one in every three adults tuned into his broadcasts, a figure that compared well with the one in two adults cited for Churchill's broadcasts (Priestley 1967: xvi; Addison 1975/1994: 118). Priestley's success was to use vignettes of wartime experience to develop his theme that there could be no going back to the social conditions that existed pre-war. Above all he spoke to and for, what he called, 'all of us ordinary people' about patriotism, about community, about the little pleasure steamers that sailed 'into the inferno, to defy bombs, shells, magnetic mines, torpedoes, machine-gun fire – to rescue our soldiers'. His homely, middlebrow appeal, that had been condemned by pre-war modernists, was re-interpreted in the circumstances of war as the voice of the people. Graham Greene, who had previously attacked Priestley's plays and novels, wrote in the *Spectator* for December 1940 that he 'became in the months after Dunkirk a leader second only in importance to Mr Churchill. And he gave us what our other leaders have always failed to give us – an ideology' (Addison 1975/1994: 119). This 'ideology' which embraced social egalitarianism, social welfare and the reconstruction of a better world after the war was rooted, similarly to Orwell's, in the assumed decency of the 'ordinary' person.[13]

On Sunday, 22 September 1940 Priestley broadcast what he called 'a very special postscript . . . about women and the war' in which he celebrated women's contribution to the 'home front':

> Now there's a familiar type of masculine mind that believes that women should have nothing to do with political and public life. Woman's place, they tell us, is in the home. It's largely the same mind, I believe, that then muddles away so that the home is put on short rations and then bombed. Privately I've believed for years the opposite of this – that a great deal of political and public life is nothing but large-scale common-sense housekeeping, and that as women have an almost terrifying amount of common-sense and the ones who are good at housekeeping are very good at it, then the sooner some of our communal and national affairs are managed by women the better . . . For this is total war; and total war is right inside the home itself, emptying the clothes cupboards and the larder, screaming its threats through the radio at the hearth, burning and bombing its way

from roof to cellar. It's ten times harder being a decent housewife and mother during such a war than it is being a soldier. You have to make a far greater effort to keep going, for you've no training and discipline to armour you. The soldier has his own respons-ibilities, but when he assumed them he was released from a great many others; whereas his womenfolk know no such release, but have more and more responsibility piled upon them. (Priestley 1967: 112–15)

Home Intelligence reports suggest that Priestley's down-to-earth egalitarianism and tolerance were shared by many of his listeners (Calder 1991: 197). In con-sequence it is likely that his plea for a fuller role for women after the war in which their 'feminine; housekeeping skills would be used in the management of national affairs' would have appeared self-evident to his audience, horrified by the 'tramp-ling, bragging, swaggering, idiotic males, silly little boys who've somehow grown to be the size of men' in Germany and Italy (Priestley 1967: 114). Nevertheless, Priestley's use of the housewife as a figure to represent both an ideal of 'femininity' as well as the actual women who were struggling with wartime upheaval and restrictions brings the private world of the 'clothes cupboard' and 'the larder' very firmly into the public domain symbolically, materially and politically. Priestley goes on to record his praise for the courage shown by 'nurses, secretaries, clerks, telephone girls, shop assistants, waitresses' but it is the housewife in whom he places his hopes for post-war reconstruction. The housewife and mother was a crucial worker in the struggle for victory but she also represented what was at stake,

And all wondering, suffering women – some of them homeless, lost, with bewildered small children in their arms – should be told here and now that that is what we're all struggling and battling for. Not for some re-grouping on the chess-board of money and power politics; but for new and better homes – real homes – a decent chance at last – new life. And every woman should remember that – keep the promise locked in her heart, and when the time comes, with one voice – and, if necessary, with that full feminine fury which is among the most awe-inspiring phenomenon – demand that the promise be redeemed, so that the children now hurried through the shelters can one day walk in the sunlight and build upon our ruins a glorious new world. (Priestley 1967: 118)

Debates about the importance of supporting families and children through housing policies, family allowances and other welfare measures were not new in the 1940s. Eleanor Rathbone had been arguing for family allowances throughout the interwar years, Margery Spring Rice had detailed the conditions under which working-class mothers tried to raise children, and social reformers of both sexes had insisted that social reconstruction required a sustained focus on the so-called private worlds of homes and families (Rathbone 1924; Spring Rice 1939; Dyhouse 1989). Since the turn of the century 'national efficiency' had demanded that motherhood and domesticity were crucial to the survival of both 'race' and nation (Lewis 1980;

Davin 1989). Throughout the 1920s and 1930s state intervention, in the form of infant welfare clinics, health visitors, school meals and the provision of milk for schoolchildren, had insisted on the importance of rearing healthy children and had made strenuous efforts to educate (working-class) mothers in hygiene and nutrition. In many ways Priestley was drawing on a well-established discourse of women and home but one that, in the circumstances of war, offered women opportunities to see themselves as major players in securing victory. In the First World War women had been exhorted to 'keep the home fires burning'; in the Second they were asked to actively participate in the struggle for a democracy that would reward them with 'new and better homes': the home fires had become the home front on which wartime victory might depend.

However, this address to, and symbolisation of, the housewife hid a fundamental fact of modern life. That is that, at least during the war, many women were, simultaneously, nurses, secretaries, shop assistants *and* housewives. The conceptual separation of women into housewife or worker was not confined to the speeches of public figures like Priestley. It was to be found in policy decisions and in official schemes that attempted to organise the practical realities of carrying out a dual role but continued to address women's needs as either the needs of the worker or the housewife/mother (Summerfield 1984, 1993a; Riley 1983). This discursive polarisation both constituted and mirrored the anxiety and ambivalence that lay beneath the glorifying, and morale raising, rhetoric of citizen housewives. On the one hand, the war effort required that women, particularly those without childcare responsibilities, became, in the terminology of the time, mobile. Thus, single women or married women without children could be conscripted and have to move away from their home towns to work in war factories, the Land Army or the armed services. On the other hand, fears that mobile and working women would abandon, neglect or lose interest in femininity abounded. According to Summerfield women:

> [w]ere required both to be at home, keeping the home fires burning as they watched and waited for their menfolk to return from the front, and they were required to 'do their bit' in the war effort, in a paid or voluntary capacity. They were expected to be carers and mothers, but they were also under pressure to be soldiers and workers. There were demands for women to wear dresses and look feminine, but also to put on uniforms, the wartime emblems of citizenship, which restrained the visible signs of feminine difference. They were represented as both loyal citizens and as treacherous subversives. (1998: 14)

Jennifer Hartley estimates that by 1943 80 per cent of married women and 90 per cent of single women were involved in the war effort in a variety of ways (Hartley 1994: 135). Wartime mobilisation recruited women into work previously understood as masculine: the armed services, manufacturing munitions and aeroplanes, maintenance work on vehicles, flying planes, driving trucks, tractors and buses, and agricultural labour. At the same time women were also exhorted to contribute their particular 'feminine' skills to the war effort and, although this enabled many married women to extend their responsibilities beyond the home, working in WVS canteens, in hospitals, in casualty clearing stations and in shops, restaurants and cafes, they were also expected to contribute through their prudent management of the household. During the war, the state involved itself in the home in ways that were unprecedented, providing nurseries for childcare, introducing food rationing, advising on nutrition and 'make do and mend', and controlling the supply of products like soap, textiles and furniture. Nevertheless, wartime attitudes to working women remained predicated on a belief that a woman's primary responsibility was to her home and family and anxieties about the erosion of this traditional role were never far from the surface even when women's work outside the home was being most celebrated (Summerfield 1996; Lant 1991).

Advertising was quick to exploit the marketing possibilities in women's dual roles but in doing so was one of the few cultural spaces in which women were addressed as both workers *and* housewives (and, of course, consumers). A 1943 *Picture Post* advertisement for Mansion Polish asserts that at a time when there is 'less time for housework . . . the quickness and ease in use of "Mansion" is helping many thousands of busy War Workers to keep their homes bright and healthy' (*Picture Post*, February 27 1943). The accompanying picture shows a woman working in a canteen and the caption reads, 'A war time necessity. One tin must do the work of Two'. The message is clear: women, like the tin of Mansion Polish, are required to do the work of two, as both workers and housewives their role is to contribute to the war effort. Advertisers drew heavily on the vocabulary of war in order to construct the housewife as a figure of national importance. The same issue of *Picture Post* carries a page of advertisements with the following captions: 'Moths are a National Menace . . . Use Mothaks all the year round and save your clothes coupons'; 'Health is a National Duty . . . Take Eno's Fruit Salt'; 'Keep Britain Ahead' by purchasing, when supplies allow, a Smith Sectric Clock. Alongside the advertisements for a range of commodities is a reminder from the Ministry of Fuel and Power that 'in the Battle for Fuel . . . No Economy is Too Small to Count'. The rhetoric of the home front addressed the housewife, who is always represented as classless, as having an essential part to play in securing the nation's future through her careful management of the family's health and well-being as well as in her consumption of domestic commodities like Smith Sectric Clocks and Mansion Polish.

Throughout the war the housewife was instructed, in government propaganda and in women's magazines, how to run her house efficiently to secure the war effort. She was shown how to make nourishing meals from meagre rations, how to care for her children's health, what clothes she should wear and how to make the most of her limited resources. The resourceful citizen housewife was encouraged and praised in morale boosting propaganda and her skills lauded at every turn. The March 1945 issue of the women's magazine *Everywoman* echoed Priestley when it asserted that in the post-war world:

> Hard facts and new trends in thought will make post-war marriage entirely different from anything society has ever known before . . . It will, of course, take a lot of the self-esteem out of men; but this is excellent, for only men with colossal self-conceit could have landed the world in the mess it is in now. If, in future, they take their wives' opinions about affairs more seriously, there is a chance of the world being a happier and safer place. (*Everywoman* 1988: 16–17)

While there is no hard evidence that women's aspirations for the future were directly influenced by this rhetoric, it is possible to speculate that many women invested their aspirations for self-identity in this newly valorized role of citizen housewife. Certainly the raft of post-war welfare reforms appeared to promise better conditions for all housewives and the pleasures of domesticity after the strains and upheavals of war must have beckoned invitingly to women, exhausted by night-time work shifts interspersed with housework and air raid alarms. As Joyce Storey recalls of her first home after the war, 'the prefab was my dream come true. The image of a cottage with roses round the door had kept the dream alive all through those weary war years' (1992: 189). For white working-class women liberation had long been envisaged as freedom from the double burden of housework and paid work: the post-war world offered them opportunities to devote their energies to a home of their own.

For white middle-class women the possibility of a modern house, designed to be labour-saving and 'servantless' offered opportunities to enjoy the role of citizen housewife free from the necessity of sharing a home with a 'rude, resentful, talkative and unmannerly' maid (Fremlin 1940: 102). Women like Nella Last, a middle-class woman in her fifties, who remembered the way in which 'pictures and furniture . . . were once polished every week', wondered 'if people would *ever* go back to the old ways', and observed in her wartime diary that she could not 'see women settling to trivial ways – women who have done worthwhile things' (Hartley 1994: 189). Last did not necessarily envisage women taking up full-time jobs and careers. But she did hope that the post-war world would offer women opportunities to engage in useful work:

> Women like myself who have been busy and useful, feeling they were 'helping' cannot find a way to help the 'peace' as we did in wartime. With 2000 women at the Labour Exchange, it would not be right to do anything they could do, yet I know many who, like myself, long to do something. (Sheridan 1990: 264)

During the war it was Nella's housewifely skills that had enabled her to be 'busy and useful' and that had given her a newly found sense of self. She helped to run a WVS canteen in her home town of Barrow-in-Furness and adapted her recipes for wartime consumption:

> I get many a chuckle at myself nowadays – no hiding away my dodges and strict economies as I used to. Instead I broadcast 'how little fat', or 'how economical' my bits and bobs of recipes are. And Gran's old recipes are going the rounds. Her piccalilli and chutney are pronounced 'marvellous'. I had no time to copy out a recipe one day, and hurriedly pushed my old tattered recipe book in my basket, to do it at the Centre. I got on with my job, and when I went into the office, a chorus of 'Would you mind me taking a recipe for . . .' greeted me. It's childish of me, I know, but it gives me such a warm feeling to find I've anything people want. I've not a lot to give, and I do so like giving. (Hartley 1994: 144)

When Nella contemplates the horrors of war and the anguish of displaced peoples she imagines what it would be like to heap a few essential items onto a handcart and leave behind her 'bits of treasures' – an old tea set, some bits of brass and a 'bowl of golden yellow tulips'. She finds herself 'admiring afresh my smooth panelled hall, my wide windows, my honey-coloured fireplace, with a wonder which is like reverence that I can keep them, while other women . . . see ruin and desolation to their loved homes. It's so *wrong*' (Hartley 1994: 187). Nella understands her home in terms of the material objects that constitute it and it is these that are so lovingly invoked as signifiers of security and comfort. Economical but tasty food, ornaments, a vase of flowers, a tea set, a coloured fireplace, the soft toys she makes for the war effort, all represent the ordered and harmonious world that war threatens but are also signifiers that allow Nella to articulate a political sensibility ('the dreadfulness of the punishment meted out to Poles and Fins and Jews leaves me feeling so puzzled') and offer her a sense of usefulness that is dignifying (Hartley 1994: 187). She concludes 'I don't envy people with money as I used to do, for most of them want it all for themselves; it's best to have a little gift of making things' (Hartley 1994: 188). Second World War rhetoric that lauded the housewife, invested a 'gift of making things', whether it be healthy meals out of limited rations or patching and darning clothes and sheets, with an importance and usefulness that offered dignity and pride to women in this role. Moreover, many women, like Nella, must have compared their situations with those of the displaced, dispossessed, maimed or killed by war, and felt a deep thankfulness that their homes and all these stood for remained relatively intact.

To conclude we might consider an advertisement for a range of household cleaners that appeared in *Woman and Home* for May 1944. This depicts a cosy living room, lit by a coal fire, with a table set for tea and two empty chairs. It appears on the inside front cover in full colour and is a full-page spread. The image invites the viewer to take up the proffered chair and to enjoy the comfort and warmth that the picture invokes. The text that accompanies the picture is as follows,

The fire has been mended, the hearth is swept, and though the lamp is lit the curtains are not yet drawn, for the world is at peace again, with nothing to fear from the dark.

Into the quiet of this pleasant room there comes the tinkle of tea-cups, faintly, as if to accompany the friendly shadows which dance around the walls. Tic-toc, tea-time! tic-toc, tea-time! and the clock prattles on.

How lovely Grandmama's silver service looks after all these years; how it gleams and twinkles in the flickering firelight—a kindly light which mantles the snowy tea-cloth with a rosy glow! Look at that portly scuttle, how he squats beside the fire, beaming all over his cheerful face – thanks to Brasso—as if he owned the place!

Yes, it is the little things that transform a simple house into a gracious home: a tea-cloth lustrous white—snowy white as only Reckitt's Blue can make it; the gleam and glint of those treasured silver pieces, radiant with pride in the polish that Silvo gave them; the grate, too, as though of polished jet, tells a tale of Zebo.

Even to-day these good companions of the cheerful home are at your service, though in that brave new world to which we look forward they will be more freely available.

Figure 2 *Woman and Home*, May 1944

The fire has been mended, the hearth is swept, and though the lamp is lit the curtains are not yet drawn, for the world is at peace again, with nothing to fear from the dark. Into the quiet of this pleasant room there comes the tinkle of tea-cups, faintly, as if to accompany the friendly shadows which dance around the walls . . . How lovely Grand-mama's silver service looks after all these years; how it gleams and twinkles in the flickering firelight – a kindly light which mantles the snowy tea-cloth with a rosy glow! Look at that portly scuttle, how he squats beside the fire, beaming all over his cheerful face – thanks to Brasso – as if he owned the place!

Yes, it is the little things that transform a simple house into a gracious home: a tea-cloth lustrous white – snowy white as only Reckitt's Blue can make it; the gleam and glint of those treasured silver pieces, radiant with pride in the polish that Silvo gave them; the grate, too, as though of polished jet, tells a tale of Zebo. Even today these good companions of the cheerful home are at your service, though in that brave new world to which we look forward they will be more freely available. (*Woman and Home* 1944)

Home is represented here as something that is created from the housewife's skilled deployment of material objects, with the modern household cleaners, Brasso, Silvo, Reckitt's Blue and Zebo as companionable replacements for servants. Home, in the form of two chairs, a fire and a table set for two, is also presented as a symbol of peace and safety. The advert appeared a year before the war in Europe ended and taps into what must have been extremely powerful yearnings for norm-ality, comfort and security. But, above all, the image and the text that accompanies it offer a vision of the future ('that brave new world to which we look forward') when commodities like Brasso will be more 'freely available' and 'simple houses', thereby transformed into 'gracious homes', will symbolise the new world for which Britain has been fighting. In this 'modern' world, middle-class housewives need not fear the disappearance of older forms of domesticity: service will be provided by household commodities. For working-class women the drudgery and dirt that once made it so difficult for them to create comfortable homes will be a thing of the past. They too can aspire to 'gracious homes' through their con-sumption of a range of domestic products that will serve them as they once served their mistresses. This is a message and an image that would have been recognised by the readers of *Good Housekeeping* and *Mrs Miniver*, as well as by the readers of *Woman and Home*, by those who attended the Daily Mail Home Exhibition, and by Nella Last. It must also have offered a vision to women like Joyce Storey who, at the end of the war, were dreaming of acquiring their own homes. This is not to suggest that the image was unproblematically consumed by, or directly imposed its ideology on, such women but that it cleverly works a cluster of meanings linked to historically specific ideas of the housewife, home, peace, and the emergence of a new and better world, and as such can tell us something about the subjectivities to which it spoke and from which it draws its iconography.

I began this chapter by stating the case for considering femininity and consumption in terms of the central part played by these in the cultural transitions of the twentieth century. First, changes in retailing and an expanding market for domestic commodities positioned women as the main consumers of such products. Department stores, chain stores and advertising targeted women and, in doing so, found it necessary to consider their needs and aspirations. Shopping for the home and family became one of the key tasks of the twentieth-century housewife. For middle-class women the job of supervising servants and managing the household that had, in the nineteenth century, been the most significant marker of middle-class status, was replaced by the work of consumption. Social status became increasingly linked to the purchase of domestic commodities and it was the job of middle-class women to create the 'ideal' homes that demonstrated this 'cultural capital'. These changes provided employment opportunities for working-class (and lower-middle-class women) in the retail sector thus enabling them to reject domestic service. Second, the proliferation of women's magazines, and the advertising that financed these, offered women of all classes a wider range of femininities from which to fashion identities. Third, the increased focus on the home as crucial to the survival of the nation that found its apotheosis in Second World War propaganda that created the figure of the citizen housewife, invited women of all classes to see their domestic role and feminine values as a useful and respected contribution to the struggle for democracy and to the post-war reconstruction of a better world.

This domestic modernity was, however, experienced differently by women of different classes and its effects varied considerably. In some ways domestic modernity could offer new opportunities for understanding and experiencing their worlds that bestowed self-esteem and dignity. In other ways there were profound losses. Manufacturers anxious that women should continue to purchase and desire the proliferating range of domestic products, required that women should remain linked to the home and to this end advertising focused almost entirely on creating an impossible 'ideal' home. In consequence standards of cleanliness and home improvement were raised and the time saved by the use of mechanised household appliances was used to maintain these. Ruth Schwartz Cowan has shown how American housewives, for example, spent the time saved by washing machines to wash clothes, towels and bedding more frequently (Cowan 1989). We saw earlier that boiling the wash to achieve whiteness was linked to cleanliness and to having expended the 'right' amount of time on the task of washing. Increasingly as synthetic fibres made boiling redundant the frequency with which washing was done became a marker of the 'good', that is hardworking, housewife. Working-class women who acquired, for the first time after 1945, a home to run, adapted to, and created their own, standards of housewifery as part of their need to consolidate a new identity for themselves as home-owning housewives. Consumer culture invited them to invest their money and their energy in the dream of the 'ideal' home and, while this positioned them as members of the society and nation that had for so long excluded them, it also created new forms of anxiety about money, material objects and selfhood. Carolyn Steedman has shown how her mother's subjectivity was constituted from her desire to possess the products of a consumer culture and her envy of those for whom such commodities were (apparently) easily attainable (Steedman 1986).

Middle-class women whose role as mistress of servants was gradually eroded in the first half of the twentieth century increasingly found themselves required to undertake household tasks that would previously have been done by servants. This, as we have seen, manifested itself in a greater awareness of the materiality and the mechanics of running a home that finds its expression in the fiction and magazines of the period. While this undoubtedly offered opportunities to exercise a brisk and cheerful competence, it also required the loss of authority that went with the, albeit limited, power to delegate household tasks to servants. Moreover, the kind of usefulness and self-respect that Nella Last experienced as a result of using her domestic skills in the public arena of the 'home front' was shortlived as educated, middle-class women in the 1960s came to recognise the price extorted for the dream of comfort, security and marriage, and the housewifely skills, upon which their mothers prided themselves, were increasingly scorned. In such circumstances consumer culture and its invitation to identify as 'Mrs Consumer' made it possible for middle-class women to acquire a certain 'cultural capital' as arbiters of what could turn a 'simple house' into an aesthetically 'gracious' home. Nevertheless, the demise of domestic service meant that middle-class women had fewer opportunities to influence their working-class sisters, at the same time as experiencing the loss of personal service and deference contingent upon this. Women, who a generation or so earlier would have served in the Victorian households of the middle classes, increasingly worked in the public spaces of shops and restaurants where they were less dependent upon the women they served and thus less likely to extend the kind of deferential service that had been the norm in privatised households. The cultural transitions that took place in the first half of the twentieth century around women's relationship to consumption engendered new forms of feminine subjectivity that expressed classed and differentiated responses to the experience of modernity. In the final chapter I want to suggest the material and imaginative legacies of these transitions that have shaped the ways in which domesticity is experienced and understood in a variety of domains, including contemporary feminism.

−4−

Legacies: The Question of 'Home' and Women's Modernity

In the introduction the definition of modernism (and modernists) that I gave was the orthodox understanding of the term as denoting a particular artistic and philosophic way of representing the world that emerged in the late nineteenth and early twentieth century in the West. In this final chapter I want to argue that the gendered dichotomies that underpin this narrowly conceived modernism persist in, and limit, the ways in which feminist scholars use the concept of 'home'. I am proposing that thinking about domesticity in terms of modernity not only rescues women from historical invisibility but, more radically, challenges conventional understandings of modernity and modernists, as well as the polarisations inherent in concepts of public and private. As Lesley Johnson has observed '[a] re-thinking of home and its relationship to modernity is necessary . . . if feminism is to destabilize those very oppositions that have been central to how womanhood has been defined in Western cultural traditions' (1996: 449). In recent years there has been considerable scholarship on the relationship between women and modernity. Wolff has urged a re-writing of modernity that includes women, Nava and Wilson have shown how women were less absent from the modernist city than is generally thought, Huyssen has proposed that modernism is based on gendered dichotomies, and Felski has pointed to the instability of concepts of modernity itself (Wolff 1985; Nava 1997; Wilson 1991, 1992; Huyssen 1986; Felski 1995). However, despite the radical challenge offered by this literature, gendered concepts of home persist in many accounts of modernity and modernism by feminist scholars, who in other areas are committed to disrupting and destabilising gendered dichotomies. If we are to contest those cultural and historical understandings of woman that link her with home, stasis, the everyday, the private, the traditional and dependency, it is vital that these dichotomised meanings of home are, at the very least, questioned.

The homologies that construct the (modernist) meaning of 'home' are organised around certain key oppositions: home/away (journey or voyage), stasis/movement, everyday/exceptional, private/public, traditional/modern, dependence/independence, feminine/masculine. Contemporary feminists have often deployed these oppositions in the emancipatory narratives that constituted the liberation proposed by second-wave feminism. 'Leaving home', in many of these narratives, is a necessary condition of liberation. Johnson cites, for example, Wilson's claim that 'urban life, however fraught with difficulty, has emancipated women more than rural life or suburban domesticity' (Wilson 1991:10). Marilyn French's *The Women's Room*, with which this book opened, narrates the heroine's journey from suburban domesticity to a liberated autonomy that is free from domestic commitment, and, although this is not achieved without pain, it is intended to be read as a universally desired feminist aspiration. Another example, cited by Johnson, is Teresa de Lauretis, who, in search of a historical feminist consciousness, invokes a similar narrative. Such a consciousness, for De Lauretis, involves:

> [l]eaving or giving up a place that is safe, that is 'home' – physically, emotionally, linguistically, epistemologically – for another place that is unknown and risky, that is not only emotionally but conceptually other; a place of discourse from which speaking and thinking are at best tentative, uncertain, unguarded. But the leaving is not a choice: one could not live there in the first place. (De Lauretis 1990: 138)

Equally, feminist histories in the 1970s and 1980s claimed that women were forced 'back home' after operating successfully in the public world of work during both world wars, and critiques of consumer culture condemned popular images that, it was claimed, bombarded women with 'false' desires for 'ideal homes'. Such histories were written in a cultural framework that envisioned domesticity as something that must be left behind if women were to become 'modern', emancipated subjects. In terms of the worlds of home and work 'staying at home' was an undesirable option; 'going out to work' was the only valid route a liberated woman could take.

This story, of course, is also echoed in the writings of modernists with little concern for women. Wyndham Lewis, the leader of the early-twentieth-century Vorticist movement, described what he called 'the modern city man' who in his city office is 'probably a very fine fellow' but who becomes 'an invalid bag of mediocre nerves, a silly child' in his suburban villa (Reed 1996: 11). Lewis, who celebrated mechanisation and technology and despised what he perceived as the emotionalism and sentimentality of nineteenth-century art, insisted that 'the best type of artist would rather give expression to the more energetic part of that City man's life – do pictures to put in his office, where he is most alive – than manufacture sentimental and lazy images . . . for his wretched vegetable home existence' (Reed 1996:11). The spaces of 'modern man' are the city and the street; domesticity, represented by the suburban villa, is the antithesis of all that is new, alive and modern. Berman, also, insists that modernity is a journey away from 'home', a journey into the unknown, a 'risky' venture that is, nevertheless, exhilarating and exciting, and one that demands we leave behind the safe haven of the familiar (Berman 1988). Writing about the anxieties that surrounded women's entry into the public sphere, Sheila Rowbotham says '[e]very time we mounted the steps of their platforms we wanted to run away and hide at home' (1973: 45). In all these formulations home is represented as the place of tradition and repression from which it is necessary to escape if full selfhood is to be achieved. Hence, the modernist self-defining subject, 'unrestrained by private or domestic respons-ibilities, possessing a rational mind freed from the distorting effects of the emotions and the needs of the body', is represented as an individual characterised by those values historically associated with the masculine (Johnson 1996: 450). What Johnson calls 'the home-and-away story of the modern subject' shaped feminist thinking in the 1960s and 1970s and its legacy remains as we struggle to concept-ualise and analyse the positive meanings that home and domesticity carry for millions of so-called 'ordinary' women (Johnson 1996: 450).

In Britain second-wave feminism drew its analyses from a socialist and Marxist paradigm of production and reproduction. Key questions involved the issue of whether women did form a distinct sex-class and this required that Marxist ideas about reproduction be extended to include women's work in the home. Such work was identified as a consequence of a rigid sexual division of labour in which women are 'responsible for the production of simple use-values in those activities associated with the home and family' while men 'are responsible for commodity production; they are not, in principle, given any role in household labour' (Benston 1968/1980: 121). For British feminists the focus of analysis was capitalism and its relationship with patriarchy, 'to act effectively we have to try to work out the precise relationship between the patriarchal dominance of men over women, and the property relations which come from this, to class exploitation and racism' (Rowbotham 1973: 152). As a result feminism in Britain, because it critiqued the oppressive nature of home and family under both capitalism and patriarchy, did so from a long tradition of socialist thought that focused on working as well as middle-class experiences. In North America, second-wave feminism drew heavily on the New Left and the Civil Rights movement, although, as we shall see with regard to Friedan, this could be severely compromised by the paranoid atmosphere of Cold War 'red-baiting' and McCarthyism. Both British and American feminism (rightly) saw childcare and household labour as key issues in any analysis of women's oppression and, from different theoretical positions, argued for radical re-thinkings of how these labours might be carried out in order to release women for, what were frequently seen as, more creative tasks. Suzanne Gail, a graduate, wrote in the 1960s of her life as a wife and mother, 'I sit crouched in a chair, feeling all that useless and unwanted power suppressed inside me' and Sheila Rowbotham has written of the tensions between the educational promises of the post-war years and the actual reality that awaited women in the form of marriage and motherhood (Gail 1965–67/1980: 110; Rowbotham 1972/1980: 198 and 2000). The dilemmas and despair of many educated women who found themselves, with little preparation, confined to tedious and exhausting work in the home should not be under-estimated. As Gail observes, 'I was humbled by the discovery that what I had considered work fit only for fools was beyond my capacity' (1965–67/1980: 105). Not only was domesticity monotonous, it could be damaging to the self-esteem of educated women, brought up with the promises of the post-war years to believe that nothing was beyond their capabilities. Ann Oakley in her important book *The Sociology of Housework* attempted, as other socialist feminists in Britain were doing, to identify the precise nature of women's relationship to home and domesticity and to explore why what was seen as a 'labour of love' was so often exploitative and oppressive (Oakley 1974). However, for millions of women, domesticity, albeit frequently boring and sometimes stifling, did not have quite the same dramatic impact and these feminist analyses that urged a re-thinking of home and all it stood for went largely unheeded in popular consciousness. Indeed, many women continued to stress that their primary allegiance was to home and family with career, job or public works fitted in around the demands of domesticity.

One of the most popular and accessible analyses of women's position was Betty Friedan's *The Feminine Mystique*, first published in America in 1963 and sub-sequently in Britain by Penguin where it went into seven editions between 1965 and 1982. Friedan, along with Kate Millett and Germaine Greer, was for many women their first encounter with feminism. Despite its specific location in American culture, *The Feminine Mystique* spoke directly to numerous 'ordinary' women in Britain. I remember, as a suburban housewife in the late 1970s, reading Friedan with a group of similar women, and I still recall the excitement we felt. Friedan's achievement was to popularise many feminist ideas that were relatively inaccess-ible to those outside academia. Although, as already stated, *The Feminine Mystique* is firmly located in post-war American culture, and much of this book has examined British culture, I, nevertheless, want to examine it in some detail. I want to do so, not only because it was popular and influential in Britain, but also because Friedan's analysis is couched in terms of the modernist account of the self-defining (masc-uline) individual and exemplifies many of the points about modernism, home and gender that I have made above. I then want to propose a wider understanding of home and modernity that neither pathologises nor pities the millions of women for whom domesticity is a primary concern and an actively created space.

The Feminine Mystique, (1963) Betty Friedan

The Feminine Mystique is generally regarded 'as a catalyst to the western feminist movement that began in the mid to late sixties', hailed as 'a time-bomb flung into the Mom-and-Apple-Pie image' and as a 'classic text of the modern women's movement' (Bowlby 1987: 61; Friedan 1963/1982 jacket covers). It begins with the premise that 'something is very wrong with the way American women are trying to live their lives today' and proceeds, as Rachel Bowlby has pointed out, rather like a thriller narrative (Bowlby 1987: 61). The story goes that behind the closed doors of post-war American suburbia a problem is growing, a problem that, in 1960, 'burst like a boil through the image of the happy American housewife' as the discontent of such women was widely reported (Friedan 1963/1982: 19–20). In the recent past, Friedan claims, feminists had fought for political rights, education and social equality. As a result of these hard-won victories women were able to enter the professions and to benefit from higher education. Then, Friedan's story continues, men returned from the Second World War desperate for stability in the form of homes, wives and children. This craving was fuelled by the mass media, psychiatrists, psychologists, educationalists, and sociologists, who pedalled a dream of women's fulfilment that could only be satisfied by husband, baby and suburban domesticity. Thus, Friedan concludes, the promise of free choice for which previous generations struggled so hard has been lost as women are duped into dropping out of college and foregoing careers in order to marry and reproduce. Friedan seeks answers to questions about how and why this has occurred and her quest takes her to Madison Avenue and the producers of advertisements and magazines, to institutions of higher education and into psychology. The rhetoric of detection is pervasive as Friedan gradually uncovers the culprits and the consp-iracy that she asserts has trapped women in a stultifying domesticity. In Chapter 7 for example she begins her analysis of why women are dropping out of higher education as follows, '[i]t must have been going on for ten or fifteen years before the educators even suspected it', and she opens Chapter 9, 'months ago, as I began to fit together the puzzle of women's retreat to home, I had the feeling I was missing something' (Friedan 1963/1982: 132, 181). 'The problem that has no name' is finally identified as the prevailing ideology of femininity (the feminine mystique) which has been used to brainwash women into accepting the role of 'happy housewife' and eschewing paid work, politics or professional activities. Finally, in a somewhat dubious analogy, she likens the suburban homes of these 'happy housewives' to a 'comfortable concentration camp' in which both boys and girls show evidence of personalities 'arrested at the level of infantile fantasy and passivity' as a result of their mothers' 'intensity of preoccupation' with their upbringing (Friedan 1963/1982: 245, 248–9). The story that Friedan tells, quite rightly, challenged women to question the assumptions of femininity and in what follows I am not trying to deny her influence and significance for Western fem-inism. What I do want to explore are the connections between her view of suburban America, gender, mass society and modern individuality for in her analysis of the situation of 'modern' American women and her exhortation to change their lives, Friedan draws on modernist paradigms and conventional narratives of the form-ation of the 'modern individual' (Johnson 1996: 451).

If the interwar period was the moment when suburban housing became widely available to lower-middle and working-class people in Britain, the period after the Second World War was its equivalent in America.[1] The mass-produced suburbs of the post-war housing boom in America offered new forms of living to middle and some working-class families of white European descent. The Federal Housing Administration provided building loans (these included conditions that effectively reserved these new neighbourhoods for white Americans, many of whom were second-generation immigrants), and loans to returning soldiers. As a result many post-war suburban towns contained a high proportion of young married couples ready to raise families but separated from extended family or the ethnic ties of the city (Spigel 1997: 219). This new design for living was heavily promoted in post-war America as offering the best (and only) way of organising everyday life and was underpinned by a growing prosperity that enabled increased consumption of domestic commodities. Suburban architecture celebrated this new era of affluence. For example, houses sported huge picture windows that emphasised the role of the home as a showcase for a developing consumer culture. Spigel quotes from a house manual of the period that asserts the housewife's need for 'an effective and glamorous background for her as a sexual being, commensurate with the amount of energy she expends on clothes, make-up and society' and Alison J. Clarke has demonstrated the significance of the Tupperware phenomenon as a symbol of post-war American suburban life (Spigel 1997: 221; Clarke 1997). '[L]ightweight, unbreakable . . . attractive in pastel jewel-like colors and modern designs', Tupperware products captured the vision and myth of suburban modernity (Clarke 1997: 156). After the disruptions of war, post-war America sought stability in the dream of a renewed family life in which men and women occupied clear roles. Women, who had found a new independence during the Second World War, were now encouraged to see their place as domestic, deferential and dependent. Yet, at the same time, there was an increased demand for women's labour in the workplace. These contradictions exacerbated fears that masculinity was under threat, a fear already prompted by women's encroachments into areas of male prowess during the war. The revival of a traditional domestic ideology, which is what Friedan is attacking, emerged from anxieties that anything less would lead to the impairment of 'masculine development [in boys and men] as individual beings in a competitive society' (Campbell and Kean 1997: 198)

Criticisms of the post-war American dream of affluence and suburban bliss were not new in 1963 when Friedan published *The Feminine Mystique*. Spigel has argued that by the late 1950s there was an established critique of suburbia on TV as well as in science fiction novels like Philip K. Dick's *Time Out of Joint* (Spigel 1997: 226). And a number of sociological studies explored what was seen as the stultifying and homogenising effects of consumerism, estate living and 'selling your soul' to the corporation.[2] In fact the popular success of the book was precisely because its propositions, albeit focused on women and their position in society, were readily recognisable to a wide constituency of readers, educated within a framework of modernist ideas and sensibilities. This included feminism which had not gone underground or disappeared in the 1940s and 1950s, as Friedan claimed, although it was to struggle in the paranoid atmosphere of Cold War politics as progressive groups of whatever persuasion were subjected to 'red-baiting'. Daniel Horowitz has documented the numerous women's and feminist groups that Friedan had access to in the late 1940s and 1950s. Many of these also espoused labour and anti-racist causes as well as women's rights issues (Horowitz 1998: 124–32). The Popular Front feminist, Elizabeth Hawes, published *Why Women Cry* in 1943 and in 1946 *Hurry Up Please* in which she recounted her work as union organiser with the United Automobile Workers. Fifteen years before *The Feminine Mystique*, Hawes was attacking the myth of the happy housewife: she 'examined how the media, especially the women's magazines and advertisers, prescribed the way women should lead their lives' (Horowitz 1998: 129). Progressive feminists of the 1940s and early 1950s were well aware that domesticity could be stultifying and frustrating for educated women and, like Friedan, they saw the solution as women's entry into the paid work force and opportunities for meaningful work.

As Horowitz has shown, Friedan herself was involved with labour, anti-racist and left-wing politics during the 1940s and early 1950s. She wrote pamphlets and journalism for the radical union, United Electrical, Radio and Machine Workers of America (known as the UE) in which she argued for the rights of women workers. She was certainly aware of Hawes's publications and wrote for the magazine *New Masses* in the 1940s when it was carrying articles about the plight of the housewife confined to domesticity (Horowitz 1998: 121–52). Friedan had a rich legacy of feminist and progressive thought to draw on. When she wrote *The Feminine Mystique* in the early 1960s she was not saying anything that hadn't been said before; her achievement was to link these earlier analyses with her theory of a 'feminine mystique' that functioned to keep women in their place. However, in 1973 Friedan insisted that until she began writing *The Feminine Mystique* she 'wasn't even conscious of the woman problem' and even when she alluded vaguely to her past in radical politics she consistently maintained that the book emerged from her own experience as a suburban housewife. Horowitz has suggested how the damaging conservative politics of McCarthyism and anti-communism forced left-wing radicals like Friedan to disavow their pasts and to reinvent themselves in ways that were acceptable to mainstream American culture in the 1950s, 1960s and 1970s:

> In 1996 and 1997, I discovered that beginning at least as early as 1940, Friedan knew a wide variety of radicals whom anti-communists investigated in the late 1940s and 1950s. I emphasize these connections not to paint Friedan with a red brush, but to suggest that

the McCarthyite attacks on people she knew may have made her fearful of redbaiting. These attacks shaped not only her politics from the 1940s on, but also American feminism in the postwar period . . . With *The Feminine Mystique* Friedan began a long tradition among American feminists of seeing compulsory domesticity as the main consequence of 1950s McCarthyism. This emphasis, while in some ways on the mark, nonetheless threw later feminists off-track. It helped prevent them from seeing that another significant result of McCarthyism was that many left-wing feminists had to go underground in the 1950s. Left-wing feminists later emerged as second-wave feminists, some of them, like Friedan, minimizing any connection to 1940s radicalism. (1998: 10–11)

Horowitz's story of the writing of *The Feminine Mystique* re-assesses the origins of the book which, he argues, go back to Friedan's childhood, her time at Smith College and, in particular, her experience as a writer and journalist with radical labour unions in the 1940s and early 1950s (Horowitz 1998: 2).

Earlier in this book I noted the lack of suburban voices in the literature on suburbia. Those who wrote or spoke about suburbia in Britain or America did so from positions outside the phenomenon they so roundly condemned. Friedan, on the other hand, represented herself as a voice from the suburbs, an advocate on behalf of those women whom experts like Stephen Taylor diagnosed as 'neurotic'. In the opening chapter of *The Feminine Mystique* Friedan recalls that,

on an April morning in 1959, I heard a mother of four, having coffee with four other mothers in a suburban development fifteen miles from New York, say in a tone of quiet desperation, 'the problem'. And the others knew, without words, that she was not talking about a problem with her husband, or her children, or her home. Suddenly they realized they all shared the same problem, the problem that has no name. They began, hesitantly, to talk about it. Later, after they had picked up their children at nursery school and taken them home to nap, two of the women cried, in sheer relief, just to know they were not alone. (1963/1982: 17)

She goes on to claim that she first 'sensed the problem, not as a reporter, but as a suburban housewife, for during this time I was also bringing up my own three children in Rockland County, New York' (Friedan 1963/1982: 18). The 'problem' that Friedan identifies is that many women were trying to live their lives 'in the image of those pretty pictures of the American suburban housewife, kissing their husbands good-bye in front of the picture window, depositing their stationwagons-ful of children at school, and smiling as they ran the new electric waxer over the spotless kitchen floor' (Friedan 1963/1982: 16). Most of the women Friedan interviewed were college-educated and it is these middle-class wives with whom Friedan is most concerned: women like herself who do not lack material advantages but for whom these do not constitute fulfilment. At one point she suggests that 'the problem' may not exist for those 'preoccupied with desperate problems of hunger, poverty or illness' (Friedan 1963/1982: 24). As a result the analysis of women in *The Feminine Mystique* does not confront the problems of women's material deprivation nor does it explore racial differences and their impact on experience. Friedan's upbringing and her commitment to labour politics meant that she was aware of racial issues as well as the deprivations suffered by urban working-class women, and she could have developed an analysis of women's oppression that included these. Growing up in Peoria, Illinois as Bettye Goldstein, the daughter of a moderately prosperous jewellery store owner, Friedan became increasingly aware of anti-Semitism. Much later she commented on this 'When you're a Jewish girl who grows up on the right side of the tracks in the Midwest, you're marginal' (Horowitz 1998: 23). Her sense of marginality and isolation culminated in high school when she was turned down for membership in a sorority because she was Jewish (Horowitz 1998: 23). Her work with the UE in the late 1940s would have brought her into contact with those who were fighting discrimination on the grounds of race as well as sex and in 1952–53 she wrote a series of articles for *Jewish Life* about the International Ladies' Garment Workers' Union in which she condemned as unjust the circumstances in which affluent women could buy and wear clothes that working-class women had laboured to produce (Horowitz 1998: 133–4, 151). Yet, she explicitly and implicitly excludes such issues from *The Feminine Mystique*. Horowitz comments on her transformation from labour journalist to free-lance writer around 1952:

> Perhaps one of the reasons Friedan was relieved to quit the world of radical labor journalism was that it was getting too hot there. She might have felt she could take cover in a more feminine and less feminist place. With McCarthyism, Friedan was once again in danger of losing her voice. Now she would begin to learn how to speak differently, a process that would eventually lead to *The Feminine Mystique*. (1998: 152)

In 1947 Friedan married Carl Friedan who was, at the time, struggling to make a career in staging experimental theatre. In 1950 with two children the Friedans moved to Parkway Village, a residential development for United Nations personnel and a one hour journey from Manhattan. Parkway Village, although similar in geographical layout to many other suburban developments of the time in America, was markedly different in its cosmopolitan mix of inhabitants. According to Horowitz, Parkway Village included diplomats, African Americans and Jews, like the Friedans. Friedan enjoyed this mix of people and promoted the Village as a model of democratic and co-operative living in her editorship of the local newspaper, *Parkway Villager*. During her time at Parkway Friedan involved herself in local issues, such as rent protests, and in her writings, actively promoted the establishment of a racially-integrated community in which women contributed equally with men. For example, during the rent protests, Friedan led the publicity committee and a woman chaired the rent committee. While the articles Friedan wrote for *Parkway Villager* drew on her earlier radical politics, she increasingly used this knowledge to write about middle-class women and the problems they encountered.

In 1956 the Friedans moved to Grand View-on-Hudson in Rockland County, a suburban community made up almost entirely of professional middle-class families. In 1976 she was to describe her time in Rockland County in terms of the 'feminine mystique': 'I chauffeured, and did the P.T.A. and buffet dinners, and hid, like secret drinking in the morning, the book I was writing when my suburban neighbours came for coffee' (Friedan 1976: 14). At the time she offered a different version. Her own response to the questionnaire she used for *The Feminine Mystique* reports that the family income was above average (between $15,000 and $20,000 per annum) to which she was contributing between $4,000 and $8,000. She employed domestic help for three to four days a week, paid for from her own earnings and while, she continued to face tensions between her wish to combine domestic commitments with, what she saw as, meaningful work, she felt herself to be gradually integrating these conflicting aspects of her life. In the questionnaire response Friedan makes it clear that, at this point in her life, she had learned to conform in superficial ways but recognised what made her different from the ordinary suburban housewife – 'she worked for the Democratic Party, preferred writing to motherhood, and resisted prejudice against Jews, African Americans, and Asians' (Horowitz 1998: 170–1). She also established and led an Intellectual Resources Pool that worked to enrich the school curriculum by bringing in writers, artists, scientists and academics who lived in the area. This involved her in writing funding proposals, and grants to the Pool paid for her part-time work as project director. As in Parkway Village Friedan was centrally involved in community projects that offered a positive picture of what suburban women could achieve and she, later, used these personal insights as the basis for her belief that motherhood and a professional career need not be incompatible. Yet, *The Feminine Mystique* represents suburban housewives as passive victims of a mass culture that dupes them into a certain version of mother and housewife – dependent, infantile, living vicariously through husband and children, and materially acquisitive. As we have seen, Friedan's life in the suburbs was not like this, and nor were the lives of many women who served on local committees, engaged in the micro-politics of suburban life, worked part-time or for voluntary agencies, or, albeit less frequently, held down a full-time job or career. Sylvie Murray has offered evidence that counters Friedan's view of suburban life in her study of Queens, New York during the years 1945 to 1960. She describes communities where political discussion and action were integrated into the everyday experiences of women and men in their homes, in the local shops, in the neighbourhood and in the community organisations that flourished in suburban areas. She argues that whilst women's presence 'was often concealed behind the public celebration of male leadership' women participated actively in a range of political activities that were characterised by 'their sense of themselves as citizens, their allegiance to the local community, their concern for national and international affairs, and, most importantly, the integration of collective and political actions in the very fabric of suburban domesticity' (Horowitz 1998: 157–8).

It was during these years in Parkway Village and Rockland County that Friedan emerged as a freelance writer, offering a critique of American suburbia that tapped into and drew on the general dislike of mass society amongst radical and left-wing intellectuals. In Britain intellectual contempt for mass society emerged from the perceived threat posed by working-class literacy: in America this contempt was exacerbated by the perceived attempts of McCarthyism to suppress 'free' thought (Carey 1992: 5). Although the new centres of cultural power developed differently in post-war North America and Britain, the growing influence of wealthy news-paper owners, the dominance of Hollywood over the film industry and the potential of radio and TV to communicate with hitherto undreamed of mass audiences generated anxieties in both countries about the monolithic power of capitalism and the emergence of a debased mass culture. In 1947 T.W. Adorno and Max Horkheimer wrote:

celebrity culture? *aspiration / emulation on*

culture now impresses the same stamp on everything. Films, radio and magazines make up a system which is uniform as a whole and in every part. Even the aesthetic activities of political opposites are one in their enthusiastic obedience to the rhythm of the iron system. The decorative industrial management buildings and exhibition centres in authoritarian countries are much the same as anywhere else. The huge gleaming towers that shoot up everywhere are outward signs of the ingenious planning of international concerns, toward which the unleashed entrepreneurial system (whose monuments are a mass of gloomy houses and business premises in grimy, spiritless cities) was already hastening. Even now the older houses just outside the concrete city centres look like slums, and the new bungalows on the outskirts are at one with the flimsy structures of world fairs in their praise of technical progress and their built-in demand to be discarded after a short while like empty food cans. Yet the city housing projects designed to perpetuate the individual as a supposedly independent unit in a small hygienic dwelling make him all the more subservient to his adversary – the absolute power of capitalism. (During 1993: 30)

Adorno and Horkheimer were writing, as refugees from Hitler's Germany living in North America, in the aftermath of the Second World War and, as Simon During comments, 'Hitler's totalitarianism (with its state control of cultural production) and the American market system are fused in their thought' (1993: 29). Their concern, not surprisingly therefore, is to identify and critique all manifestations of state and capitalist control that result in the loss of freedom and individuality. To this end their writing deploys powerful metaphoric structures that construct organised capitalism as a violent and invasive attack on individuality and freedom. Thus the culture industry 'impresses the same stamp' on all its products, be they public buildings, films, radios, magazines or private houses. In doing so the individual is made 'subservient to his adversary' which is 'the absolute power of capitalism'. The individual is thus positioned as subject to and victim of an implacable enemy who is 'coercive' and 'manipulative'. When Adorno and Horkheimer insist that the 'need which might resist central control has already been suppressed by the control of the individual consciousness' they are drawing on the language of 'brainwashing' and 'conditioning' that was associated with Cold War politics and linked to the manipulations of mass advertising in which people were persuaded to satisfy what were labelled as 'false needs' (Adorno and Horkheimer 1947/1979: 31).[3] Friedan was able to link this animus against, what was seen as, a growing homogeneity, conformity and anti-intellectualism, to the position of middle-class women. Her suburban housewives exhibit all the attributes ascribed to the 'masses' by the Frankfurt School, represented as passive victims of a culture that brainwashes them into docility, acquiescence and dependency.[4] She uses the same rhetoric of coercion and imposed power as Adorno and Horkheimer, insisting that women 'must refuse to be nameless, depersonalized, manipulated', brainwashed into limiting 'sex-roles' by a mass media who peddle a false dream of fulfilment (Friedan 1963/1982: 268).

One of the impulses behind Friedan's writings in the late 1950s and 1960s was the desire to sustain and maintain the kind of intellectual and political life that she believed was the only way to ensure self-realisation and to resist assimilation by a coercive and dominant culture. Individuality and identity are key issues in *The Feminine Mystique*:

> the core of the problem for women today is not sexual but a problem of identity – a stunting or evasion of growth that is perpetuated by the feminine mystique. It is my thesis that as the Victorian culture did not permit women to accept or gratify their basic sexual needs, our culture does not permit women to accept or gratify their basic need to grow and fulfil their potentialities as human beings, a need which is not solely defined by their sexual role. (Friedan 1963/1982: 68)

Identity for Friedan does not denote a sense of self rooted in race or gender or sexual orientation. Rather she uses the term in the psychological meaning it acquired in the 1950s to suggest an individualist sense of self that defined itself in terms of 'uniqueness' and thereby could be set against the pressures of conformity and homogeneity. In particular she draws on the work of A.H. Maslow who formulated the idea that once basic physical survival has been ensured, people need to exercise all their capabilities to the full: '[t]he unused capacity or organ can become a disease centre or else atrophy, thus diminishing the person' (Friedan 1963/1982: 274). Friedan's work for the Intellectual Resources Pool in Rockland County had confirmed her belief in the importance of personal development, something, she believed, could only be achieved by education. In particular she saw the struggle for self-definition as difficult for women whom 'the feminine mystique' decreed 'are not expected to grow up to find out who they are, to choose their human identity' (Friedan 1963/1982: 69). A mature 'identity' for Friedan connotes a certain intellectual ability and political awareness that will be used to counter, what she sees as, the alienating tendencies of suburban modernity. As a result *The Feminine Mystique* is structured around metaphors of growth and stunting, hunger and satisfaction, and contrasts are set up between developed man and under-developed woman that draw on the same cultural stereotypes deployed in the gendering of mass culture that has been discussed in earlier chapters.

Maslow's description of individual 'growth', quoted approvingly by Friedan, reads like a classic account of modernity:

> Growth has not only rewards and pleasure, but also many intrinsic pains and always will have. Each step forward is a step into the unfamiliar and is thought of as possibly dangerous. It also frequently means giving up something familiar and good and satisfying. It frequently means a parting and a separation with consequent nostalgia, loneliness and mourning. It also often means giving up a simpler and easier and less effortful life in exchange for a more demanding, more difficult life. Growth forward is in spite of these losses and therefore requires courage, strength in the individual, as well as protection, permission and encouragement from the environment, especially for the child. (Friedan 1963/1982: 274)

It is this dangerous, exhilarating journey that Friedan is exhorting women to take, 'a turning point from an immaturity that has been called femininity to full human identity' (1963/1982: 70). Insofar as she wishes women to leave behind their 'feminine' past and to enter fully into the experience of modernity, she challenges those accounts of modernity that relegated women to the margins of culture. The problem is that, while she undoubtedly wants women to seek their own identities *as women*, Friedan's image of the 'full human identity' that should be their ideal, is a masculine one. Until recently only men, she states, 'had the freedom and the education necessary to realize their full abilities, to pioneer and create and discover, and map new trails for future generations' (Friedan 1963/1982: 73). However, she goes on, in the nineteenth century 'pioneer' feminists began 'to forge new trails for women' (Friedan 1963/1982: 71). These 'trails' were 'unexpectedly rough' as women sought to push back the 'frontiers' that limited their experience and win 'the battles' for civil and political rights; as they set out on their 'journey away from home . . . in search of new identity' (Friedan 1963/1982: 71–87). The language used here constructs a certain version of American masculinity (the pioneer, frontiersman) as the model to be adopted in the search for a modern 'human identity' with home and femininity representing a restrictive, immature and outdated culture from which women must escape. Moreover, Friedan implicitly links her own work with the 'pioneering' spirit that motivated feminists, like Elizabeth Cady Stanton:

> The call to that first Woman's Rights Convention came about because an educated woman, who had already participated in shaping society as an abolitionist, came face to face with the realities of a housewife's drudgery and isolation in a small town. Like the college graduate with six children in the suburb of today, Elizabeth Cady Stanton, moved by her husband to the small town of Seneca Falls, was restless in a life of baking, cooking, sewing, washing and caring for each baby. (1963/1982: 81)[5]

Ironically, Stanton, unlike Friedan, vehemently extolled 'feminine' virtues, '[t]he need of this hour is not territory, gold mines, railroads, or specie payments, but a new evangel of womanhood, to exalt purity, virtue, morality, true religion, to lift man up into the higher realms of thought and action' (Elshtain 1981: 232). In contemporary America, the frontiersman has become, according to Friedan, those 'able, ambitious men' who work in the city and are, in her view, fully mature human individuals. There is no attempt in *The Feminine Mystique* to problematise the equally pervasive myth of masculine success in which 'manliness' is conceived as 'a good business suit, ambition, paying one's bills on time, enough knowledge of baseball to hand out tips at the barbershop' (White 1983: 147). As Elshtain comments, '[h]er book is a paean of praise to what Americans themselves call the "rat race": she just wants women to join it' (1981: 251). In exhorting women to seek particular (masculine) forms of modern individuality, Friedan's polemic continues to reproduce the gendered dichotomies that see the values of home as modernism's other – comfort, ordinariness and dependency.

While Friedan argues for women's entry to full human status, the language consistently sets up oppositions between masculinity (public, active, mature, forward-thinking, critical) and femininity (private, passive, immature, backward-looking, conformist) that ensure that access to a 'full human identity' in the modern world means denying the feminine and assimilating to the masculine. *The Feminine Mystique*, while it undoubtedly allowed many women to understand their lives (the letters Friedan received speak of relief and gratitude for her recognition of their experiences), also ensured that suburban women were seen as passive victims of a 'false consciousness' that could easily be remedied by a good dose of education. Friedan had no time for voluntary or charitable work or for local evening classes: to find their new identities women needed university or college education. In other words they could only be freed from their domestic prisons by becoming the grateful recipients of white, Western, male thought and culture. It also ensured that liberal feminism in America, if not Britain, would continue to centre its analysis of women on the problems of middle-class domesticity to the neglect of urban working-class women and racial issues which, arguably, could have proved equally potent starting-points for a newly formulated feminism in the 1960s. Friedan's alignment with (white, male) intellectual thought that positioned domesticity, suburbia and mass culture as feminine and therefore inferior meant that *The Feminine Mystique* spoke only to and for middle-class, educated women whose needs are assumed to be the needs of all women. Those women whose identity and self-worth are linked to motherhood, domesticity, the neighbourhood community and local ethnicities are invited to see themselves as either the pitied victims of 'false consciousness' or as outdated relics of an oppressive past. Thus, there is no space in which the aspirations and deprivations of huge numbers of women in the twentieth century can be explored. Friedan aligns herself with those canonical male narratives, in which battling to contain the perceived threat posed by mass culture to a certain form of intellectual and creative thinking, is represented as the only valid response to modernization.

Friedan drew on rhetoric and ideas that were already circulating in intellectual thought and in American mass culture to formulate her attack on the limiting oppressions of domesticity. Because she spoke a language that was already familiar and recognisable to a wide spectrum of Americans she was readily assimilated as a radical voice speaking out on behalf of women. However, *The Feminine Mystique* is unable to deal with the uneven and complex nature of suburban domesticity as well as the complicated relationship between media institutions, the audience to whom they offered their products and the freelance writers, some of whom, like Friedan, were suburbanites, because of the gendered dichotomies that underpin her thought and hence her determination to see suburban domesticity as always oppressive for all women. Ironically, its tendency to homogenise suburbia and the women who live there follows precisely those tendencies that Friedan so passionately deplores in the modern world, denying identity and individuality to the women she describes.

'Back to the Home': Post-War Culture in North America and Britain

Much historiography of women in post-war America and Britain has accepted Friedan's narrative unquestioningly: the generally accepted story is that women retreated into domesticity in the 1950s and only emerged with the advent of the women's movement (of which Friedan's text was part) in the 1960s, with the whole era characterised as a low point for feminism and a much lamented regression. For example, Helen Dennis's discussion of Sylvia Plath begins by describing the 1950s as 'the decade of reaction, when "Rosie the Riveter" returned to the suburbs and "hubby" did his best to become "one-dimensional man"' (2000: 74). However, taking issue with Friedan's assertions that mass culture imposed 'the feminine mystique' on millions of women, Joanne Meyerowitz has demonstrated that women's magazines did not simply celebrate or peddle an uncritical acceptance of domesticity, and her edited collection of essays on the period counters the stereo-typing that places all women in suburban domesticity, offering histories of single women, lesbians and political activists as a corrective (Meyerowitz 1993; 1994). Meyerowitz argues that magazines offered images and stories about successful career women who juggled domestic commitments and professional work, that they ran articles in which the problems of domesticity were discussed and, that they consistently advocated individual achievement as an acceptable goal for women. Her point is that the domestic ideology attacked by Friedan was never complete and that it was usual to find contradictory points of view in the same magazine. Meyerowitz concludes that women's activities in the 1950s were more complex and varied than has often been acknowledged and that those who spoke *either* for an uncritical return to domesticity *or* for women's rights to jobs and careers were in the minority. Mainstream magazines offered 'multiple messages, which women could read as sometimes supporting and sometimes subverting the "feminine mystique"' (Meyerowitz 1993: 1480).

Meyerowitz's study of magazines discusses how mainstream media culture in America frequently 'expressed overt admiration for women whose individual striving moved them beyond the home' (1993: 1458). Publications like *Ebony*, aimed at African-American readers, and 'middlebrow' magazines, such as *Reader's Digest*, carried stories about women who had achieved public success, who had unusual talents or overcame adversity to achieve this success. For example, Meyerowitz cites an article detailing the success of Dorothy McCullough Lee who had become mayor of Portland, Oregon by, it would seem, single-handedly defeating a powerful and corrupt opposition. Lee is praised in the article for her 'relentless drive' against organised crime and is described, without further comment, as a 'violent feminist' who has 'intense concern with the status of women'. The article concludes that Lee is 'headed for national distinction'. At the same time the author Richard L. Neuberger describes Lee as 'an ethereally pale housewife' who wears fancy hats. The juxtaposition of femininity and public service was not unusual for the time and while, it was undoubtedly irritating for powerful, high-achieving women to be labelled as housewives and discussed in terms of their appearance, articles, like the one on Lee, suggested that it was both possible and desirable for women to transcend suburban domesticity. Energetic women who juggled domestic commitments and achieved success in career, job or community work were frequently celebrated in the pages of these 1950s magazines (Meyerowitz 1993: 1459). Above all magazines praised and endorsed hard work. The same article told its readers how 'the mayor lives, breathes, eats and sleeps her job'; other articles, cited by Meyerowitz, praise the energy, 'ceaseless activity' and devotion to work that characterised high-achieving women. Nowhere, in these mainstream magazines, was it suggested that such women should retreat into domesticity, although neither were they expected to 'neglect' their domestic commitments. The ethos of hard work was central to the thinking of the mass media at this time: housewives were criticised if they indulged in those activities generally associated with the affluent, 'lady of leisure'. Playing bridge, excessive shopping, holidays on the Riviera were seen as 'idleness' and set against hard work undertaken in the home and in the workplace. This appeal to housewives as professional, efficient, hard-working citizens is one that we have seen operated in Britain in the 1930s and 1940s and undoubtedly tapped into many women's desires, both before and after the Second World War.

In Britain, during the war, there were regular meetings between the editors of women's magazines and government ministers in attempts to persuade magazines to engage in propaganda targeted at women. This politicisation of women's magazines, which has not occurred since, represented a recognition on the part of the state that popular culture can be a powerful tool for disseminating information and ideas. After the war this collaboration continued and magazine editors worked with the new Labour government to carry messages about its social policies and to inform readers about social legislation that was of particular concern to women. Mary Grieve, the editor of *Woman* from 1940 to 1962, recalled the ways in which women's magazines engaged with the post-war world:

> When the war ended, the social Acts, the Education Act, Acts like holidays with pay meant that suddenly vast numbers of people were interested in these new things. Whereas before the war it was a class distinction: you went for a holiday or you went for a day trip. So you couldn't write in our magazine about a week going down the French canals, however desirable and enlarging that might have been. But now you could.
>
> The National Health Service meant that women, the mothers who'd never had any doctoring really – their husbands did because they were on the panel, their children did – the mothers had very little. But when she could have medical attention, she began to be interested in the subject, and medical articles burgeoned in all the magazines. They were not there before, because medical attention was not in her experience. (Ferguson 1983: 21)

British women's magazines in the post-war period did not simply impose an ideology of femininity nor did they always exhort their female readers to return to domesticity, as has often been claimed, any more than their American counterparts did. They offered an uneven mix of messages that both shaped, and were shaped by, the subjectivities of their women readers. For example, the magazine *My Home* carried a series of articles on 'careers with a future' from 1950 onwards.[6] These included air hostess, occupational therapist, children's nurse, hairdressing, hospital almoner, librarian, PE teacher, laundry manageress, midwife, journalism, dairy work, make-up artist, petroleum chemical industries and local government work. The range of occupations covered in these articles, which gave information about pay, training and qualifications, as well as details of the kind of work involved, was wide, incorporating jobs in both the professional and the service sector. Moreover, although marriage and domesticity remained a central element in the magazines' ideology, single career women were treated with respect and admiration. A story in *My Home* for January 1950 tells the story of a woman who is matron of a hospital and single. She is presented as 'an austere spinster who had reached a pinnacle in her profession'. She has 'fine, dark eyes' (always a signifier of moral worth in popular fiction of the period) and is represented as a strong, compass-ionate woman who encourages her junior nurses to become qualified and to take their work seriously. Nevertheless, the story is about how her compassion and strength stem from the death of her fiancé in a car crash, thus enabling her to understand the importance of romantic love and marriage to the junior nurse she helps. Throughout the 1950s *My Home* published stories like this alongside the articles mentioned above as well as the usual features on cooking doughnuts and making lampshades. It also included book reviews that discussed biographies, autobiographies, novels, and travel books and in one instance, an article on Aristotle. Magazines like *My Home* were concerned to draw women's attention to the world outside the home at the same time as presenting that world from the viewpoint of a femininity defined by marriage and motherhood. The overriding message is 'make up your mind to do something and do it. Try hard enough and all things can become possible' (*My Home* 1950). In the post-war world, alongside the egalitarian and collective sentiments of social welfarism, there ran an equally powerful discourse of individualism and personal responsibility that is mirrored in the address of magazines, like *My Home*, to its women readers.

For young women growing up in 1950s Britain and America, Hollywood, as well as magazines, offered versions of femininity that could transport women to a multiplicity of possible worlds. They could be Marilyn Monroe or Audrey Hepburn, but they could also imagine themselves as war heroes or space adventurers. As Rowbotham observes 'amidst the pastel shades and the thick-pile carpets of 1950s' new prosperity, heroic aspirations, images of adventure, sacrifice for a noble cause, courage and daring somehow crept into the production of a feminine self' (1999: 287). By the 1960s, when women born immediately after the Second World War came to adulthood, the concern with security and stability, engendered by specific historical circumstances, had, if not disappeared, at least been temporarily displaced by a sense of excitement and possibility. Women of all ages and classes continued to seek spaces in which they might negotiate the tensions between the necessary safety of mundanity and the need for individual fulfilment. At different times, in different places and between different groups, safety or risk may pre-dominate: for some feminists who came to adulthood in the 1960s, the social climate in Britain and America engendered the exciting 'promise of a dream', to coin Rowbotham's phrase (Rowbotham 2000). This was a dream that meant 'leaving home' and all that that meant. While it has long been understood that men worked out these dilemmas of modernity in the public spaces of modern life, it has been less usual to find any recognition that, first, women engaged with similar tensions and, secondly, that they did so in relation to specific feminine subjectivities.

Feminine Subjectivities and Modernity

Feminism's reliance on narratives of 'leaving home', as the discussion of *The Feminine Mystique* suggests, has meant that 'feminine' desires for home as safety, connectedness and continuity have received little attention in academic scholarship. Yet any discussion with women outside the academy reveals that the need for intimacy, security and stability must be met if we are to function effectively in the modern world. Indeed, the need for 'home', wherever and whatever it may be, is equally important, if differently understood, for men. And, as I have been arguing in this book, the desires represented by home are differentiated historically and socially. Home meant (and means) different things to working-class and middle-class women.

Mavis Kitching, born in 1916, grew up in the jewellery quarter of Birmingham, a congested inner-city area, which in the early twentieth century, consisted of a mix of small factories, workshops, residential housing and shops. Mavis's father was unemployed due to illness and her mother worked as a cleaner in various places in order to keep the family. In 1948 Mavis and her husband George were rehoused in a new council house on the south-west perimeter of the city. Time and again in her story Mavis recalls the shoes and clothing that she received, as a small child, from a local charitable organisation, 'you were given Daily Mail clothes, a big D.M. on the side of your boots, and your dresses were like prison dresses'. She also remembers how she was tormented in the school playground as the recipient of charity. The D.M. on her boots marked her out as 'different', an object of charity to be patronised by those whose philanthropy provided the boots and clothes, but equally an object of derision and ridicule amongst her peers in the playground. Mavis vowed that 'my kids will never have D.M. clothes' and 'I would work my fingers to the bone rather than them have to have Daily Mail clothes.' Being 'poor' also meant being given a holiday by the Girl Guides, 'the guides paid for me, they all put together so that I could go with them. I liked it all the way through.' For Mavis poverty meant exclusion and dependency: this, in turn, bred anger and resentment against her tormentors, gratitude to her benefactors, and overall a sharp awareness of the importance and power of money. When Mavis moved to her new council house she acquired a treadle sewing machine. Her pleasure in this, one of her first possessions as a married woman, expresses a profound sense that she has at last found a place where she is safe from the vicissitudes of her childhood, a place in which Daily Mail clothes are replaced by clothes of her own making. Mavis insists that she loves homemaking and housework, 'people laugh at me – some people say they don't like housework but I love it. I love doing it, knitting, sewing. It's my favourite thing sewing and altering.' Mavis grew up understanding that she would receive nothing unless she 'earned' it either through hard physical work or through psychological endurance. Acquiring a council house and a sewing machine enabled Mavis to provide comfort and clothing for herself and her family. Making clothes and maintaining a home were for Mavis visible symbols that she had 'earned' the right to be included in a society that had so often sought to label her as 'poor' and 'different'.

Mavis loved her new council house, representing as it did the better future she had always hoped for. Council tenancies, home ownership, the ability to purchase a wider range of domestic products, and welfare reforms made possible the dreams of millions of women like Mavis in the years after the Second World War. Modern homes were places not only of safety and belonging but also places where women, like Mavis, could actively make spaces of comfort and pleasure through the exercise of their creative skills in homemaking, knitting, and sewing. Such skills were a source of considerable pride and offered self-dignifying opportunities for subjectivities formed from a mix of exclusion, anger, deference and envy. Many older women, like Annie Stables quoted in the introduction, condemn the disappearance of housekeeping skills amongst younger women. To understand why we need to understand the meanings such skills had for women of this specific generation for whom the opportunity to be a housewife in a home of one's own was a mark of self-worth and belonging. However, it is equally important to remember that this 'better future' was granted to working-class women on certain terms. Mavis recalled how when she and George first moved into their council house 'a visitor used to come. She would turn your bedclothes back and lift your bed up and look underneath to see if there was any fluff or anything . . . And they fumigated all your furniture from down town before you come into here. They always made sure you was clean.' Being a 'good' housewife was to be associated with cleanliness which was itself a mark of social status. A council tenancy required certain standards of housekeeping that were closely monitored by middle-class visitors and other tenants: those unable to keep their homes in 'a good, clean condition' ran the risk not only of losing the tenancy but also the respect of neighbours. Poverty was frequently associated with dirt and disorder. Hence, washing nets, scrubbing doorsteps, boiling the wash to achieve whiteness and sweeping under beds were not only practical ways of combating disease and dirt but were also symbolic demonstrations that, even if you were not very affluent, you did not belong to the class of people known as 'the poor' .

The story of Jean Slater in Chapter 1 reminds us that disease and death were everyday occurrences for many working-class women. Like Jean, Mavis's parents died when she was nineteen, and she found herself responsible for six younger siblings. As a child she contracted scarlet fever. Two of her brothers died 'in the Army' and her first boyfriend died in India. Like Jean, Mavis's sense of herself is rooted in her knowledge that she has survived when so many didn't. For women like Jean and Mavis physical existence is fragile and precarious: to have survived childhood, childbirth, war and adult diseases is cause for pride, and frequently understood as the result of hard work, endurance, and a certain stoicism. The welfare reforms of the post-war era made significant inroads into the pervasive climate of death and disease, and the hopes for a lasting peace enabled women and men to imagine a future that was not dominated by fear and injury. In order to grasp the particular pleasures that modernity offered these women, it is necessary to recognise the ways in which dirt, disease and otherness constituted the elements from which they were invited to create subjectivities. Modernity, for them, signified cleanliness, health and belonging, and was made materially manifest in clean bodies and clothes, fit, healthy children, the ability to purchase domestic commodities, and a comfortable house in the suburbs. For many working-class women, the post-war world offered opportunities to actively create 'modern' homes that provided this hygienic, ordered and healthy environment. As such it became possible for them to see themselves as active agents in the creation of a 'better future' and a modern world through their work in the home.

The relationship of middle-class women to modernity varied from that of their working-class sisters in that their subjectivities were formed from different elements. By the end of the 1950s middle-class women had lost their servants, although the more affluent might still be able to afford part-time, non-residential help. With the loss of servants went the loss of a certain authority linked to the role of mistress in the home and, as we have seen, this might create anxieties around power and status. Middle-class college educated women who came to adulthood just after the Second World War had grown up in a world where servants were taken for granted, and in which the status and authority of the middle-class mistress was still reasonably secure. By the 1950s this was no longer the case. June Macdonald, a middle-class housewife, recalls her changing awareness of social class:

> I was acutely aware that, for the first time in my life anyway, everybody during the war was more or less equal. Of course one was aware of hierarchy in the job, but the moment you got outside and you were confronted with a clippie in charge of a bus, she was in control and you did what she told you, and shop assistants were suddenly very powerful people because things were in short supply. (Hinton 1994: 139)

Not only did their authority over working-class women appear weakened but they were also expected to do their own housework and possibly hold down a job or career. Moreover, although, in theory, most professional careers were now open to educated women, juggling motherhood and career continued to mean that many middle-class women chose one or the other. In 1966 Hannah Gavron published *The Captive Wife*, in which she argued that mothers, and in particular middle-class mothers, were increasingly self-conscious about their role in childcare and the demands this made on their right to autonomy and privacy (Gavron 1966). As we have seen middle-class women believed they had a right to privacy, to opportunities for self-actualisation, and to what, Woolf called, 'a rich inner life'. Modernity may have allowed them more privacy as they were no longer required to share their homes with servants, but it also left them with the drudgery and tedium of housework. As Gavron reported 'nothing has prepared young wives for the relentless boredom of scrubbing floors and ironing shirts' nor had it prepared them for the demands of childcare (1966: 132). One response was to seek a feminist explanation to the situation in which such women found themselves. As I have discussed this took different forms in Britain and North America.

However, not all middle-class women experienced their housewifely role simply as exhausting or stultifying. As we have seen, the women who contributed to the 1946 radio debate on domestic help spoke 'as housewives' with a particular role to play in the future of the nation. Post-war reconstruction was concerned above all else with restoring social stability at home as the means to increased prosperity and future advancement. The nature of marriage, the role of mothers, the importance of adequate housing, the health of women and children, the provision of childcare, the work of the 'housewife', financial support to mothers and families were all issues fiercely debated by successive governments as well as by pressure and special interest groups in the period. The focus on domesticity and its minutiae by government and official bodies was unprecedented and, although the outcomes were not always favourable to women generally and specific groups in particular, issues around women's roles informed debates about industrial productivity and the responsibilities of the welfare state. The fact that domesticity was such a key issue in the late 1940s and early 1950s enabled many middle-class women to speak 'as housewives and mothers'. A particular example was the British Housewives League that protested against the Labour government's policies on food rationing in the late 1940s and early 1950s. This highly organised pressure group held marches and rallies that gained considerable attention and offered a public space in which some middle-class women could speak politically from their identities as housewives, identities that had been strengthened by the part played in the war by the 'home front'. Such women found a voice 'as housewives' and were able to use this to press their claims that the domestic spaces, within which everyday life was experienced should be valued, recognised and properly organised, as well as to challenge outdated notions of femininity. Mrs Lovelock, one of the founders of the British Housewives League, protested consistently and vociferously that women were no longer willing 'to be beasts of burden' nor would they accept the 'domineering, petty tyrants who treat women like children' and place their own convenience and profit above the needs of women and families (Hinton 1994: 139). Moreover, she insisted that the League, was a non-partisan body dedicated to putting 'into public life the same spirit shown by women in home life, unselfishness and readiness to serve'; that women were better placed than men to 'know what's worth preserving in Britain and what wants changing' (Hinton 1994: 142). Such confidence suggests that, at this particular historical moment, women, like Mrs Lovelock, a Labour voter in the 1945 election but conservative in many ways, were able to see themselves as having a central and crucial part to play in the formation of a modern and 'better' Britain.

Finally, for millions of women of all classes, but in particular the working-class, the modern home represented a space in which children could be brought up free from the harsh discipline, material deprivation or unhealthy environments of the past. In her autobiography, *Jipping Street*, Kathleen Woodward describes her mother's life in the late nineteenth century:

> Six children she reluctantly bore, and she was in the habit of saying in a curiously passionless tone that if she had known as much when her first child was born as she learned by the time she bore her sixth, a second child would never have been . . . to me it was clear that if we children had never been born mother's life would have been as an absurd dream of continued ease. (1928/1983: 7)

Kathleen Woodward's mother made no pretences, 'regretting each [child] come to a world filled with anxiety and numberless hours of toil' (Woodward 1928/1983: 7). Perhaps the most significant change for women in the twentieth century has been the spread and development of birth control. By 1960 it was increasingly possible to control pregnancies, and children, rather than being seen as another unwanted mouth to feed, were, in Carolyn Steedman's words, 'repositories of hope, and objects of desire' (1986: 108). Jean Slater's daughter, born at the end of the Second World War, was seen as a symbol of a brighter future, and the son Hannah Armstrong bore when she returned to Yorkshire after her 'adventures' in the south was, in her words, 'the love of her life'. Steedman suggests that the 1950s were 'a watershed in the historical process by which children have come to be thought of as repositories of hope, and objects of desire' (1986: 108). In Britain, in the 1950s, children (and the reproductive capacities of the mothers who bear them) became central to the programmes of successive governments for rebuilding Britain, not as it had been in the recent past, but as a 'modern' nation. At the same moment young women, thwarted by the war years of separation and anxiety, began to plan the families that would establish a sense of a future for themselves as individuals. As Johnson observes with regard to post-war Australia,

> Children as the repositories of hope, for whom safe places – homes with particular characteristics – were needed, represented the focus of a set of gendered desires in the 1950s, not for the past, for tradition, but for a commitment to and an expectation that 'as housewives' women were part of the nation – citizens in the fullest sense – and part of its future. (1996: 459)

Thus Friedan's account of women in post-war America relies on a certain version of modernist thinking that is historically and gender specific. In doing so it obscures the diverse ways in which women understood, negotiated and articulated their relationships to modernity. The working-class women who rejected domestic service in favour of employment in shops, factories and offices; the middle-class women who struggled to formulate a new identity and found a new voice as housewives; women, like Hannah, Jean and Mavis, who saw that a certain kind of 'modern' marriage could secure a future for their children and a home in which bodily and personal needs could be attended to; Joyce Storey planning the décor of her new council house; the women who read magazine fiction in which the everyday dilemmas of modern living were given expression; my mother proudly representing herself as a mother and housewife but later succumbing to severe depression; the university educated feminists who struggled to analyse the experiences of women in Britain and America: all these women were as 'modern', in their different ways, as the élite masculine subjectivity conventionally understood as the paradigmatic 'modern individual'. This is not to celebrate uncritically certain values of home. All too often domesticity can be a space of violence and abuse, of insecurity, of frustration and tedium. However, in the first half of the twentieth century, modernity for millions of women was about working to create a space called 'home' in which violence, insecurity, disease, discomfort and pain were things of the past. This could provide women with a sense of citizenship and a stake in the future. Most importantly working to create 'better' homes offered many women the opportunity to see themselves as having a central role in achieving, what is believed to be the project of modern social existence, the right to define their own futures and the capacity to be in control of their own lives. In focusing on the home as the space where this might be articulated, women were not only active participants in the modern world but challenge those narrow conceptions of modernity that understand the modern only in terms of the undomestic or the avant-garde. A version of the modern which 'imagined itself away from home, marching towards glory on the battlefields of culture' (Reed 1996: 7). Hence, the attempt in this book to write a history of the home and its relationship to modernity, is part of a wider project that in contesting the fixity of modernist notions of home might enable us to re-think the ways in which we integrate our need for relation-ship, continuity and comfort with our equally powerful desires for autonomy, change and the new. How, in other words, we create spaces in which the best values of public and private, home and away are no longer polarised, but function together to produce that 'better future' that is the continuing project of modernity.

Notes

Introduction

1. As Nava has noted it is surprising given the feminist work of recent decades that the gendered assumptions that underpin the classic narratives continue in recent accounts of modernity. She cites, for example, Frisby 1985 in which she notes there is no mention of gender or sexual difference (Nava 1997: 39).
2. In the twentieth century Freud was, of course, to argue that the price of 'civilisation' could be neurosis: 'if civilization imposes such great sacrifices not only on man's sexuality but on his aggressivity, we can understand better why it is hard for him to be happy in that civilization. In fact, primitive man was better off in knowing no restrictions of instinct. To counterbalance this, his prospects of enjoying this happiness for any length of time were very slender' (1930/1995: 752). In the first half of the twentieth century there were growing fears that modern men and women had become 'over-civilized' and were losing any ability to relate to or understand 'natural' instincts.
3. Such constructions of American selfhood also, of course, exclude those for whom history, ancestry, ethnic genealogy and heritage may constitute a very different version of identity and culture.
4. This quotation is from John Smith, Speech at the Birmingham Temperance Meeting, Birmingham, 1835.
5. Masterman recognises many good qualities in his 'Suburbans' but is also critical of what he perceives as the homogeneity of suburbia. For a useful discussion of the ambivalences in Masterman's essay see Creedon 2003.
6. Edward Shorter has argued that improvements in women's health were a significant factor in the emergence of an active feminist movement (Shorter 1982).
7. See, for example, Attfield and Kirkham (eds) 1989; de Grazia (eds) 1996; Gledhill and Swanson (ed.) 1996; Steedman 1986, for a range of studies that begin to explore the links between material changes in everyday life and the formation of consciousness.
8. Much of the material in this section was originally published in Giles 2002.
9. Dawson's concept of 'composure' has been insightfully applied by Penny Summerfield to the stories told by women about their work in Second World War Britain (Summerfield 1998: 16–23).

Chapter 1 'Something that Little Bit Better': Suburban Modernity, Prudential Marriage and Self-Improvement

1. Recent research has demonstrated that there are alternative stories to tell about late-nineteenth-century suburbia. See Creedon 2003; Hapgood 2000.

2. Modernist art with its emphasis on the unique sensibility and the shock of the new is intended to shake us out of our familiar and conventional views of the world.

3. It is important to remember that there were numerous forms suburbia could take and although certain characteristics are common to all suburban development in Europe and America – out of town, at a distance from workplaces and having their own leisure and shopping facilities – there are differences between English council housing and American housing programmes, between the suburbs surrounding London and those to be found in smaller towns, between new town developments such as Stevenage and exclusively upper-middle-class areas such as Alderley Edge and Wilmslow in Cheshire, between the suburbs of Los Angeles and those of smaller Midwest towns.

4. Simon Dentith has discussed the radical and socialist principles that under-pinned the Garden City Movement and asks how far those aspirations survived in the practical realisation of such schemes (Dentith 2000).

5. In particular, I have in mind here the essays in Roger Silverstone's edited collection, *Visions of Suburbia* 1997. But see also Creedon 2003; Webster 2000.

6. Novels and paintings frequently represented fallen women throwing themselves from a city bridge or finally collapsing under one of the London bridges as they face death or disease, states that are mythologised as the end of the road for sexually licentious women. See Nead 1988.

7. Of course women writers were not exempt from this modernist aesthetic. Modernist art and writing represented the 'high' culture in which they wished to participate. To do so they were required or chose to adopt the 'masculine' subjectivity from which this aesthetic was produced.

8. Born in 1903 in India, Eric Blair was the only son and middle child of three. In 1904 his mother returned to England and settled in Henley-on-Thames in Oxfordshire. Eric grew up, until he was eight, amongst women, only seeing his father briefly during this time. A passage in one of his notebooks, written towards the end of his life, conveys some sense of this experience,

> The conversations he overheard as a small boy, between his Mother, his aunt, his elder sister and their feminist friends. The way in which, without ever hearing any direct statement to that effect, and without having more than a very dim idea of the relationship between the sexes, he derived a firm impression that women *did not like* men, that they looked upon them as a sort of large, ugly, smelly and ridiculous

animal, who maltreated women in every way . . . It was not until he was about thirty that it struck him that he had in fact been his mother's favourite child. It had seemed natural to him that, as he was a boy, the two girls should be preferred. (Crick 1982: 56)

9. Some of the material in this section was previously published with a different focus in *Signs: The Journal of Women in Culture and Society* (Giles 2002).

10. Fears about venereal disease reached panic proportions during and immediately after the First World War. The Royal Commission on Venereal Diseases (1916) reported that 10 per cent of men and 5 per cent of women had contracted syphilis and many more had gonorrhoea (Bourke 1994: 39–41). The emotional costs were enormous: 'I know myself of a case where a woman has suffered untold agonies through the disease given to her by an unfaithful husband. Her children also suffer from a skin disease, and are puny and sickly looking, and yet he has never struck her. Outwardly, he is apparently all that a man should be' (Women's Co-operative Guild member as cited in Bourke 1994: 41).

11. Nostalgia – the yearning for an idealized and uncomplicated past – is often linked with political conservatism (Wright 1985; Samuel 1994). However, as Carolyn Steedman has demonstrated, nostalgia has never been the sole preserve of the political right. Some versions of left-wing and Marxist thought have drawn upon an imaginary and idealized version of the proletariat in those forms of political rhetoric that celebrate the solidarity, stoicism and collectivism of 'traditional' working-class communities (Steedman 1986, 1992: 36–8).

12. Danby is a small rural village on the North Yorkshire moors.

13. *Random Harvest* tells the story of a First World War officer who, suffering from shell-shock and amnesia and unaware that he is already married, falls in love and marries a music hall singer. He is later shocked into remembering that he is head of a noble family and his first wife, whom he does not remember, becomes his secretary. Eventually, another shock brings back memory and happiness. It is a classic Hollywood fiction about romance, sexual desire and social status.

14. Orwell criticised magazines like *Oracle* and *Peg's Paper* for providing a 'fantasy-world' centred on 'pretending to be richer than you are' that offers 'the bored factory-girl or worn-out-mother-of-five a dream-life' (Orwell 1939/ 1957: 199). The two magazines he mentions are in the same category as *Red Star Weekly* (see below).

15. *Red Star Weekly* was a popular weekly magazine, targeted at working-class women, that offered melodramatic and sensational stories often set in exotic locations. For a useful discussion of this genre of women's magazines see Fowler 1991: 50–71.

16. Throughout the 1930s the distinctions between the affluent 'modern' South and the depressed industrial North were part of the mythology of England. See in particular Priestley 1934/1984: 371–80.

17. Anonymous reviewer for *Signs: the Journal of Women in Culture and Society.*

18. In York 104 acres of land were set aside for allotments, in High Wycombe the figure was 68 acres, and in Liverpool 5,000 allotments were available for rent (Rowntree 1941: 387; Rowntree and Lavers 1951: 402; Caradog-Jones 1934: 295).

Chapter 2   Help for Housewives: Domestic Service

1. This chapter is an extended and reworked version of an article previously published as 'Help for Housewives: Domestic Service and the Reconstruction of Domesticity in Britain, 1940–50', *Women's History Review*, 10, 2, 2001.

2. All the texts cited above argue that increased opportunities in shop, factory and office work made it possible for women to reject domestic service as an employment option. However, young women from the depressed and rural areas of Britain where employment opportunities in retailing and office work were fewer continued to seek work as domestic servants by migration to the centres of affluence in the Midlands and South-East, to seaside and spa resorts, and to the residential areas of large cities like Birmingham and London.

3. See the *Lady* for 10 April 1930, 11 April 1940, 12 April 1945, 5 January 1950.

4. See Black 1918, Butler 1916, Fabian Society Women's Group Papers 1914. For a discussion of these initiatives see Dyhouse 1989: 107–44.

5. The Central Committee on Women's Training and Employment (CCWTE) provided domestic service training schemes for unemployed working-class women in urban industrial areas from 1921 onwards. The Domestic Workers Union was set up in 1938 and attempted to regulate wages and conditions of service. The Union was mainly based in London and its membership even in 1940 remained small. The Charter laid down minimum wages for resident, non-resident and part-time workers, rules about accommodation, uniform, visitors and food, as well as holiday entitlements.

6. All the household manuals that I have looked at offer advice on the legal position with regard to the dismissal of servants, suggesting the prevalence of anxieties about dishonesty and disobedience.

7. Lottie, Nelly Boxall's friend, was employed by Virginia and Leonard before working for Adrian Stephen, Clive Bell and then Vanessa. Lottie and Nelly

were very close and even when not living in the same household visited each other regularly, exchanging notes on their employers through what Woolf called their 'secret society' (Lee 1997: 355).

8. There is in Fremlin's description of residential domestic service an only barely concealed, suggestion that the conditions of service may result in the forming of lesbian relationships and Hermione Lee notes that Nelly Boxall and Lottie Hope may have been lovers – they insisted on sharing a bed while working for the Woolfs (Lee 1997: 355).

9. As a result of *The Seven Chars of Chelsea* Fremlin was invited by Tom Harrisson to become an observer and interviewer for Mass Observation. Her work for Mass Observation continued throughout the war and afterwards.

10. For the documentary film movement see Baxendale and Pawling 1996: 17–45. For Mass Observation see Calder and Sheridan 1984: 2–6.

11. For an insightful discussion of pronatalism in the 1940s see Riley 1983: 150–96.

12. Note how the domestic workers are called by their surnames in contrast to the other women in the discussion.

13. Fremlin left the Communist Party when the Nazi–Soviet pact was announced. In her interview with Angus Calder she said 'Everybody who was anybody was in the Communist Party . . . that was where all the fun was' but maintained she had 'no overwhelming convictions' (Fremlin 1980).

14. The EVW schemes were set up to recruit women to domestic work in public institutions such as sanatoria and hospitals. There were rules limiting the kind of households that could apply to employ these workers. Doctors, clergymen and farmers were usually given priority. See Webster 1998: 32–9; Settle 1946.

15. From the 1930s to the 1950s the *Lady* carried numerous advertisements for 'cake-makers' in cafés. It is frequently suggested that ex-cooks should apply for such posts.

Chapter 3 Getting and Spending, Identity and Consumption

1. Mark Abrams was a marketing theorist and researcher who carried out *A Survey of Press Readership* for the IIPA in 1939. See Jeffrey and McClelland 1987.

2. See, however, Nava 1997; Ryan 1995.

3. Some owners of department stores, recognising the significance of the suffrage movements in the first decades of the twentieth century, supplied goods in the symbolic purple, white and green colours of the suffragettes. See Nava 1997: 72.

4. In 1939 Mark Abrams *Survey of Press Readership* revealed that 54 per cent of the *Daily Mail*'s readership was female, the majority of whom were middle-class, middle-aged and elderly. See Jeffrey and McClelland 1987: 38–9.

5. In 1937 620,000 attended the Exhibition and 1,329,644 in 1957. Thereafter attendances decreased. See Ryan 1995: 5.

6. An income of £250 per annum was the generally accepted dividing line between the working and middle classes in the 1930s, that is approximately five pounds per week.

7. A survey of consumer expenditure on laundries and dry cleaners carried out in 1949 revealed that 49 per cent of women questioned preferred to do laundry at home. See Kemsley and Ginsburg 1949: 3–6.

8. This manuscript is tellingly entitled 'The Crisis: War in Diaries'. The crisis referred to here is not simply the Second World War but the post-war world for which 'we are planning a world of public services that shall be ever more efficient and more widely available; of houses and flats that are to be ever more easily run' and in which the problem of 'how to reconcile personal, individual relationships . . . with a state of society which is aiming at reducing individual interdependence to a minimum' looms ever larger. The 'identity crisis' for middle-class housewives is not only perceived as part of this wider problem, but is intended by Fremlin to be seen as emblematic of it.

9. 1938–1945 circulation figures for *Good Housekeeping* were 99,000 and for *Woman and Home* 301,000. *Good Housekeeping* came out monthly and cost three shillings (15p) in 1922, *Woman and Home* was also a monthly magazine but only cost sixpence (2p) in 1929. Circulation figures are not available for *Woman's Sphere* but it was also a monthly magazine that cost sixpence in 1936. See White 1970: Appendix IV, 325

10. The first issue of *Good Housekeeping* in September 1922 ran an article on 'The Law as a Profession for Women', in 1926 there was an article on 'Super-women in business' and in 1927 a feature on 'Women's Clubs'.

11. The problem page of *Woman's Sphere*, December 1936, has letters from women living in Hertfordshire, Staffordshire, Berkhampstead, Shropshire and Croydon.

12. Billie Melman has pointed out that the 'relation between the role of magazine fiction and the social status of the magazine-reading public has been noticed. The space given to fiction was in inverse proportion to the class of readers. The "higher" this class, the smaller the story component' (Melman 1988: 113).

13. It should be noted that Priestley was as vociferous as Orwell in condemning 'the England of arterial and by-pass roads, of filling stations and factories that look like exhibition buildings, of giant cinemas and dance-halls and cafes, bungalows with tiny garages, cocktail bars, Woolworths, motor-coaches, wireless, hiking, factory girls looking like actresses, greyhound racing and dirt

tracks, swimming pools, and everything given away for cigarette coupons' for its 'depressing monotony' and its lack of 'zest, gusto, flavour, bite, drive, originality' (Priestley 1934/1984: 375–80).

Chapter 4 Legacies: The Question of 'Home' and Women's Modernity

1. Suburban areas in the United States experienced a 48 per cent growth rate in the 1950s and 1960s while the growth rate for cities was 10 per cent (Giddens 1989: 564).
2. The studies are John Keats, *A Crack in the Picture Window* (1956), William Whyte, *The Organization Man* (1956) and Lewis Mumford, *The City in History* (1961) cited in Spigel 1997: 226.
3. Vance Packard's *The Hidden Persuaders* was the most well-known proponent of this view.
4. In the same period in Britain F.R. and Q.D. Leavis, from a different political perspective, condemned the preferences of the majority of the population for the products of the mass media (Leavis 1930; Leavis 1932). In 1957 Dwight Macdonald wrote that 'mass man is a solitary atom, uniform with and undifferentiated from thousands and millions of other atoms who go to make up "the lonely crowd" as David Reisman well calls American society' (Macdonald 1957: 60).
5. Friedan's reference to Stanton's abolitionist politics suggests a coded reference to her own past in radical politics.
6. *My Home* was a monthly magazine, costing 2/6d (12½ p), but unlike *Woman and Home* which cost the same and came from the same publishing house, Fleetway, it carried less fiction and more features (White 1970: 325).

Bibliography

Official Documents

Ministry of Health minute, 23 September 1942, Public Records Office Lab70.
Markham, V. and Hancock, F. (1945), *Report on the Post-War Organization of Domestic Employment*, Cmnd 6650, London: Public Records Office.

Interviews and Letters

Bevin, Ernest to Brown, Ernest, 26 January 1943, Public Records Office Lab70.
—— Proposal, 5 July 1943, Public Records Office Lab70.
Celia Fremlin, interview with Angus Calder, 17 March 1980, University of Sussex, Mass Observation Archive.
—— interview with Nick Stanley, 18 September 1981, University of Sussex, Mass Observation Archive.
Annie Stables, interview with Karen Boddycombe, August 1999
Doris Arthurs, interview with Judy Giles, February 1987.
Edith Dickens, interview with Judy Giles, January 1987.
Eileen Hutchings, interview with Judy Giles, February 1987
Hannah Armstrong, interview with Karen Boddycombe, August 1999.
Jean Slater, interview with Karen Boddycombe, August 1999.
Mavis Kitching, interview with Judy Giles, February 1987.
Pauline Charles, interview with Lindsey Murray-Twinn, April 1994.

Magazines and Periodicals

Birmingham Post, 8 November 1930.
Everywoman, 1988.
Lady, 10 April 1930, 11 April 1940, 12 April 1945, 5 January 1950.
Listener, 11 April 1946, 464–6.
My Home, January 1950.
Picture Post, 27 February 1943.
Woman and Home, May 1929, May 1944.
Woman's Sphere, December 1936.

Books and Articles

Abrams, M. (1959), 'The Home-Centred Society', *Listener*, 26 November, pp. 914–15.

Addison, P. (1975/1994), *The Road to 1945: British Politics and the Second World War*, London: Pimlico.

Adorno, T. and Horkheimer, M. (1947/1979), *Dialectic of Enlightenment*, London: Verso.

Alexander, S. (1992), 'Feminist History and Psychoanalysis' in E. Wright (ed.), *A Dictionary of Psychoanalysis and Feminism*, Oxford: Basil Blackwell.

Alexander, Sally. (1994), 'Memory, Generation and History: Two Women's Lives in the Inter-War Years' in her *Becoming a Woman and Other Essays in 19th and 20th Century Feminist History*, London: Virago.

Andrews, M. (1997), *The Acceptable Face of Feminism: The Women's Institute as a Social Movement*, London: Lawrence and Wishart.

Ashplant, T. (1987), 'Fantasy, Narrative, Event: Psychoanalysis and History', *History Workshop Journal*, 23: 165–73.

—— (1988), 'Psychoanalysis in Historical Writing', *History Workshop Journal*, 26: 102–19.

Attfield, J. (1989), 'Inside Pram Town: A Case Study of Harlow House Interiors, 1951–61' in J. Attfield and P. Kirkham (eds), *A View From the Interior: Feminism, Women and Design*, London: The Women's Press.

Attfield, J. and Kirkham, P. (eds) (1989), *A View From the Interior: Feminism, Women and Design*, London: The Women's Press.

Auslander, L. (1996), 'The Gendering of Consumer Practices in Nineteenth Century France' in V. De Grazia (with E. Furlough) (ed.), *The Sex of Things: Gender and Consumption in Historical Perspective*, California: University of California Press.

Baren, M. (1996), *How it all Began, Up the High Street*, London: Michael O'Mara Books.

Baudelaire, C. (1863/1964), *The Painter of Modern Life and Other Essays*, J. Mayne (trans. and ed.), Oxford: Oxford University Press.

Baxendale, J. and Pawling, C. (1996), *Narrating the Thirties, a Decade in the Making: 1930 to the Present*, Basingstoke: Macmillan.

Bell, A. Oliver and McNeillie, A. (eds) (1977–84), *The Diary of Virginia Woolf*, 5 vols, London: Hogarth Press.

Bennett, T. and Watson, D. (2002), *Understanding Everyday Life*, Oxford: Blackwell.

Benjamin, W. (1973), *Charles Baudelaire; Lyric Poet in the Era of High Capitalism*, London: New Left Books.

Benson, J. (1994), *The Rise of Consumer Society in Britain 1880–1980*, Harlow: Longman.

Benston, M. (1969/1980), 'The Political Economy of Women's Liberation' in
E. Malos (ed.), *The Politics of Housework*, London: Allison and Busby.

Berman, M. (1988), *All that is Solid Melts into Air: The Experience of Modernity*,
Harmondsworth: Penguin.

Berry, P. and Bishop, A. (1985), *Testament of a Generation: The Journalism of
Vera Brittain and Winifred Holtby*, London: Virago.

Black, C. (1918), *A New Way of Housekeeping*, London: Collins.

Bourdieu, P. (1984), *Distinction: A Social Critique of the Judgement of Taste*,
London: Routledge and Kegan Paul.

Bourke, J. (1994), *Working-Class Cultures in Britain 1890–1960*, London:
Routledge.

Bowden, S. and Offer, A. (1996), 'The Technological Revolution that never Was:
Gender, Class and the Diffusion of Household Appliances in Interwar England'
in V. De Grazia (with E. Furlough) (ed.), *The Sex of Things: Gender and
Consumption in Historical Perspective*, California: University of California
Press.

Bowlby, R. (1987), '"The Problem with no Name": Rereading Friedan's *The
Feminine Mystique*', *Feminist Review*, 27: 61–75.

Braithwaite, B., Walsh, N. and Davies, G. (1986), *Ragtime to Wartime. The Best of
Good Housekeeping 1922–1939*, London: Ebury Press.

Briggs, A. (1970), *A History of British Broadcasting in the United Kingdome, Vol
III: The War of Words*, Oxford: Oxford University Press.

Brittain, V. (1928), *Women's Work in Modern England*, London: Noel Douglas.

—— (1932/1984), 'I denounce domesticity' in P. Berry and A. Bishop (eds)
*Testament of a Generation: The Journalism of Vera Brittain and Winifred
Holtby*, London: Virago.

—— (1953), *Lady into Woman: A History of Women from Victoria to Elizabeth II*,
London: Andrew Dakers Limited.

Burnett, J. (1986), *A Social History of Housing 1815–1985*, London: Methuen.

Butler, C.V. (1916), *Domestic Service: An Enquiry by the Women's Industrial
Council*, London: G. Bell.

Cahoone, L. (1988), *The Dilemma of Modernity: Philosophy, Culture and Anti-
Culture*, Albany: State University of New York Press.

Calder, A. (1991), *The Myth of the Blitz*, London: Jonathan Cape.

Calder, A. and Sheridan, D. (eds) (1984), *Speak for Yourself: A Mass Observation
Anthology 1937–49*, London: Jonathan Cape.

Campbell, C. (1987), *The Romantic Ethic and the Spirit of Modern Consumerism*,
Oxford: Blackwell.

Campbell, C. and Falk, P. (1997), *The Shopping Experience*, London: Sage.

Campbell, N. and Kean, A. (1997), *American Cultural Studies*, London:
Routledge.

Caradog-Jones, D. (ed.) (1934), *The Social Survey of Merseyside*, London: Hodder and Stoughton.

Carey, J. (1992), *The Intellectuals and the Masses*, London: Faber and Faber.

Carter, E. (1984/1993), 'Alice in the Consumer Wonderland' in A. Gray and J. McGuigan (eds), *Studying Culture: An Introductory Reader*, London: Edward Arnold.

Chopin, K. (1899/1993), *The Awakening*, Harmondsworth: Penguin.

Chorley, K. (1950), *Manchester Made Them*, London: Faber and Faber.

Clarke, A.J. (1997), 'Tupperware: Suburbia, Sociality and Mass Consumption' in Silverstone, R. (ed.), *Visions of Suburbia*, London: Routledge.

Clephane, I. (1935), *Towards Sex Freedom*, London: The Bodley Head.

Cooper, L. (1936), *The New House*, London: Gollancz.

Cowan, R.S. (1989), *More Work for Mother: The Ironies of Household Technology from the Open Hearth to the Microwave*, London: Free Association Books.

Creedon, A. (2003), 'Representations of Suburban Culture 1890–1914', Unpublished Ph.d, University of Leeds.

Crick, B. (1982), *George Orwell. A Life*, Harmondsworth: Penguin.

Cunningham, G. (2000), 'The Riddle of Suburbia: Suburban Fictions at the Victorian *Fin de Siècle*' in R. Webster (ed.), *Expanding Suburbia: Reviewing Suburban Narratives*, Oxford: Berghahn Books.

Curran, J., Smith, A. and Wingate, P. (eds) (1987), *Impacts and Influences: Essays on Media Power in the Twentieth Century*, London: Methuen.

Davidoff, L. and Hall, C. (1987), *Family Fortunes: Men and Women of the English Middle Class, 1780–1850*, London: Hutchinson.

Davin, A. (1989), 'Imperialism and Motherhood', in R. Samuel (ed.), *Patriotism. The Making and Unmaking of British National Identity*, London: Routledge.

Dawson, G. (1994), *Soldier Heroes: British Adventure, Empire and the Imagining of Masculinities*, London: Routledge.

De Beauvoir, S. (1949/1988), *The Second Sex*, London: Picador.

De Grazia, V. (with Furlough, E.) (ed.) (1996), *The Sex of Things: Gender and Consumption in Historical Perspective*, California: University of California Press.

De Lauretis, T. (1990), 'Eccentric Subjects: Feminist Theory and Historical Consciousness', *Feminist Studies*, 16, 1: 115–50.

Delafield, E.M. (1930/1984), *The Diary of a Provincial Lady*, London: Virago.

Dennis, H. (2000), 'Gender in American Literature and Culture' in R. Maidment and J. Mitchell (eds), *The United States in the Twentieth Century: Culture*, London: Hodder and Stoughton/Open University.

Dentith, S. (2000), 'From William Morris to the Morris Minor: An Alternative Suburban History' in R. Webster (ed.), *Expanding Suburbia: Reviewing Suburban Narratives*, Oxford: Berghahn Books.

Donald, J. (1999), *Imagining the Modern City*, London: The Athlone Press.

Du Maurier, D. (1938/1975), *Rebecca*, London: Pan Books.

During, S. (ed.) (1993), *The Cultural Studies Reader*, London: Routledge.

Dyhouse, C. (1989), *Feminism and the Family in England 1880–1939*, Oxford: Blackwell.

Edynbury, R. (1938), *Real Life Problems and Their Solutions*, London: Odhams Press.

Elshtain, Jean B. (1981), *Public Man, Private Woman: Woman in Social and Political Thought*, Princeton: Princeton University Press.

Fabian Society Women's Group Papers (1914), Committee to Reorganize Domestic Work.

Felski, R. (1995), *The Gender of Modernity*, Cambridge, Mass.: Harvard University Press.

—— (1999–2000), 'The Invention of Everyday Life', *New Formations*, 39: 15–31.

Ferguson, M. (1983), *Forever Feminine: Women's Magazines and the Cult of Femininity*, London: Heinemann.

Foley, W. (1986), *A Child in the Forest*, London: BBC, Ariel Books.

Fowler, B. (1991), *The Alienated Reader. Women and Popular Romance Literature in the Twentieth Century*, London: Harvester Wheatsheaf.

Fraser, N. (1992), 'Re-thinking the Public Sphere: A Contribution to the Critique of Actually Existing Democracy' in C. Calhoun (ed.) *Habermas and the Public Sphere*, Cambridge, Mass.: MIT Press.

Fremlin, C. (1940), *The Seven Chars of Chelsea*, London: Methuen.

—— (1943/1987), *War Factory*, London: The Cresset Library.

—— (1944), 'The Crisis: War in Diaries', unfinished, unpublished manuscript, Mass Observation Archive, University of Sussex.

French, M. (1978), *The Women's Room*, London: Sphere Books Ltd.

Freud, S. (1930/1995), 'Civilization and its Discontents' in P. Gay (ed.), *The Freud Reader*, London: Vintage.

Friedan, B. (1963/1982), *The Feminine Mystique*, Harmondsworth: Pelican.

—— (1976), *It Changed My Life: Writings on the Women's Movement*, New York: Random House.

Frisby, D. (1985), *Fragments of Modernity: Georg Simmel, Siegfried Kracauer and Walter Benjamin*, Cambridge: Polity Press.

Gail, S. (1965–67/1980), 'The Housewife' in E. Malos (ed.), *The Politics of Housework*, London: Allison and Busby.

Gavron, H. (1966), *The Captive Wife*, London: Routledge & Kegan Paul.

Gay, P. (ed.) (1995), *The Freud Reader*, London: Vintage.

Giddens, A. (1989), *Sociology*, Oxford: Blackwell.

Giles, J. (1995), *Women, Identity and Private Life in Britain 1900–50*, Basingstoke: Macmillan.

—— (2001), 'Help for Housewives: Domestic Service and the Reconstruction of Domesticity 1940–50', *Women's History Review*, 10, 2.

—— (2002), 'Narratives of Gender, Class and Modernity in Women's Memories of the Mid-Twentieth Century in Britain', *Signs: The Journal of Women in Culture and Society*, 28, 1: 21–41.

Gillis, J. (1997), *A World of Their Own Making: A History of Myth and Ritual in Family Life*, Oxford: Oxford University Press.

Gittins, D. (1982), *Fair Sex: Family Size and Structure, 1900–39*, London: Hutchinson.

Gledhill, C. and Swanson, G. (eds.) (1996), *Nationalising Femininity: Culture, Sexuality and the British Cinema in the Second World War*, Manchester: Manchester University Press.

Glucksmann, M. (1990), *Women Assemble: Women Workers and the New Industries in Inter-War Britain*, London: Routledge.

Gordon, L. (1984), *Virginia Woolf: A Writer's Life*, Oxford: Oxford University Press.

Gray, A. and McGuigan, J. (eds), *Studying Culture: An Introductory Reader*, London: Edward Arnold.

Griffith, E. (1938), *Modern Marriage and Birth Control*, London: Gollancz.

Greenwood, W. (1933/1993), *Love On the Dole*, London: Vintage.

Grossmith, G. and W. (1892/1998), *The Diary of a Nobody*, Oxford: Oxford World's Classics.

Habermas, J. (1989), *The Structural Transformation of the Public Sphere: An Inquiry into a Category of Bourgeois Society*, Cambridge, Mass.: MIT Press.

Hall, C. (1982), 'The Butcher, the Baker, the Candlestick-Maker: The Shop and the Family in the Industrial Revolution' in E. Whitelegg et al. (eds), *The Changing Experience of Women*, Oxford: Martin Robertson.

—— (1992), *White, Male and Middle-Class: Explorations in Feminism and History*, Oxford: Polity Press.

Hapgood, L. (2000), '"The New Suburbanites" and Contested Class Identities in the London suburbs, 1880–1900' in R. Webster (ed.), *Expanding Suburbia: Reviewing Suburban Narratives*, Oxford: Berghahn Books.

Harrison, B. (1995), 'Women and Health' in J. Purvis (ed.), *Women's History: Britain, 1850–1945*, London: UCL Press.

Hartley, J. (1994), *Hearts Undefeated: Women's Writing of the Second World War*, London: Virago.

Hinton, J. (1994), 'Militant Housewives: The British Housewives' League and the Attlee Government', *History Workshop Journal*, 38.

Holtzmann, E. M. (1983), '"The Pursuit of Married Love": Women's Attitudes towards Sexuality and Marriage in Great Britain, 1918–1939', *Journal of Social History*, 16, 39–51.

Horn, P. (1975) *The Rise and Fall of the Victorian Servant*, London: Gill and Macmillan.

Horowitz, D. (1998), *Betty Friedan and the Making of the Feminine Mystique: The American Left, the Cold War and Modern Feminism*, Massachusetts: University of Massachusetts Press.

Hughes, M.V. (1940/1979), *A London Family Between the Wars*, Oxford: Oxford University Press.

Humphries, S. and Gordon, P. (1993), *A Labour of Love: The Experience of Parenthood in Britain 1900–1950*, London: Sidgwick and Jackson.

Huyssen, A. (1986), 'Mass Culture as Woman: Modernism's Other' in T. Modleski (ed.), *Studies in Entertainment: Critical Approaches to Mass Culture*, Bloomington: Indiana University Press.

Jack, F. and Preston, P. (c.1930), *The Woman's Book*, London: The Woman's Book Club.

Jackson, A. (1991), *The Middle Classes 1900–1950*, Nairn, Scotland: David St John Publisher.

James, E. (1962), 'Women and Work in Twentieth Century Britain', *Manchester School of Economics and Social Science*, XXX, September.

Jeffrey, T. and McClelland, K. (1987), 'A World Fit to Live in: The *Daily Mail* and the Middle Classes 1918–1939' in J. Curran, A. Smith and P. Wingate (eds), *Impacts and Influences: Essays on Media Power in the Twentieth Century*, London: Methuen.

Jennings, H. (1945), *A Diary for Timothy*, Basil Wright/Crown Film Unit.

Jephcott, P. (1943), *Girls Growing Up*, London: Faber and Faber.

Johnson, L. (1996), 'As Housewives We Are Worms': Women, Modernity and the Home Question', *Cultural Studies*, 10, 3: 449–63.

Jones, H. (ed.) (1994), *Duty and Citizenship: The Correspondence and Political Papers of Violet Markham, 1896–1953*, London: The Historians' Press.

Keating, P.J. (1976), *Into Unknown England 1866–1913: Selections from the Social Explorers*, London: Fontana.

Kemsley, W.F.F. and Ginsburg, D. (1949), *The Social Survey: Consumer Expenditure on Laundries, Dyeing and Cleaning, Mending and Alterations, and Shoe Repairing Services*, London: Central Office of Information, British Library of Political and Economic Science.

Kristeva J. (1981/1991), 'Women's Time' in R. Warhol and D.P. Herndl (eds), *Feminisms: An Anthology of Literary Theory and Criticism*, New Jersey: Rutgers University Press.

Lambert, C. and Weir, D. (eds) (1975), *Cities in Modern Britain*, London: Fontana.

Langhamer, C. (2000), *Women's Leisure in England 1920–60*, Manchester: Manchester University Press.

Lant, A. (1991), *Blackout. Reinventing Women for Wartime British Cinema*, Princeton: Princeton University Press.

Leavis, F.R. (1930), *Mass Civilization and Minority Culture*, Cambridge: Minority Press.

Leavis, Q.D. (1932), *Fiction and the Reading Public*, London: Chatto and Windus.

Lee, H. (1997), *Virginia Woolf*, London: Vintage.

Lefebvre, H. (1971), *Everyday Life in the Modern World*, London: Penguin.

Lewis, J. (1980), *The Politics of Motherhood: Child and Maternal Welfare in England, 1900–1939*, London: Croom Helm.

Lewis, R.W.B. (1955), *The American Adam*, Chicago: Chicago University Press.

Lewis, R. and Maude, A. (1949), *The English Middle Classes*, London: Penguin.

Light, A. (1991), *Forever England: Femininity, Literature and Conservatism Between the Wars*, London: Routledge.

Llewellyn Davies, M. (1931/1977), *Life as We Have Known It*, London: Virago.

Ludovici, A.M. (1923), *Woman: A Vindication*, London: publisher unknown.

Lury, C. (1997), *Consumer Culture*, Cambridge: Polity.

Macdonald, D. (1957) 'A Theory of Mass Culture' in B. Rosenberg and D. Manning White (eds), *Mass Culture: The Popular Arts in America*, New York: Macmillan.

Mackay, H. (1997), *Consumption and Everyday Life*, London: Sage/Open University.

Maidment, R. and Mitchell, J. (2000), *The United States in the Twentieth Century: Culture*, London: Hodder and Stoughton/Open University.

Markham, V. (1953), *Return Passage*, Oxford: Oxford University Press.

Marx, K. (1973), The Eighteenth Brumaire of Louis Bonaparte in *Surveys from Exile*, Harmondsworth: Penguin.

Mass Observation (1939a), *Clothes Washing: Motives and Methods: Interim Report; Laundry Usage*, MO Reference 2315, MO Archive, University of Sussex.

—— (1939b), *Report on the Psychology of Housework*, MO Archive, University of Sussex.

Masterman, C. (1909/1960), *The Condition of England*, London: Methuen.

McBride, T. (1976), *The Domestic Revolution: The Modernisation of Household Service in England and France 1820–1920*, London: Croom Helm.

Melman, B. (1988), *Women and the Popular Imagination in the 1920s*, Basingstoke: Macmillan.

Meyerowitz, J. (1993), 'Beyond the Feminine Mystique: A Reassessment of Postwar Mass Culture, 1946–1958', *The Journal of American History*, March: 1455–82.

—— (1994), *Not June Cleaver: Women and Gender in Postwar America, 1945–1960*, Philadelphia: Temple University Press.

Mitchison, N. (1975), *All Change Here*, London: Bodley Head.

—— (1979), *You May Well Ask*, London: Gollancz.

Modleski, T. (ed.) (1986), *Studies in Entertainment: Critical Approaches to Mass Culture*, Bloomington: Indiana University Press.

Montefiore, J. (1996), *Men and Women Writers of the 1930s: The Dangerous Flood of History*, London: Routledge.

Nava, M. (1992), *Changing Cultures: Feminism, Youth and Consumerism*, London: Sage.

—— (1997), 'Modernity's Disavowal: Women, the City and the Department Store' in C. Campbell and P. Falk (eds), *The Shopping Experience*, London: Sage.

Nead, L. (1988), *Myths of Sexuality: Representations of Women in Victorian Britain*, Oxford: Blackwell.

Nicholson, N. (1979), *The Sickle Side of the Moon. The Letters of Virginia Woolf 1932–35*, London: Chatto and Windus.

Oakley, A. (1974), *The Sociology of Housework*, London: Martin Robertson.

Oliver, P., Davis, I. and Bentley, I., (1981), *Dunroamin: The Suburban Semi and its Enemies*, London: Pimlico.

Orwell, G. (1937/1986), *The Road to Wigan Pier*, Harmondsworth: Penguin.

—— (1939/1957), 'Boys' Weeklies' in *Selected Essays*, Harmondsworth: Penguin.

—— (1939/1987), *Coming Up for Air*, Harmondsworth: Penguin.

O'Shea, A. (1996), 'English Subjects of Modernity' in M. Nava and A. O'Shea (eds), *Modern Times: Reflections on a Century of English Modernity*, London: Routledge.

Parsons, D. (2000), *Streetwalking the Metropolis: Women, the City and Modernity*, Oxford: Oxford University Press.

Passerini, L. (1979), 'Work Ideology and Consensus under Italian Fascism', *History Workshop Journal*, 8: 84–92.

Perks, R. and Thomson, A. (eds) (1998), *The Oral History Reader*, London: Routledge.

Pollard, S. (1983), *The Development of the British Economy 1914–1980*, London: Edward Arnold.

Pollock, G. (1988), *Vision and Difference: Femininity, Feminism and the Histories of Art*, London: Routledge.

Portelli, A. (1981) 'The Peculiarities of Oral History', *History Workshop Journal*, 12: 96–107.

Popular Memory Group (1982) 'Popular Memory: Theory, Politics, Method' in Richard Johnson et al. (eds), *Making Histories: Studies in History-writing and Politics*, London: Hutchinson.

Priestley, J. (1934/1984), *English Journey*, London: Heinemann.

—— (1967), *All England Listened: The Wartime Postscripts of J.B. Priestley*, New York: Chilmark Press.

Rathbone, E. (1924), *The Disinherited Family*, London: Edward Arnold.

Reed, C. (ed.) (1996), *Not at Home: The Suppression of Domesticity in Modern Art and Architecture*, London: Thames and Hudson.

Reiger, K. (1985), *The Disenchantment of the Home: Modernising the Australian Family 1880–1940*, Oxford: Oxford University Press.

Riley, D. (1983), *War in the Nursery: Theories of the Child and Mother*, London: Virago.

Rogers, H. (1998), '"The Prayer, the Passion and the Reason" of Eliza Sharples: freethought, women's rights and republicanism, 1832–52' in Eileen James Yeo (ed.), *Radical Femininity: Women's Self-Representation in the Public Sphere*, Manchester: Manchester University Press.

Rowbotham, S. (1972/1980), 'The Carrot, the Stick and the Movement' in E. Malos (ed.) (1980) *The Politics of Housework*, London: Allison and Busby.

—— (1973), *Woman's Consciousness, Man's World*, Harmondsworth: Penguin.

—— (1999), *A Century of Women: The History of Women in Britain and the United States*, Harmondsworth: Penguin.

—— (2000), *Promise of a Dream: The Sixties Remembered*, London: Allen Lane/ Penguin.

Rowntree, B.S. (1901), *Poverty, A Study of Town Life*, London: Macmillan.

—— (1941), *Poverty and Progress: A Second Social Survey of York*, London: Longman, Green and Co.

Rowntree, B.S. and Lavers, G.R. (1951), *English Life and Leisure: A Social Survey*, London: Longmans, Green and Co.

Ryan, D. (1995), 'The Daily Mail Home Exhibition and Suburban Modernity, 1908–1951', Unpublished Ph.D, University of East London.

Samuel, R. (1994), *Theatres of Memory*, London: Verso.

Sawyer, M. (2000), *Park and Ride: Adventures in Suburbia*, London: Abacus.

Scott, G. (1998a), *Feminism and the Politics of Working Women: The Women's Co-operative Guild, 1883 to the Second World War*, London: UCL Press.

—— (1998b), '"As a War-Horse to the Beat of Drums": Representations of Working-class Femininity in the Women's Co-operative Guild, 1880s to the Second World War' in Eileen James Yeo (ed.), *Radical Femininity:Women's Self-Representations in the Public Sphere*, Manchester: Manchester University Press.

Settle, A. (1946), 'From a Woman's Viewpoint', *Observer*, 28 April, 21 July, 6 October.

Sheridan, D. (1990), *Wartime Women. A Mass Observation Anthology*, London: Mandarin.

Shorter, E. (1982), *A History of Women's Bodies*, New York: Basic Books.

Silverstone, R. (ed.) (1997), *Visions of Suburbia*, London: Routledge.

Simmel, G. (1903/1971), 'The Metropolis and Mental Life' in his *On Individuality and Social Forms*, Chicago: University of Chicago Press.

—— (1911/1984), trans. Guy Oakes, *Georg Simmel: On Women, Sexuality, and Love*, New Haven: Yale University Press.

Smith, B.G. (1998), *The Gender of History: Men, Women and Historical Practice*, Cambridge, Mass.: Harvard University Press.

Spender, D. (1984), *Time and Tide Wait for No Man*, London: Pandora.

Spigel, L. (1997), 'From Theatre to Space Ship: Metaphors of Suburban Domesticity in Postwar America' in R. Silverstone (ed.), *Visions of Suburbia*, London: Routledge.

—— (2001), *Welcome to the Dreamhouse: Popular Media and Postwar Suburbs*, Durham and London: Duke University Press.

Spring Rice, M. (1939), *Working Class Wives: Their Health and Conditions*, Harmondsworth: Penguin.

Steedman, C. (1986), *Landscape for a Good Woman*, London: Virago.

—— (1992), *Past Tenses: Essays on Writing, Autobiography and History*, London: Rivers Oram.

Stein, S. (1985), 'The Graphic Ordering of Desire: Modernization of a Middle-Class Women's Magazine 1914–1939', *Heresies*, 18.

Storey, J. (1987), *Our Joyce*, London: Virago.

—— (1992), *Joyce's War 1939–1945*, London: Virago.

Struther, J. (1939/1989), *Mrs. Miniver*, London: Virago.

Summerfield, P. (1984), *Women Workers in the Second World War: Production and Patriarchy in Conflict*, London: Croom Helm.

—— (1993a), 'Training Women for War Work 1939–45', *Journal of Gender Studies*, 2, 2.

—— (1993b), 'Women and Social Change in the Second World War' in B. Brivati and H. Jones (eds), *What Difference Did the War Make?*, London: Leicester University Press.

—— (1996), '"The Girl that Makes the Thing that Drills the Hole that Holds the Spring . . .": Discourses of Women and Work in the Second World War' in C. Gledhill and G. Swanson (eds), *Nationalising Femininity: Culture, Sexuality and the British Cinema in the Second World War*, Manchester: Manchester University Press.

—— (1998), *Reconstructing Women's Wartime Lives*, Manchester: Manchester University Press.

Taylor, P. (1978), 'Women Domestic Servants, 1919–1939: The Final Phase', Unpublished MA thesis, University of Birmingham.

—— (1979), 'Daughters and Mothers-Maids and Mistresses: Domestic Service Between the Wars' in J. Clarke, C. Crichter and R. Johnson (eds), *Working-Class Culture: Studies in History and Theory*, London: Hutchinson.

Taylor, S. (1938), 'The Suburban Neurosis', *Lancet*, 26 March, 759–61.

The Book of Good Housekeeping (1944), St Albans: J.W. Vernon and Co. Limited.

The Home Counsellor (1936), London: Odhams.

Tosh, J. (1996), 'New Men? The Bourgeois Cult of Home', *History Today*, December: 9–15.

Twain, M. (1884/1966), *The Adventures of Huckleberry Finn*, Harmondsworth: Penguin.

Walkowitz, J. (1992), *City of Dreadful Delight*, London: Virago.

Webster, R. (2000), 'Introduction: Suburbia Inside Out' in R. Webster *Expanding Suburbia: Reviewing Suburban Narratives*, Oxford: Berghahn Books.

Webster, W. (1998), *Imagining Home: Gender, 'Race' and National Identity 1945–64*, London: UCL.

White, C. (1970), *Women's Magazines 1693–1968*, London: Michael Joseph.

White, E. (1983), *A Boy's Own Story*, London: Picador.

White, N.R. (1998), 'Marking Absences. Holocaust Testimony and History' in R. Perks and A. Thomson (eds), *The Oral History Reader*, London: Routledge.

Williams, P. (1991), *The Alchemy of Race and Rights*, Cambridge, Mass.: Harvard University Press.

Wilson, E. (1985), *Adorned in Dreams: Fashion and Modernity*, London: Virago.

—— (1991), *Sphinx in the City*, London: Virago.

—— (1992), 'The Invisible *Flâneur*', *New Left Review*, 191, 90–110.

Winship, J. (1987), *Inside Women's Magazines*, London: Pandora Press.

Wolff, J. (1985), 'The Invisible *Flâneuse*: Women and the Literature of Modernity' in her (1990), *Feminine Sentences*, Oxford: Polity.

Woodward, K. (1928/1983), *Jipping Street,* London: Virago.

Woolf, V. (1906/1985), 'Phyllis and Rosamund' in S. Dick (ed.), *The Collected Shorter Fiction of Virginia Woolf*, London: Hogarth Press.

—— (1927) *To the Lighthouse*, London: Hogarth Press.

—— (1929), *A Room of One's Own*, London: Hogarth Press.

Wright, P. (1985), *On Living in an Old Country*, London: Verso.

Yeo, E. Janes (ed.) (1998), *Radical Femininity: Women's Self-Representation in the Public Sphere*, Manchester: Manchester University Press.

Zmroczek, C. (1994), 'The Weekly Wash' in Oldfield, S. (ed.), *This Working-Day World*, London: Taylor and Francis.

Zola, E. (1972), *Nana*, trans. Holden, G., Harmondsworth: Penguin.

Index

Index

Index